I'M NOT CRAZY

I'M NOT CRAZY

THE TRUE STORY OF FRANCES DEITRICK'S FLIGHT FROM A PSYCHIATRIC SNAKE PIT TO FREEDOM

Frances I. Deitrick

NEW HORIZON PRESS
Far Hills, New Jersey

Library of Congress Catalog Card Number: 91-66896

Deitrick, Frances I.
  I'm Not Crazy

ISBN: 0-88282-103-2
New Horizon Press

1996 1995 1994 1993 1992 / 5 4 3 2 1
Manufactured in the U.S.A.

For my family
and
Mr. John Charles

"Someone must have traduced Joseph K. for without having done anything wrong, he was arrested one fine morning."
—Franz Kafka
THE TRIAL

AUTHOR'S NOTE

These are my actual experiences. The personalities, events, actions, and conversations portrayed within the story have been reconstructed from interviews and research, utilizing letters, personal papers, and the memories of participants. In an effort to safeguard the privacy of certain individuals, I have changed their names and, in some cases, altered otherwise identifying characteristics and chronology. Events involving the characters happened as described; only minor details have been altered.

ACKNOWLEDGEMENTS

The contents of this book were especially hard for me to write because they are so very, very, true. But if I had written it any other way, the meaning would have been lost. I never intended to hurt anyone with any of its contents but I know I have; still, there were truths that had to be told. Above all, I feel a deep necessity to express to my family my eternal, heart-felt gratitude for their priceless and non-wavering support.

There are also two extremely exceptional doctors, Dr. Mahar and Dr. Perrine, whom I wish to thank. They were the first to believe in me as a real person and to defend my rights. They acted as sparks to ignite my own conscious, as well as others, consciousness about the entire situation. They have proved, time and time again through their professionalism and expertise, to be top in their fields. I thank God they were and still are my doctors.

Although at the time I felt nothing but hatred and anger toward many of the doctors and staff at "Brookhollow" (not the real name), I now realize that medicine is a human science and they did their best in difficult and unusual circumstances.

There still remains a very special person who not only deserves my deepest thanks, but who also indirectly assisted with the completion of this book, Mr. John Charles, my eleventh-grade English teacher. Many years ago he instilled a special motivating factor in an extremely insecure little girl. He firmly believed, and showed through both his words and actions, in my ability to write and asked that I dedicate my first book to him. At the time his comment seemed a fantasy but, now, even though it's ten years later, I want to thank you, Mr. Charles, and do just that.

ONE

Though I was determined to confront him, I hated the icy, narrow road I had to take to Steve, my ex-fiancé's, house.

There was a one-lane bridge, two sets of railroad tracks, and a multitude of curves and hills. The hills alone made my stomach clench. I steeled my nerve and conquered the first set of obstacles: the one-lane bridge and railroad tracks were behind me. Now came the steepest hill along the road. I inched down it at only twenty miles per hour, stopping at the one and only stop sign on the entire route.

Suddenly, from nowhere it seemed, I was blinded by the headlights of a truck reflected in my rear view mirror. I tried braking, hoping it would pass me. My car seemed to lurch forward. "The brakes aren't working," I murmured desperately. I began furiously pumping the pedals, but nothing seemed to slow the car.

Suddenly, my ears roared with the impact of the collision. The car began spinning around and around, finally careening into the middle of the intersection facing oncoming traffic. On impact, my body wrenched forward, my head slammed into the steering wheel. Minutes passed. I was conscious, but petrified, riveted to the seat.

More time passed. How long I was unsure. Fleeting

thoughts and desperate feelings passed through my mind. *Should I try to move or sit still until someone came?* My eyes darted back and forth, unable to focus. *Was there blood? Was I hurt? What about the other guy? What had happened?*

I heard only dead silence.

Looking through the windshield, I saw an approaching police car. Tears came as I squinted, then opened my eyes wide trying to see more clearly. The police car looked strange, like a child's toy car. Jumping out of my own vehicle, I waved frantically to attract the policeman. He pulled to the side of the road and got out. Only then did I notice that the truck which had hit me had been pulled into a nearby parking lot. Turning now to look at my car, I saw the rear end was completely smashed in.

The tall, dark-haired officer started talking.

"Move that car," he said firmly.

"There's no way I am going to get back in that car," I objected.

"I'll move it then," he said. Reaching for the door handle, he peered inside and began muttering.

"You locked the door!" he exclaimed. I stood there trembling. *Oh, my God! Now what?*

"I think I have an extra set of keys," I stammered.

My hands were trembling so I could hardly open my purse to search. After a few seconds I managed, but looking inside, it seemed to me that all the objects were floating around as if they'd been thrown into a bottomless well.

As I searched for the extra set of keys, I rambled on to the officer, "I've always been told to leave the car right where it was if I were ever involved in an accident. Isn't that right? Aren't you supposed to leave it right there?"

"Not in the middle of an intersection," he replied caustically.

His tone raised my adrenaline flow. I bit my lip. *Is this man really a police officer? They shouldn't talk in that tone.*

Finally, I pulled the elusive keys from my purse and handed them to the officer. As he drove the car onto the road's shoulder I watched his every move. That done, the officer called me over and began asking questions about the accident. When I didn't reply, he stared at me intently.

"Do you want me to call an ambulance?"

I shook my head. "There's no reason. I'm not hurt. Neither is the other driver."

He walked over to his car and started talking into the CB. Left alone with the other driver, we started to talk. Rather, I rambled and he talked. I had no idea what I said or why. I hopscotched from one thing to another without taking a breath. I was telling him, "My tires are new; Steve lives up the road; my parents grew up on farms in Pennsylvania; I had blood drawn the other night." Words were pouring out non-stop. When conversation seemed pointless, I started pacing back and forth. Every once in a while, I'd walk a complete circle or etch out drawings in the ground with the tip of my shoe.

The officer interrupted my reverie, "Could you both come over to my car?"

He had not said a word when I blurted out, "I must have stepped on the gas a little too much." Then, as if to myself, I added, "Why am I saying that? I don't know what happened."

A woman came running down the side of the road shouting, "I saw what happened."

I shouted back to her, "We don't need you." *Why did I say that?*

The officer asked to see our licenses. The other driver left to get his while I stayed at the patrol car.

"Could you call Steve for me," I asked, still trembling.

The officer placed the call, but reported that there was no answer. Next, I asked him to try my sister Jackie; again no answer. I began shaking. I needed a familiar face. I asked him to try another number where Steve might be;

they didn't know where Steve was. Finally, I asked him to try my parents' number; there was no answer. I was in tears.

Where is everyone? I resumed pacing, now and then shuffling my feet or walking in circles.

The other driver was back now. The officer looked at his license, then asked for mine. My fingers shook as I tried to pull it out of my wallet. Failing in this attempt, I handed the whole wallet to him. He refused it and suggested I sit down and try to find it myself. Sitting in the back of the police car, I kept riffling through my purse. Finally, with a wide smile, I handed my license over to him.

The officer jotted down a few notes from our licenses, and then gave each of us forms to complete. My head hurt so much that, I couldn't comprehend his instructions. "Look, I have to get some air," I said. Gasping, I got out of the car, trying to take heavy breaths to calm myself enough to fill out the forms. The words jumbled before my eyes. I couldn't read them, much less answer questions. I went back to my own car and called the officer over.

"Could you explain how to fill this out?"

Pointing at each little box on the form, he said, "Your first name goes here. Your last name here. Your address over there . . ." He went back towards his car.

Before I could complete the forms, strange sensations rippled through my body. I felt weak and dizzy. Spasms ran up my neck and back. Then I stiffened up like a board and became nauseated. Doubling over I cried out, "What's happening? I need help. I need Steve." I leaned on the horn nonstop to attract attention. Within seconds, the officer stuck his head in the window.

"Help!" was all I could manage.

"Do you want me to call an ambulance?" he asked.

"Yes!" I screamed.

"What's going on?" the other driver called out.

"Shock," the officer replied.

TWO

It seemed like only minutes passed before two men dressed in white started climbing into my car. The sound of their voices startled me, one behind me and one in front. They were talking to me, telling me their names. They began strapping all kinds of harnesses on me; one around my neck, another my head, and then my back. The next thing I knew, I was out of the car being carried somewhere on a stretcher.

"Where am I going?"

One of the men patted my hand. "You'll be all right. We're taking you to a hospital."

Time passed. Now flat on my back, my coat and shoes were gone; all the straps were gone except for the collar around my neck. It hurt! I was inside a building lying upon some kind of a table. The room was white and sterile. A man standing at my feet was running something up and down one of my soles.

"Where am I?" I asked hoarsely. "I have to get out of here!"

I tried to move, but couldn't. Then a woman and man wearing white coats came in. The man asked me my name. The woman asked if I was pregnant. They asked me questions about what happened. The only thing I told them was

I had to go to the bathroom. The woman walked out of the room and came back with some sort of a pot in her hand.

"Can you pull your pants off?" she asked.

"I went to college. I have a B.S. in Business. I used to be sharp, I think I can manage that," I replied, as I tried to snap my fingers, but couldn't.

Then she put a bedpan under me and they left.

My bladder was about to burst, but I couldn't urinate in some little pot. As I lay there, half-conscious, the man in a white coat walked in again. He palpated my stomach. The woman did the same.

"Can you tell me your name?" she asked in a whisper.

"Frances I. Deitrick," I said slowly.

"Do you want us to call anyone?" she asked.

"Where am I?" I asked.

"You're at First Memorial," she replied.

"Am I really?" I shook my head trying to focus. I told her to call Steve and gave her his number.

"He isn't there. Is there anyone else?" she asked when she returned.

"Jackie! Call my sister, Jackie," I said. "230-0516."

She wasn't there either. I told the woman to try Jackie at work. She wasn't there either.

"I need her! She'll make sure everything is done right."

The woman, who turned out to be a nurse, then asked if I wanted her to call my parents.

"No!" I replied without a thought.

She left and I was alone. My mind drifted.

When I woke, I felt the urgent need to go to the bathroom. I rang the bell and when the nurse entered, I asked, "Can I please use the bathroom? She refused, but mumbled something about a catheter.

"What's that?"

I soon found out and did it ever hurt, even though the rest of my body was numb.

The next thing I knew I was being wheeled down a hall-way.

"Where am I going?" I asked the orderly. Steve, my ex-fiancé was standing against a wall, but he was shrouded in a mist, or so it seemed. Then he started to disappear. The orderly pushed the gurney through a door. Reaching my arm toward him, I heard Steve say, "You'll be fine. I'm here for you."

The liar, I thought reflecting on Steve, and drifted off again.

The male nurse standing at the foot of the long table said in a metallic voice, "You're in X-ray." Then I saw aluminum foil covering the ceiling.

"This can't be X-ray," I cried. "I've been in an X-ray room before and it didn't look like this." I started screaming.

My paranoia was mounting. I couldn't move. I couldn't think.

Within minutes, a grey-haired woman with steel-rimmed glasses joined us. She seemed more authoritative than the nurse. She stood at my feet and he at my head.

"What are you doing?" I yelled. "Are you trying to kill me?" They began talking animatedly to each other, but I could make out only bits of the conversation, snatches of words like "drug dose," "possible abuse" and "schizophrenia." I tried to tell them there was something wrong with me; I wasn't crazy. But no one listened. I was fading in and out of a semiconscious state. I dozed off again.

The next time I awoke I was back in my original room, floating in and out of reality and speaking in short, abrupt statements. When a nurse with red hair whom I'd never seen before walked in, I demanded that she call my parents. A minute later, I was apologizing for my rude demand. I told her I didn't know what I was doing there or what was happening to me. My whole body ached and my head pounded like a drum.

The nurse said she would call my parents and that my sister, Jackie, had called while I was in X-ray. I felt better now because Jackie would make sure I received the best treatment. The nurse left. Then, I drifted.

Still semi-lucid, I began to feel vibrations in my head. They grew stronger and stronger as I lay there. My head seemed to be growing and then shrinking. *I'll prove to them I don't belong here.* Climbing out of bed, I ran to the nurses' station. "I am having brain seizures," I cried, "Won't you help me?"

"You really shouldn't be out of bed," the disinterested nurse sighed. "Now, why don't you be a good girl, turn around and go back to your room. I'll be there in a minute with some medicine the doctor left to calm you."

I pleaded with her to listen to me and get the doctor. She turned a deaf ear. Then, I told her to forget the medicine.

"I don't need that type of medicine."

I headed back to my room.

Things seemed to be going from bad to worse. First, I was flat on my back. Waves of pain hit me. As the pain intensified I began curling myself up, grabbing at my knees, and then releasing my grip. As abruptly as it started, it stopped.

Surprised, I noted "My neck brace is gone. Why? Have I died? Who cares! Now is my chance to escape."

Before that chance arose, another doctor was on the scene. He inserted a needle into my arm, and taped it into place.

Frantically, I tried to rip the needle out, only to be stopped by the doctor.

"Why? What is it? What are you trying to do? You won't kill me without a battle," I protested. "Somehow I'll escape all this," I cried out.

Once again I was being pushed down a corridor. At one stop, someone behind me called to a doctor. I heard the name Jackie.

"Is my sister here? I need her." I scanned the hallway but she wasn't there. *Were they keeping her away on purpose?*

The table I lay on was pushed next to a wall and a curtain was drawn around it. The doctor and Steve walked in. The haze from my bedroom floated in this room also. The doctor began to speak; his voice sounded as if we were both inside a bubble.

Am I being gassed? What's wrong? Why me? Is it AIDS? I have to know. Can I trust the doctor to tell me honestly what's going on? It's worth a try. I'll start with easy questions. If his answers are convincing, I'll keep going.

"Do I have AIDS?" I asked as I interrupted the doctor.

"No. There's nothing wrong with your body. It's all in your mind," he replied.

What? I didn't believe him.

"I need Jackie. Her, I'll believe." In an attempt to satisfy my need, I began pounding my fist on the table as I yelled, "I want Jackie!"

The doctor didn't reply. He simply began to rub my temples.

"Why isn't anyone answering me?" I kept asking, tears spilling from my eyes.

I was alone. The collar was back around my neck. I couldn't seem to move very well and my back ached.

Then, someone strolled into the room. I saw an outline of a body and assumed it was the doctor. "I'm sinking," I gasped. He didn't reply. Instead, he ran his fingers up and down my spine. When he reached a certain spot on my neck, he stopped and pressed hard against it as he asked, "What do you feel?"

Every fiber of my being raced as I replied sarcastically, "Adrenaline." Then I fainted.

Coming to again, a doctor was rubbing my temples

and asking, "Did you have your seatbelt on in the accident?"

What accident?

"Yes," I replied as if it was the toughest word in the world to pronounce. *Why did I say that? I wasn't sure it was true.*

Then he asked, "Can you tell me what happened in the accident?" I squinted my eyes and opened my mouth to speak.

Rubbing my chin I replied, "I have no idea."

My response seemed to please him, "It's better if you don't."

"Look," I protested. "I'm in terrible pain. Something is terribly wrong. Just tell me what it is. I can deal with it. It's not knowing that's so awful."

"Perhaps it's all in your mind," he said in a Buddha-like voice.

"The hell it is!" I yelled, grabbing at his shirt to shake some sense in him. I clawed at him with my nails. He broke away, running out of the room.

Escaping became my major goal. Finally, I got up and shakily made my way to the building exit. I stood there, looking out at the sun-filled world, debating whether or not to risk the chance of running. It was an easy decision. I opened the door and walked right out. As I headed down the sidewalk, I heard someone call my name. Pausing, I looked back. It was the woman in the white coat. I hesitated and she caught up with me. "Stop trying to kill me," I said. "Get me some help." She took me by the arm and propelled me back inside.

Wrenching my arm back I headed for freedom again. This time I almost made it to the end of the sidewalk before I was cornered—by the same woman. She took hold of my arm again and began to cajole me. As we walked, she told me there was someone who wanted to talk with me in another part of the hospital building around the corner. Then, an ambulance halted in front of us and we stopped walking.

Two burly attendants came from the front of the ambulance to help me get in. The woman followed while I protested, "I don't want to." But they propelled me inside, and the doors began to close. "I have to get out of here." I tried, but they held me back. After driving a short distance, we stopped. The two men took hold of my arms and helped me out of the ambulance, but kept tight grips on my arms. "What? Where are we going? Why? I don't want to go with you," I yelled. I began to struggle to free myself from them. They only tightened their grips as they quickened their pace. Soon, my feet weren't even touching the ground, I continued to struggle and scream.

They carried me into a red brick building. We traveled down a long corridor before we stopped in front of a door. Plastered on the wall was a poster which read "You are living in the Ninth Ward. Today is Saturday, December 12, 1987. The season is Fall."

While the two men held me, the woman stepped in front of us. She unlocked the door and opened it only long enough for the men to literally throw me in. I felt as if I was flying. I was barely inside when the door closed as quickly as it had opened. I had no idea where I was or why. I rattled the door. It was locked.

Then I panicked. Shrieking in horror I crouched to my knees screaming, "Noooooo! Noooooo!" It was a combination of fright, anger, and confusion. My high-pitched cries echoed through the building as I backed away from the door.

"My God, help me!" Turning, my spine was like a jellyfish. I lost all balance, and toppled to the floor.

THREE

I must have passed out. I woke shuddering, still crumpled on the floor. My head throbbed, my heart vibrated like a leaf. I forced myself to look around. The room was almost bare, the only furniture was a worn iron cot, two scarred wooden chairs, and a small dresser. My eyes searched for the window from which disconnected bits of light darted across the floor. When I found it, I gasped. Across the window stretched iron bars.

I tried to raise myself off the floor, but my body felt as if it belonged to a ninety-year-old woman. And, my God, how my head throbbed! Finally, I got myself up and managed a few steps before my legs began to weaken and I let myself fall where I was. I couldn't stand the pain of moving another inch.

Am I becoming paralyzed? I moved my hand to the back of my neck. *It feels funny.* I rubbed it.

I massaged my legs, hoping that would make them feel better. As I did, I noticed how swollen they were. "I don't understand," I whispered. Tears began to stream down my face.

Although the massage was somewhat soothing, when I tried to stand I couldn't bend my knees in order to pick myself up.

Frozen with fear I remained sitting on the floor. After

about fifteen minutes, my legs began to feel better and I managed to stand. My head beat with a rhythm of its own.

I was standing and listening to my name being called. I looked behind me. There was no one there. To my right, a silhouette of a man appeared. Standing in the middle of the open doorway, the man called to me.

"May I come in, Fran?"

My mouth dropped.

"You can trust me," he said.

I wouldn't budge. He came in, leaving the door open. He positioned the two chairs directly inside the door frame. He called.

"Come on over, Fran. You can sit right here and we'll talk."

He was convincing.

"This better not be a trick," I said, as I headed over to the chair and sat down.

Side by side we sat there. He started off by telling me his name: Dr. Irving. My heart was racing. I needed a soothing drink to calm me down.

"Can I have a glass of milk?"

Dr. Irving called to someone to bring me a glass of milk. When it arrived, I gulped half before realizing it wasn't doing any good. So I asked for a glass of cranberry juice.

"Maybe it's my bladder," I said.

When it arrived, I quickly drank some and realized it wasn't working either. Next, I asked for a glass of orange juice. It didn't do the trick either, so I placed it with the others on the floor. I began to ask for something else when I was interrupted by Dr. Irving.

"But, Fran, you already have quite a collection of drinks."

"None of them work," I replied.

The instant I said this he began calling for a glass of

water. *Why does he want me to drink water?* Even though my better judgment warned me against it, I slowly drank the liquid and, to my surprise, I felt calmer.

Then, Dr. Irving began to talk in a soothing tone.

"Won't you walk around the room with me now?"

I hesitated for a moment, then got up to go with him. In the center of the room, I stopped and looked back at the door.

"It's not closed yet," I said.

"That's right," he nodded and brought me over to a bed.

"This is *your* bed, Fran."

I looked back at the door. *Still not closed.*

He brought me over to a dresser.

"This is *your* dresser, Fran."

I wasn't replying to anything he said. I only kept my eye on that door. He opened a drawer.

"This is *your* comb."

I asked, frightened, "Is the door closed yet?"

"This is *your* bathroom," he said. We were almost back to the door and it wasn't closed. Dr. Irving picked up the two chairs and moved them further into the room and sat down. I followed.

"See, you can trust me," he said.

"I don't," I said trembling.

As we sat there, my stomach began to growl. "Could I have something to eat?" I asked timidly.

"How long has it been since you've eaten?" he asked.

I couldn't remember. I didn't even know what time it was or, for that matter, what day. I made no reply, but heard him call for a tray anyway. They put it on a table right nearby. I scurried over to it and began to wolf it down.

"Everything tastes like bananas. Why?" I asked him. He shook his head. As I placed my fork down, out of the corner of my eye I caught the movement of someone lumbering toward me through the door. Looking in that direction I withdrew in panic.

There stood a girl with a helmet on her head held in place by straps under her chin. She carried a doll in her arms. She was short and fat. Her eyes were slanted upward, but you could tell they shouldn't have been. She came closer. Her walk was a lopsided gait and one arm flung loosely. Utter nonsense was spewing out of her mouth.

"Get away from me," I yelled.

As I screamed, I dropped the tray. Its contents scattered over the floor.

I began to cry.

"Don't worry, Frances. It was just an accident. We can get you another," Dr. Irving said softly.

My eyes were on the girl. Near hysterics, I cried out, "Get away from me!"

Dr. Irving motioned to the girl to leave.

"I don't belong here," I cried out.

Dr. Irving came to my side. "I'm sorry about that. She only wanted to be your friend."

"What happened to her?" I asked.

"She was in a car accident. She's never been the same since," he replied.

"A car accident! That's what I had. Is that going to happen to me?"

He shook his head. "No, Frances, it isn't."

I leaned over to get closer to Dr. Irving and asked, "Can I take a shower and brush my teeth?"

"You can take a shower, but you can't brush your teeth," he said.

Why? I wondered, but I didn't ask him.

Dr. Irving called out a name and a short, plump, Hispanic-looking woman walked in. I turned away from her.

"I don't need her."

He turned to me and said, "She'll have to go to the showers with you."

"How humiliating. How embarrassing. I don't want her to go. I can do it myself," I pleaded.

"If she doesn't go, you can't take a shower," he said in return.

I had no choice. I was dying for a shower; she'd have to go. I was given a single towel, almost the size of a hand towel, soap, shampoo, and conditioner. With this in hand, the woman and I headed for the showers.

I was expecting a nice, hot, soothing shower. When the shower room door opened, my hopes for this diminished. I saw before me a hand-held, fake shower head. The water drizzled down, drop by drop, and was lukewarm.

Slowly, I tried to bathe my body. When I finished, the woman started to check me over. She started with my mouth and made her way down.

"Why am I going through this?" I asked miserably.

In spite of the shower, I didn't feel as good as I hoped. My head still hurt and I was lethargic.

"What's wrong with me?" I asked the attendant. She didn't reply. I was still determined to find out where I was and why. I made my way down the hallway, at the end of which stood Dr. Irving.

Just the person I wanted to see, I thought.

I was three-fourths of the way to him when he commented, "You look much better." Determined to go straight to the heart of the matter, I ignored his comment.

But, before I had a chance to ask my first question, Dr. Irving took control of the situation and led me back to my room.

"We're going to keep this door unlocked now, Frances," he said patronizingly, as if he were talking to an errant child.

"Look," I said to Dr. Irving once we were inside. "I'm terribly ill. I know this isn't a regular hospital. You have to tell me where I am and why."

His eyes were fixed on me.

"This is First Memorial Hospital. We have placed you in a section for those who are emotionally ill."

"But I'm not emotionally ill," I interrupted.

"We believe you are," Dr. Irving said firmly. "That is why you are here."

"I know my legal rights," I insisted. "You can't keep me here."

Without replying, Dr. Irving excused himself, saying he had other patients to see.

I walked over to the bed and lay down, afraid to close my eyes in case they locked the door again. Thoughts were leaping through my mind. I couldn't lie there anymore. I got up and headed out the door.

On the wall, just as I remembered, was the poster which read "You are living in the Ninth Ward." Now it said, "Today is Saturday, December 12, 1987. The season is Fall."

My eyes filled with tears.

"I don't belong here," I said vehemently.

Looking down the hall, I spotted a telephone and breathed a sigh of relief. Rushing over, I picked it up and, using my credit card number, I dialed my parents' home number. The phone was ringing . . . one . . . twice . . . half a dozen times. No one was answering. Finally, the answering tape came on. Disheartened, I left a message and hoped they would understand.

Then, I went back to my room.

As I lay on the bed, my head continued to throb nonstop. Tears filled my eyes. *Maybe I am crazy*, I thought despairing. I fell asleep with this last thought.

At six o'clock the next morning, Dr. Irving awakened me.

"Your mother and sister Eileen are here," he said grimly. "I've spent the last hour trying to convince them you ought to remain here, in isolation, for your own good. But they insist on taking you out."

"I'm saved," I said gratefully, as my sister Eileen

walked in followed by Mother. They stared at me with round, disbelieving eyes.

"Mom," I sobbed, sitting up. "Mom, why am I here?"

Mother walked over to the bed and took my arm.

"Come on, Baby. Come on. We're going home."

____F_OUR____

N ever had my house or family looked so good to me. I was so glad to be there. For the first few days, my parents, my sisters, Eileen and Connie (who came by to visit all the time), and I adopted a holiday mentality. We spent all our time asking how it all could have happened and rejoicing in just being back together again.

But, after this short interval, as usually happens with most families, our everyday problems returned with a nagging intensity.

"Please, don't stay upstairs in your room all the time, Fran," my mother pleaded.

"Mom, please," I pleaded back. It never dawned on me that everyone else in my family now thought I might be retreating to my room to contemplate suicide. Of course, I didn't pay attention to the signals.

Sure, I knew how worried they all were. Especially now. The breakup of my engagement, losing my job, the accident, my recent frightening hospitalization. The stress points were enough to permanently traumatize anyone. But even though this was the case, I felt I was strong enough emotionally to overcome it all and get back to my normal self.

After all, I had always been considered stable, resilient, and happy-spirited. My parents and teachers called

me "a golden girl"—always striving to please, always obedient. I loved life and at only twenty-five, was tall, attractive, and had a college degree. Though my ex-fiancé constantly pointed out that I was overprotected, daddy's and
mommy's little girl, I was considered to have a lot going for
me, more than most.

Still, as the days passed, I felt more and more miserable. In the mornings, I could not get out of bed and would
sleep all day. When I finally did get up, I didn't want to see
anyone.

Then I—not to mention my family—started to notice
behavioral changes. My "entertaining personality" seemed
to be undergoing a complete 180-degree change. My
brother, who lived in New York (but called regularly), began referring to me as a total bitch. I had no idea what
caused these changes, but I knew I hated the feeling and
had to do something about it.

One day, while smiling into a mirror, I noticed one of
my back teeth was getting black. Ordinarily, a visit to the
dentist would solve the problem—not this time. I became
hysterical, sobbing as if my best friend had just died. This
was not me. I kept telling myself, *Get a grip, Fran. Get a
grip.* I tried to believe what everyone, including myself, was
saying: "In time this will pass; time heals all wounds."

Then it happened—my ex-fiancé, Steve, called. He
wanted to see me that day. I was overjoyed, yet petrified.
We went to dinner, where we both apologized with tears
flowing down our faces. I felt almost normal again. The
way our words flowed made my hopes reach an all-time
high. I knew in my heart right then that it would only be a
matter of time before I became Mrs. Steven Sanders. That
night, I slept better than I had in months.

For the next few days, I floated around in a marvelous
and beautiful daydream. I was in seventh heaven but, best
of all, I was Fran again. Days later, reality struck. Steve
hadn't called. *Why not?* I kept wondering. *Was he afraid my
parents would answer?* I knew they hated him.

Our relationship had been rocky and sometimes

Steve's temper exploded. He had even slapped me a few times and my parents knew it. I still cared about him. I began calling him. Every time I tried, there was either no answer or he wasn't home. My emotions were doing flip-flops. *Why isn't he calling? Why?* I felt myself sinking again.

More than a week passed and still no phone call. During each day of that week, I regressed further back toward the chaotic state of mind I had just conquered.

"This is beneath you, Fran," my sister Eileen heatedly told me. Not only had I begun dwelling on my broken engagement, but other strange occurrences happened as well.

My body seemed to be changing. Standing up, I couldn't keep my balance. My fingers and knees were weak and stiff at the joints. My eyes couldn't focus. My throat was dry and constricted, I would constantly put my hand over it to be sure I could still swallow. When I mentioned all this to my parents or sisters, they laughed and said, "You look fine to me."

All kinds of thoughts about what was wrong with me passed through my head. I knew one thing, it was more than depression over Steve. Still, there was no doubt that I felt his loss acutely. Christmas was coming; the first in six years without Steve.

It was tough putting thoughts of Steve aside to concentrate on myself, but I knew I must. My frightening hospitalization was over, but my fearful symptoms were growing. That very afternoon, I called my doctor and set up an appointment for the first available date—a week and a half away.

"It can't be anything serious," I murmured to myself. "Probably just my diet."

That night, I decided to heal myself and surprise the doctor by changing my old diet and becoming a healthy person. I was a picker, not an eater. I didn't balance my foods, often eating just meat one day and only fruit the next.

Several minutes later, I announced to no one in particular, "I'll go shopping and buy the most nutritious food." I decided to go right away, even though it was one o'clock in the morning. There was a twenty-four hour grocery store only a mile away.

The late hour didn't bother me. It was the best feeling in the world, knowing I was going to solve all my problems. I overflowed with energy.

When I reached the top of the stairs I heard my mother yell, "Where are you going?"

Do I dare tell her? I wondered. *No.*

"For a walk, I can't sleep," I yelled back.

At the grocery store, I could see no one other than the stock boys and cashiers. I picked up a handbasket and started shopping.

"Produce first, it has to be fresh," I mumbled. The basket overflowed as I filled it in the produce department.

"This will never do," I said to myself.

Then I got a bigger cart. Now, I was ready to conquer the entire store. My next stop was the dairy section, where I checked every expiration date to ensure freshness.

Next, I rummaged up and down every aisle, pulling more and more things off the shelves. The more I bought, the freer I felt. It was the best feeling in the world, one I had never experienced before. Wanting to keep the mood going, I grabbed additional packages. As I pushed the cart down the aisles, I danced like a ballerina.

Finally, I decided I had enough food and made my way to the checkout area. I was satisfied with all my purchases except the cheeses, three different kinds hardly seemed enough. *Perhaps I should go back and get some more?* I thought. I quickly rejected this idea, the cashier had started to ring up my order.

As I leaned over the basket to put the last few items on the counter, a prickling sensation spread throughout my body. It was strangely pleasant and I stayed bent-over the cart to enjoy the feeling. Even after the sensation faded, I kept leaning and started laughing hysterically because I felt so great. Rather begrudgingly, I stood up straight to place the last item on the check-out belt.

Simultaneously, with a huge smile across my face, I yelled, "I'm free!"

I was unaware of my surroundings until the cashier totalled my purchases, which came to one hundred and thirty dollars. Without blinking an eye, I paid the bill and danced off.

Back home, I put everything away. With a feeling of self-satisfaction, I went to bed. As soon as I was back under the covers, I realized that I had forgotten the most important item—olive oil. "Olive oil is healthier than vegetable oil. I have to have it!" I said out loud. Once again I was in action.

Outside of my room stood my mother. "Where are you going?" she asked.

"To the store," I replied.

"Well, why don't you tell your father that? He's worried," She demanded.

"I'm in too much of a hurry to stop," I said.

I did not go to his room. In order to get to the store as fast as possible, I yelled out my destination while heading down the stairs.

Back at the store, I decided to pick up more cheese, along with the olive oil. I made my way to the dairy case, where I stood staring, unable to make up my mind. Finally, I grabbed one of each kind.

"There, this should last us awhile."

Dancing my way to the aisle containing oil, I did a pirouette in front of the shelves. I grabbed a gallon of the best olive oil. This was an easy decision. I had to shuffle everything around to carry it all, and used my chin to steady the top items.

As I passed the produce section, my eye was caught by the tangerines, kiwis, and other exotic fruit. "I must have some of this," I decided. Staring at each different kind, I wanted them all; but I couldn't carry everything and settled for a few fruits.

Then, a voice from behind asked if I needed help. I turned to see a tall, hairy man in a red-print sports shirt. I didn't reply to his question, merely shot him a sideward glance and trotted off to the checkout counter. I looked back only once and he was there. Then I got in line and the man was there right behind me.

I began trembling. *Is he going to follow me outside and attack me?* I wondered.

"That will be forty-six seventy-two, ma'am. That'll be forty-six seventy-two, ma'am. Ma'am, ma'am, ma'am!" the checker said.

"Ma'am, please," the checker implored, looking at me strangely. Then she asked me if I was worried about having enough money. I didn't reply. I kept looking at the man behind me.

"Ma'am, you're holding up the line," she rather abruptly stated.

"What does she mean?" I wondered. "She just finished my order."

Another voice from behind offered to pay my bill.

I paid the cashier and left, making it to my car with no problem. While I was putting the groceries in the trunk, a car drove slowly by and stopped directly behind me. The same man popped his head out of the window. I froze where I stood.

"Oh, shit!" I mumbled, "Trouble."

Shaking his head, he wished me a Merry Christmas and drove off. I got into my car and drove home.

By the time I finished putting my latest purchase away, the refrigerator was packed solid; so were the freezer, the cupboards, and the counters.

I walked upstairs as quiet as a mouse. Even more silently, I opened my bedroom door. I looked down, saw someone in the bed, and jumped backwards one mile. It was my mother.

"What are you doing here?" I asked.

She shook her head, "Oh my God, Fran. What is the matter with you? Are you crazy or something?" She ran out of the room.

I passed my hands over my head and face while these

questions kept running through my mind. Involuntarily, more thoughts surfaced. *Why does everyone hate me? Why did Steve maltreat me? Why isn't my life any good?*

My heart was beating faster and my hands were pulling harder and harder at my hair. I was completely lost. I thought about my new health kick and forgot my mother's words. Then my thoughts changed mid-stream and I ran downstairs to the kitchen to recheck my purchases.

My mother and father were waiting for me. "What is all this?" my mother exclaimed, staring at the food piled everywhere. I didn't say anything. Besides, it wasn't a real question.

I wondered why they were up so early; it was five-thirty. This meant I had spent four and a half hours in the grocery store! It didn't seem that long.

All three of us were standing in the kitchen in complete silence. My father was the first to speak, "Are you crazy? We can't afford all this expensive stuff."

Next, it was mother's turn, "You're taking it all back now!" Without stopping for a breath, she rushed to the phone and made a call. When she returned, she told me, "I just got off the phone with the store. I said that you bought groceries for me that I can't use, and I want you to return them. Right now!"

I couldn't get a word in. I turned and left, steaming. "It was a gift," I called back.

I walked into the store ashamed and embarrassed. I had to wait until someone came in who could handle the return. Standing at the end of a register with my head hung low, I leaned on the cart. My eyes felt as if they were sinking deep into my head. Everything was covered with a mist, as if in a dream. It didn't seem as if I were really there. I was standing at the beginning of a tunnel watching what happened at the other end. Finally, the assistant arrived and I returned the groceries.

I didn't want to go back home, but did. An intense argument, with my shopping as the highlight, broke out the instant I set foot into the foyer.

My mother pulled me down the hall and told me, "I'm furious."

"Why?" I objected.

An eerie silence filled the small room. I started to say something but she cut me off. "Frances, just be quiet please."

More silence. Then moaning noises came from my father, in the kitchen. These steadily grew louder. He was repeating over and over, in a high-pitched cry, "What's happening to my daughter? She was always such a perfect child. So caring, so obedient. I can't stand this anymore."

My eyes and ears bolted into complete awareness. My body started shaking. "What's wrong? I don't understand," I said running up the stairs to my room.

"Neither do we," my mother called.

Even though I tried to attribute all my health and emotional problems to diet, other troubling things were happening as well. I found myself saying the first thing that popped into my head, no matter what the question. I walked around in a complete daze, never replying to questions, or, for that matter, even hearing them. I wasn't doing it intentionally. I seemed to have no control.

Things were getting steadily worse. My parents, who couldn't understand how I was acting or why, were constantly picking on me, "Get a job, Fran. Get on with your life, Fran." These comments only aggravated the already unstable condition I was experiencing.

All I wanted was to concentrate on one thing: to feel better. Everything else would just have to wait. But my parents couldn't seem to understand how sick I felt, how miserable about everything that had just happened. Moreover, I didn't need the added confusion their demands created for me.

I tried to explain that I needed to get my health straight before I tackled another job or began a new life.

But, because they were agonizing about me, my explanations fell on deaf ears. We had gotten along well before, now we argued even over petty things. Moreover, I felt a sense of constant guilt and so did they; because, though they loved me, they had always been overprotective of me, and I was a subservient child.

One evening, as I walked away from still another angry exchange, my emotions suddenly aboutfaced from the complete furor that I'd felt only a few minutes before. I thought of how grateful I should be to both my parents for everything they had done for me. I turned, marched right up to my father and blurted out:

"Dad, I love you and I appreciate everything you and Mom have done and are doing for me."

When I finished, I walked away quickly and sat back down on the couch. In my mind, a whole conversation had taken place. I had won my father over and now he would be able to see things my way. While I sat there, I grew more and more dissatisfied with all the flare-ups that transpired. *Something more has to be done, although I'll have to think about it.*

I decided a walk would be the perfect thing to help me think. Up I got and off I went without saying a word to anyone. I ended up walking to my sister Connie's house. Upon my arrival, I had forgotten why I wanted to go there in the first place. *This isn't like me. I've always had a memory like an elephant.* I reassured myself by thinking, *It's just my diet and, when I fix that, my memory will be in prime shape.* I had to say something, so I started to talk to Connie about the letters I had been writing to Steve.

Her only comment about this was, "Is Mom intercepting them?"

This thought was rather disturbing to me.

"How dare she?" I said.

Then Connie replied, "Why don't you just ask Mom?"

Within seconds of this suggestion, I was out the door and on my way home to question my mother. She was in bed when I got there. I didn't care. I marched right up to my parents' room and flung the door open.

I blurted out in an inquisitive, demanding tone, "Mom, are you intercepting my letters to Steve?"

She was shocked. Her eyes opened wide; there was stuttering and, before she had a chance to reply, I slammed the door and was gone.

Back in my room, I lay in bed for awhile. Again, I began to think about how much my parents had done for and given me—and what little I did to show them my appreciation. Recently, at a home interiors party, I had bought two cute wall hangings, each containing a loving phrase. Deciding these would be perfect make-up gifts, I immediately jumped out of bed and strode off to present my tokens of appreciation. Once again, I stood at their door. This time, I knocked and then went in.

Smiling from ear to ear, I proudly presented my gifts, as if they were the world's most precious gems. Along with the wall hangings, I very genuinely said, "I love you both."

My parents stared at me wordlessly, not knowing what to make of my mood swings. I didn't let their rejection faze me. I simply smiled, turned around, and walked out. By the time I reached my room again, my mind was on a brand new subject.

Though I lay down, I couldn't fall asleep. My chest hurt. And, now, I was having trouble breathing. I didn't care what anyone said, there was something wrong with me. I just didn't understand why they wouldn't help. I felt completely alone; no one would listen.

Suddenly, I knew just the right person—Steve. I could hardly wait until the next morning. But somehow I made it through the night. My parents and sisters went out food shopping.

After they left I called and let Steve's phone ring a dozen times. There was no answer. Finally, I went back to bed and fell into a troubled sleep. I did not awaken until midday, which passed uneventfully into another night.

The next morning, my headache returned. I decided to go out for a walk, reasoning that some fresh air would clear my throbbing head.

It was close to ten by the time I got home. As I walked into the house, I was praying I hadn't missed a call from Steve. I had to be the first one to answer the phone. If my parents found out it was him, they'd hang up. I couldn't have that. Luckily, no one was home.

Time passed. I must have fallen asleep and missed the call anyway, if it came at all; the next thing I remember was hearing the beeping of the smoke alarm.

My back was hurting like hell, and although I could barely move, I forced myself up. Dragging myself down the stairs, one halting step at a time, I looked around. The entire room appeared covered by haze. Reaching the kitchen telephone—and trying to remain calm—I called the fire department and got out of the house as quickly as I could. My body trembled as I escaped.

Within minutes, police cars and firefighters drove up.

"There's no sign of a fire," a tall, dark-haired fireman assured me. "The smoke alarm needs new batteries."

"Well, I'm not going back in there," I cried.

Suddenly, my head began to vibrate. I placed my hand over the back of it in an attempt to stop the vibrations.

"I'm having brain seizures," I began to cry over and over again.

One of the police officers walked up to me.

"Would you like to go to the hospital?" he questioned.

"Yes," I nodded. "Please."

I crawled into the back of the police car. I was unable to remain sitting straight; my head weighed a ton. Slowly, I slithered lower and lower, until finally, I was lying flat on my back. I didn't know where I was or where I was going.

As my head rocked from left to right, I began asking a million questions one right after another. I never received a reply. I had no idea why, I was making sense to myself. I didn't understand and started to ask even more questions about everything imaginable in an attempt to satisfy my curiosity. Still, I received no reply.

We were in a large brick building. I was standing again with no idea where I was or who the people were around me. I was only able to make out outlines of bodies. This scared me. My heart started to beat faster, adrenaline flowed, and the brain seizures returned. My head felt as if it were about to fall off. I placed my hand on the back of my neck in order to stop the seizures and keep my head in place.

As I did this, I began to pace back and forth, announcing, "My brain, my brain is exploding."

I went from person to person explaining what was happening to my head. Then, I saw my sister and mother and a packed suitcase. I ran up to them with the officer at my side.

"Sign in," my mother begged.

I didn't understand.

"Please, Fran. Just sign in."

The officer grabbed my arm. I wrenched away and headed back to the room from which I had just come. The room was full of people, just sitting there.

Where am I? What are all these people doing here? I stood leaning against the wall and stared insipidly. As suddenly as I stopped, I started up again. Starting back to the examining room, I couldn't remember which one it was.

As I went along, I stopped several times at different doors, sometimes opening them to check inside. At others, I stood in front of the door to examine it to see if it were the right one. I was in a maze. The harder I searched, the more lost I became.

Someone ran up to me and took hold of my arm. It was my sister Eileen, who led me into a tiny room with two chairs, a small table, and a bench. My head was aching.

Immediately, I laid on the bench and made myself comfortable. Eileen and my mother sat on the chairs. No one was saying anything.

"What are we doing here?" I asked Eileen.

"Waiting for the doctor," she replied.

Five minutes later, I asked again, "What are we doing here?" The same reply was given.

It wasn't too long after that I asked once more. This time both my mother and Eileen turned to me and, very methodically, replied, "We're waiting for the doctor."

I got up, took my clothes off, and replaced them with a wrinkled medical gown. Then I lay back down. My head began vibrating again.

Silence filled the room. My mother was sitting on a folding chair over in the corner crying. In the distance, sirens started going off. The shrieking sound sent tremors through my body.

Then a white-garbed doctor with a graying, aristocratic look, walked in and, in an abrupt voice, ordered my mother and Eileen to leave.

FIVE

I sat upright when the doctor started to talk. He began to fire questions at me. Elongated and misshapen words flowed to my ears. I had no idea what he was talking about. I waited impatiently for him to examine me. He never layed a single finger on me.

"I thought you're supposed to examine my head," I said angrily.

He continued to question me.

"Do you hear voices? Have you been seeing colors and strange forms? Have you seen a psychiatrist?"

I stared up at him, tears welling up in my eyes. *Obviously, he thinks I am crazy. What is the use?* I turned my head to the wall, refusing to answer. Still he kept questioning me, but I said nothing.

"I'll be right back," he said in an exasperated tone and left.

After he went out, I lay back down. I felt like there were worms in my stomach, trying to get out. I couldn't let anyone see this. I flew into the bathroom. I was afraid to look into the bowl as I sat there on the toilet. When I did dare, I discovered there was nothing there.

As I tried to make my way back to the room from which I had come, I noticed another room full of people, all of them just sitting there. *Where am I?* I thought, suddenly confused. *What are all these people doing here?* Absolutely still, I leaned against the wall and stared vacantly. As suddenly as I stopped, I started walking again, moving in the direction of the examining room.

All the doors looked the same. I couldn't remember which one I wanted. As I went along, I stopped several times at different doors. Sometimes I opened them to check inside; at other times, I just examined the door to see if it was the right one. I was in a maze. The harder I searched, the more hopelessly lost I got.

As I rounded one corner, I noticed what seemed to be the room full of people that I had seen previously. Only this time, they all had gray hair and wrinkles. Even the walls were different colors. "Time has moved without me," I murmured, "We're in the future."

As I made my way down the hallway, a girl came walking toward me. "I know her!" As she came closer, I realized it was Liz, my friend for many years. She looked older. That convinced me we were many years into the future.

When she was directly in front of me, I only asked, "What year is it?"

With a half-cocked look she replied, "1987, Fran."

"Are you okay?" I nodded.

"I'm late, gotta run. Talk to you later." She rushed on.

I was more confused now than earlier. *What's happened since I've been gone? Will I ever fit in?*

Very slowly, using the wall to feel my way, I tried to make my way back to the examining room. It was as if I was caught in a fog, a zombie in a fog. Isolated. Alone. I was feeling extremely tired and weak by this time. This made my worries of being alone disappear rather quickly and I shifted to finding a place to rest.

I continued walking until eventually I stumbled upon a row of tables lined up against a wall, one right after another, each separated with a curtain. I had no idea where I was but, at that point, I didn't care.

I had only one thing on my mind, rest. I climbed up on one of the tables and lay down. I felt as if I wasn't even there. I had no knowledge of anything or anyone being around me. My mind was out of control. Thoughts were flashing left and right.

Murmurs caught my ear, "Doctors are so scarce now, you have to wait hours to be seen. If one comes at all."

The waiting went on interminably and no one had examined my aching head. I looked around. *Maybe so many people are sick these days, they have to be lined up one right after another. Maybe my family froze my body when I died in hopes that someday they'd find a way for life to return to the dead. Maybe, I'm still frozen and they're waiting to take parts of my body.* I tried to shake off the strange thoughts which crowded into my head.

The next thing I knew, my mother and sisters were back at my side.

"I'm terribly thirsty," I said. Mother helped me off the table and began leading me somewhere. As we walked along, I saw absolutely nothing; it was as if I were asleep. Suddenly, a water fountain emerged and I stopped to try the water. It was ice cold and tasted better than any other water I had ever had. I explained this to my mother and sisters.

Mother shook her head questioningly, "Of course the water is good here. Why wouldn't it be?" She continued leading me and motioned my sisters to follow. Without realizing what I was doing, I obeyed, feeling as if there wasn't a muscle flexing or relaxing in my body. I was moving as though I were intoxicated.

We were back in the examining room. I headed to the bench once more. For some time, the room was silent even though all of us were there. This silence was disturbed suddenly when the doctor and another woman walked in.

They began to speak animatedly with my mother. Although I was close enough, I couldn't hear what was being said. Then my mother got up and left with the doctor.

When she returned, my sister Connie got up and left. After a while, Connie returned and Eileen left.

I watched all of this without ever questioning it. Though I thought to myself, *I wonder what's going on? Why aren't I included?*

When Eileen returned there was another white-coated man with her. As he entered the room, everyone else left. I didn't understand. He helped me off the table and asked me to come sit next to him. The instant I sat down he began asking me questions. Questions I didn't understand. After several "I don't know" and "huh?" replies he stopped.

Suddenly, I felt a sharp pain in my chest. I clutched at it. Along with this pain there was another sharp twinge shooting up my arm. I didn't know what was going on. I just sat there stupefied as the pain got worse. Then the vibrations in my head began. They pulsed until I began screaming, "Help, I think I'm having a heart attack."

The doctor ran into the hall. He came back with two nurses and a cart. They hooked me up to a heart monitor and took my blood pressure. When I asked them what it was their only reply was "high."

This scared me even more. "What does it mean?" I cried.

"Anxiety, probably," the doctor replied reading the monitor. They seemed to all be staring at me. I shook my head wearily. "No, it's more than that. Please, please help me," I insisted hysterically.

The doctor began to palpate my stomach. "Is it my appendix?" I asked. But he only responded that I had gas. I didn't believe him.

Then he asked if I smoked. I told him that within the last three days, I had not only smoked, but had smoked close to a carton.

He pointed out that this could be the cause of my present problems. And, if I cut down I shouldn't have this experience again. He also began to comment about the children of older Catholics. I entered my own world in the middle of his monologue, and never heard the ending.

I felt my fingers and knees coming apart at the joints. I even began to see my eyes moving in directions they had never moved before. Then my throat began to feel strange as if it were growing. I put my hand over it to feel the difference. All kinds of thoughts were going through my head as to what was wrong with me. I asked. "Is it AIDS? A thyroid disease? Is it my diet?" He kept shaking his head. "Is it my head?"

The doctor looked at me intently. "Do you have family problems?" he asked scrutinizing me.

I shook my aching head, "I don't know; we fight a lot, maybe they're all out to get me."

The doctor gave me a funny look and escorted my mother out of the room. While they were gone, the back of my head pulsed with pain. My body shook, my eyes opened wide, and my breathing became erratic. It felt like my head was going to explode. I screamed hysterically. They hurried back into the room.

"You have to help me," I pleaded.

My mother, sisters, the doctors, and a nurse gathered around me. The nurse bent over and gave me a shot.

The gray-haired doctor, who hadn't examined my head spoke, "Frances, we're going to keep you here a few days for observation," he said in that authoritarian tone I had begun to both fear and recognize.

I wanted to object but my brain seemed at a standstill. Neither my mind nor my body was working. I lay there with a distant stare, nodding. A stretcher appeared and they loaded me on it. I was already growing dizzy, sleepy.

A few hours later, I awoke in a strange bed. The room was freezing. I curled up more in the blanket. I still wasn't getting any warmer. My teeth began to chatter, my body trembled. My door was still open.

I called out to anyone within hearing distance for more blankets. There was no response. I tried again. This time, two nurses came rushing into the room. "I can't get warm. I need more blankets," I stuttered.

"It's over seventy in here," one nurse said to the other.

"Hypothermia," was her response.

They pulled at the blankets, changed my clothes and sheets. This all happened in a blur. I not only couldn't see very well what they were doing, but didn't understand why. *What have I done to deserve this? What's hypothermia?* When they were finished and out of the room I felt much better and was able to fall back asleep.

I wasn't asleep very long before I was awakened by the vibrations in my head. They were growing stronger and stronger as I lay there. My head was pounding. I pushed the button beside my bed and called into the speaker.

"Please, I really am having brain seizures. Won't you help me?"

"We'll be in in a minute," answered a monotone voice.

I began to plead with her to listen to me and call the doctor. A few minutes later, she appeared with another syringe and—over my objections—she plunged the needle into my arm.

At six the next morning, I woke and began to stare at the room around me. My head ached. *Where the hell am I?* I thought fearfully. I remembered, the hospital. They were going to help me.

I tried to calm myself. Shakily, I sat up on the side of the bed, trying to orient myself. The first thing I did was feel my head—it was normal to my touch. *How does it look?* I wondered. Slowly, I crept out of bed and made my way to the dresser. Holding onto the furniture for steadiness, I looked into the mirror. My head appeared normal.

I tried to relax and scrutinized the room. It looked bare except for the bed, a night table, and tray table.

I was interrupted by a nurse who held out a menu for me. "Order breakfast. Circle each item you want," she said.

I put the list on the dresser top and started to read it. All the words started to move together. I couldn't decipher any of it. *Should I say something?* I wondered. I decided against it. I simply made circles every once in awhile. Without saying anything, I handed the menu over to the nurse.

"Could I take a shower?" I asked.

"Not until after breakfast," she said. "I'll be back to get you." Something in the way she said it sent shivers up my spine, as I was reminded of my last hospitalization.

I waited until she left and made my way to the door. Looking outside I saw the sign. My God, I was back in Ward Nine. I began screaming and crying and frantically pushed the call button.

The nurse reappeared. "You'll have to behave yourself," she said sternly, "or you won't go home for Christmas."

SIX

"**W**on't go home for Christmas," the words echoed in my ears. *What did she mean? What was happening to me? Why had they put me here? Was this punishment for something I'd done?*

Thoughts of the summer's events began to flash through my mind. I began to babble without being able to stop myself. "The time Steve slapped me and I called the police. Maybe this all has something to do with Steve," I murmured. "He's getting revenge."

"Maybe it has nothing to do with Steve." I shook my head.

"Maybe it's my family. It could be that my sister Connie is getting revenge because of the fights we've had." The last one had sent the family into an uproar. "Maybe my whole family hates me." I began shaking again.

The nurse stood at the door and watched me, impatiently tapping her fingers against the papers she held.

I became angry and was ready to say something to her; I stopped myself in time, and she left a short while later.

Over the loudspeaker, breakfast was called. I had no idea where it was being served. Slipping out my door, I decided to wait and see what direction everyone else was taking. I couldn't ask; what if I had already done this? I had to appear normal.

I waited, and observed the people passing. "There's the girl with the helmet. That's what I'm going to look like." Shivers went up my spine with this thought. Then a few people started walking down the hallway and turned into a room at the end. "This has to be breakfast," I murmured.

I followed them into a small room; two carts were piled high with trays. Each cart was accompanied by a man calling out last names with every tray he picked up. I waited in line while listening, "Sloan, Hagen, Andrews, Von Bueren, Deitrick." *That's me. What do I do?*

I copied what everyone else did and walked into the dining room. At the entrance I stood searching, deciding where to sit. Most of the people were elderly, and most looked straggly, unkempt, and unbathed.

I sat down at a table by myself, lifted the cover off the tray and laughed. My breakfast consisted of pepper, cold cereal, hot water, and a fork! I placed the cover back on the tray and sat there disdainfully. *This can't be happening. There's nothing wrong with me.*

Noticing a lunch menu at my side, I decided to give this one a try. It wasn't much easier to read than the breakfast menu had been; somehow, though, I managed. As I replaced the menu, a dark-haired man with spittle on his chin made his way over to my table and sat down. Unable to speak, I sat there with a blank stare on my face, not knowing how to get rid of him. *What does he want?* I wondered.

He looked as though he hadn't slept, taken a bath, or shaved in weeks. He began to eat his breakfast in silence. The food dribbled out of his mouth as fast as he was shoveling it in. It was running down his face and onto his shirt. I felt sick to my stomach and left.

Back in my room, I lay down on the bed. Soon enough

I grew bored with this and decided to explore my new domicile. A tour of the hallways convinced me it wasn't much. There was one floor, a locked room, a reading room, a television room, a room with nothing but chairs in it, the showers, cafeteria, and a laundry room.

Ending my search, I went back to my room to rest. The day dwindled away as I laid there. I felt terrified. I moved only out of necessity to use the bathroom. At the end of the day a nurse came in to tell me I had a phone call. *Someone is going to save me,* I thought with tear-filled eyes.

It was Connie. She did all the talking. I didn't understand. She told me they were trying to get me out of there and into a private psychiatric hospital.

"Why do I need to go there?" I pleaded. "What are you doing to me? There's nothing wrong with my mind. Why do I need a mental hospital? I need a medical doctor," I insisted.

"You can't get out of there unless you go to the other place, we're trying to help you," she said. I still didn't understand, but I told her I'd go if it got me out of here.

"It'll be a few days before all the arrangements are made. Hold on until then," she added and hung up.

What was she talking about? Why had she started to hate me? Didn't I have a family anymore? I was too nervous to rest. Instead of going back to my room, I went into the reading room and thumbed through their selection of books. There wasn't much and I decided to try something else.

I shuffled from room to room. Some were filled to capacity with strange-looking patients. There was no way I'd go into one of them; the people scared me. They were just sitting with wild expressions, some curled up in corners. Other rooms were empty and forbidding. I tried not to think about what went on in them and headed back to my room.

Lunch came and went. My selections weren't so bad this time and I was starved. I ate every drop. After lunch, I heard they'd be letting us make cookies soon. "Something to do," I murmured enthusiastically.

I was one of the first to smear my hands in flour. Several others joined. Nothing much was said and no one else knew how to make cookies. I became frustrated with their ignorance and went back to my room. *I don't belong here.*

Hours passed as I stared at the ceiling trying not to think of my surroundings. I was merely existing. The clock struck nine. I thanked God, at least now I had something to do, I could go to sleep.

Later that night, I woke up freezing once again. The vibrations were back also. I wrapped one of my heavy blankets around my head in an attempt to gain both warmth and to stop the vibrations. Then I began to feel as if I were shrinking. My stomach started churning, it felt as if I was about to lose everything in it.

I pressed the call button and cried for help. While I waited for the nurse, my eyes started moving. I couldn't control myself. I thought I was dying from lack of air. A thin, blonde nurse arrived.

"I don't feel good," I said breathlessly. "I'll take the doctor's medicine." She nodded, left, and returned within a few minutes.

"There's your pill," she said. "But first, tell me how you feel." She looked like she couldn't have cared less. And I thought, *if I tell them, they'll never let me go.*

"I just don't feel good," I said slowly.

"Well, sit up and take the pill," she intoned.

I couldn't move. "Could you put the pill in my hand instead?" I asked haltingly. I reached up with my hand to take the pill. As she was putting the pill in my hand, it slipped through my fingers.

"Listen," she said, "you did that on purpose so you could hide it. I have to account for that pill and I want it back right now."

"What are you saying?" I asked in tears. "I didn't do that. I just don't feel good, I want to take the pill. I don't know where it is." She left.

When she returned, she was accompanied by a portly nurse wearing her hair in a bun. She came to my side.

"Now Ms. Deitrick, give that pill back." I gave her the same response. "Get out of that bed," she ordered. "We're going to perform a search."

"Please don't make me get up, I'm feeling awful." My words were to no avail. They picked me up and removed me from the bed. That done, the fat nurse went over and slammed the door. My terror returned. They tore the bed apart, checking every nook and cranny, but could find no pill.

"Get undressed right now," the portly nurse commanded.

Tears spilled down my cheeks. "I didn't do anything," I pleaded.

"If you don't strip in one helluva hurry, we'll bring someone in who can do it for you," she threatened.

"Who?" I asked, beginning to undress. They performed a thorough search, and yet, no pill. They left. I crawled back to the bed, sobbing, *"Why me!"*

I couldn't fall back to sleep, I was wound up so tightly that my neck spasmed. This added tremendously to the pain and suffering I was already experiencing. Then my mind started to play tricks on me. I thought I saw Steve walk in. The walls started to move in and out.

Finally, the bed began to move up and down. I thought there was someone underneath waiting to get me. I was lost within myself. The bones in my feet began to ache. I placed them up against the wall. *Elevation will do them good.* My feet began walking the wall, the bottom half of my body eventually followed.

I lowered my self back down and then began to repeat the process. I did this several times, not intentionally, it was happening on its own. Finally, my entire body was laying flat on the bed and I fell asleep.

Early the next morning, the blonde nurse came into my room to take my blood pressure. I wouldn't let her touch me. *I can't trust anyone around here anymore.* After she left, I tried to get out of bed to use the bathroom. My head weighed a ton, I had no strength in my arms or legs. I gave up trying. Then I felt a strong urge to urinate.

I rolled myself out of bed and slowly made my way to the bathroom. When I opened the door, I received the shock of my life. There stood a man, closing his zipper. He was tall and thin with a gaunt look. He grinned when he saw me, exposing his toothless mouth.

I slammed the door closed, leaning up against it. *What's he doing in my bathroom?* I didn't have the energy to inquire into this, so I stood there waiting. After some time had passed, I opened the door a crack to find out what was going on. He wasn't there anymore! *Where did he go?*

I sauntered over to the toilet. *I know he was here.* I surveyed the entire room, trying to reassure myself. *Don't worry about it, Frances. Use the bathroom and get out of here.* I made sure I never touched the seat. *He may have had AIDS*, I thought. I went back to bed and laid down.

The distinguished doctor who had interviewed me in the examining room came in, grabbed a chair, and sat down alongside my bed.

"I'm Doctor Holden," he said. "How are you this morning?" he asked.

"Fine. How are you?" was my response. *How could I find out about the man I had seen?* "Can anyone use my bathroom who wants to?" I asked.

"No. The only other person who uses this bathroom is in the connecting room," he responded.

"I wasn't imagining that awful man," I said. "I have to share my bathroom with somebody like that?" He changed the subject.

"You know you'll be leaving us tomorrow," he said.

"I get to go home?" I questioned.

"No, your family has decided you would be better off at a private facility called Brookhollow. I told you you'd only be here a few days," he said.

"Can't I leave tomorrow and go home?" I asked.

"No. You can't leave tomorrow unless you go to

Brookhollow. But you'll go there as a voluntary patient,"
was his response.

"What does it mean, a voluntary patient? What am I
now?"

He got up, pushed the chair aside and said, "I'll see
you later."

As I left my room for lunch, I ran straight into a man
who looked exactly like Burt Reynolds. He demanded I sit
down in the chair to have my blood pressure taken. I sat
down. He reached to take hold of my wrist. I jerked it back.
What's he going to do to me?

In a soft gentle voice he said, "Everything will be all
right. I only want to take your blood pressure." I let him
hold my wrist. Then he went to take my purse which was
clutched under my arm. I snatched it first and held it
tightly to my chest.

"I have to put it in the office," he said, taking my
blood pressure and letting me go.

After lunch, I wandered the halls for what seemed like
hours. I ended up back on my bed. *This is ridiculous. How
did I get here? It's almost Christmas. I should be shopping.
Why are they keeping me here?* I got up again and went to
the door to stare out the window. *The next best thing to
being outside.* As I stood there, Dr. Holden came to my side.

"What are you thinking about?" he asked.

"I'd tell you if I was out there," I said glancing out the
window. "I'd feel much better out there," I added as tears
began to run down my face.

"Why don't you tell me what's on your mind," Dr.
Holden suggested.

Immediately thoughts popped into my mind.

"I thought this all happened because of the accident
but now I think it's my family. They're out to get me.
They're controlling me. I hate them. I don't want to go to
Brookhollow. I don't want to be here. They do! There's
nothing wrong with me. They're punishing me. Don't you
understand?"

"You don't want to go to Brookhollow?" he asked.

Is he going to keep me here? "I want to go. No, I don't. Yes, I do. I don't know!" I replied, "anyway, it's my own damn business where I go and who I go with. They don't want me with Steve. They're keeping me here so I don't see Steve." I returned to staring out the window. He stayed right at my side.

Soon enough, I was back lying on the bed. I couldn't wait for tomorrow to come. I would be able to forget about this place. *Someone would believe me at the new hospital, someone would help me.* I held tightly to that hope and fell asleep and slept straight through until the next morning.

Right after breakfast that day, group therapy was called. *What's that?* Everyone was gathered into a room, where we all were told to form a circle with our chairs. The lady who was directing started talking to a red-haired, freckle-faced young man on the opposite side of the room.

"Why don't you give us your name and tell us something about yourself?" she asked.

"My name is Donny, I think I kill people," was his reply.

That was all I needed to hear; I got up and headed for the door. The director tried to stop me but I was out the door before she was able to bar the way. I headed back to my room.

"These people are crazy. I don't belong here. I'm not crazy," I cried out.

The male nurse, whom I referred to as Burt, stopped me to tell me I had a phone call. It was my sister Connie again. She wanted my Social Security number and told me they would be here around four.

As soon as I was off the phone, Dr. Holden arrived. He told me I was now a privileged patient and I had a new room. He led the way to it and I was astonished. There was no heavy metal door. I noticed a huge picture window which overlooked a flower garden. I even had a roommate. My new bed was actually comfortable and the pillow was soft.

I wasn't in my new room long before I was called to

the phone once more. I went to the pay phone; however, no one was on the other end. Burt motioned me over to the phone behind the desk. *Wow, this must be important, I get to use his phone.* It was a person from admissions at Brookhollow.

"Can you tell me what happened?" he asked.

"I don't know," I replied. Confused, "I don't know why I'm here. I've tried to tell them I'm sick."

"I have some official State forms I need to fill out. I need some information from you," he interrupted. "Think for a minute," he said.

There was silence for a few minutes.

"I think I am at First Memorial. I'm not sure though."

He abruptly replied, "I'll put down disorientation and confusion," he said. Then he added, "We'll see you in a while," and hung up.

I had two hours before I would leave. I went to start packing the extra clothes my mother had brought. As soon as I was off the phone, while I was packing, a woman carrying a folder came walking into my room. She introduced herself as a social worker. *I'm not on welfare. What does she want with me?*

She began to ask all sorts of personal questions. I was annoyed but answered anyway. *If it gets me out of here faster, I'll do it.* I lay down on the bed as we were talking, placing my head on the pillow.

Suddenly, everything began to get blurry, as though I was in a dream. I could still hear the woman's voice, but I couldn't see her. I stopped responding.

As I lay there silent, I heard her say, "There's no reason why you shouldn't be out there working."

"I'm not crazy," I shouted, "why is all this happening to me? Why?"

She left and Dr. Holden entered. My mind was concentrating on the reasons why I should not be there as he approached. He stopped in the middle of the room.

"I don't want to go to Brookhollow," I forcefully

stated. "My family wants me there. They're trying to drive me crazy. There's nothing wrong with me," I added.

"All the arrangements have been made. I think it would be best if you went. Your family will be here any minute. I need you to come into my office to answer some questions," was his response.

I got up and followed him to his office. Standing at the entrance were my sisters, Eileen and Connie. They walked into the office behind us. I sat as close to Dr. Holden as I could get. Both Eileen and Connie sat across from us.

Eileen's hands were trembling as she spoke. "We think this is best for Frances. We don't know what's wrong with her," she said as her voice quivered.

"I don't think it's best for me," I screeched.

Dr. Holden cut short this outburst, "She sees this as a form of manipulation." Then he turned to me and said, "They look like a nice family to have. If you can't trust your family, who can you trust?"

I looked away. *He's on their side. He's in on it with them.* I signed some papers, picked up my suitcase, and headed for the door.

SEVEN

We had a forty-minute drive to Brookhollow ahead of us. My sisters and I gabbed as if we were on our way to a shopping mall instead of to a mental hospital. The last few days were banished from my memory and I felt happy, until we arrived at our destination, an ugly building of mottled gray stone. There were metal grates on the windows. I sat in the back seat staring at the place, horrified at the thought of having to go in.

"This is crazy," I objected, looking at both sisters. "Why are you taking me here?"

Eileen looked weary and was trembling, "We have to, Fran. That was the only way they'd release you. Look, all we want is for you to get better. We don't know what's wrong. We all have to trust the doctors."

I did everything I could think of to forestall the inevitable. Eventually we were standing at a set of double doors. We passed through the first one with no problems. The next door was locked, and we had to wait for a dark waxy-haired receptionist to open it. There was no key—she used some sort of mechanism behind her desk. I saw her lean over, then came a horrendous buzzing noise, and we were able to pass through the doorway.

We made ourselves comfortable in the waiting area.

Our silence was interrupted by the receptionist who, pointing with polished red nails in our direction, motioned us to sign in. One by one we did this.

Back in my chair, I began to feel lightheaded and my body went limp. It was as if I wasn't even there. *I'm not going to say anything, they'll think I'm crazy!* Then I began sinking into my chair. I thought I was going to hit the floor, when I was retrieved by a man's husky voice.

"I'm John Slattery," he introduced himself. "I'm from the admissions department, would you fill out these forms? Unfortunately, you'll have a longer wait than expected because your doctor isn't in yet."

"My doctor?" I said questioningly.

I took the forms and began tackling the questions one by one. I was able to fill in my name and date. The others confused me. I didn't understand what they were asking or why so I left them blank.

I thumbed through magazines in the waiting room. Slattery came back, relieved me of my forms, looked them over, and asked, "Who filled these out?"

"I did," I replied almost as a question.

"Very good!" he replied as though I had just completed a masterpiece. I scrutinized him. He was about thirty-five, tall and lean. I shook my head at his foolish response. *What does he think I am?*

As he stood riffling through the papers, he directed us to an upstairs room, where the doctor would meet us. "The doctor's name is Dr. Kamari."

As we headed down the hallway, Eileen tried to ease my anxiety by commenting about the doctor's distinguished, foreign-sounding name. She said, "With a name like that, he will be very nice, if not overly gracious, and has to know what he is doing.

For the entire time she was talking, I was thinking. *What do I need a psychiatrist for anyway? I'm ill, why doesn't anyone listen. She doesn't know what she's talking about. He'll be just like everyone else if not worse.*

"How can you tell from a name?" I asked. "He won't listen and he won't let me go home. I hate him already."

Once we were seated in the room, the doctor walked in. He wasn't what I had expected. He was tall and dark with graying sideburns and wire glasses perched on his nose. His voice was very nice and calming, and his manner was cordial—the complete opposite of what I had envisioned.

He sat down at a desk next to my seat and began asking me questions. Eileen interrupted one of my answers to give her own viewpoint. "Please Eileen, mind your own business," I blurted out, demanding she stay out of it. She wouldn't listen and kept on talking.

I couldn't stand it. They didn't understand and now the doctor wouldn't either. I flew out of my chair and started a fierce argument with her. Shortly after, Connie joined in. All three of us were now standing, screaming at each other. Dr. Kamari got up, commented about this being a family problem and left. Eileen and Connie left with him.

Alone in the room, all I could think of was how much I wanted a cigarette. I went out into the hall in search of a place to have my cigarette. As I looked, I ran across a pinch-faced attendant and asked her if I could have a cigarette there.

"There's no smoking in this section," she said abruptly.

I exploded once again. This made her decide to let me have a cigarette and she unlocked a bathroom inside of the room I had just left. As I stood in there having my cigarette, Connie, Eileen, and Dr. Kamari returned. A few steps behind them walked a balding man carrying a box of chocolates.

"Wouldn't you like one?" he said kindly.

My anger subsided as I took a piece of candy. After thanking him, I sat down. He and Dr. Kamari were also seated, one on my left and one on my right. *What are they going to do to me?* I wondered, becoming fearful.

The other man introduced himself as Dr. Keogan. He began to tell me a story of how his son had gotten into a car accident. And, even though X-rays had been taken, a minute crack in his skull was later discovered by a MRI scan.

"Is this what's wrong with me? Do I have a crack in my skull? Is that why I'm here?" I asked beseechingly.

He shook his head and continued, explaining what an MRI scan did as he moved directly in front of me. He assumed a kneeling position and asked me to watch the chocolate on his finger. He moved his finger left and right, up and down. I kept my eye on it during every move. *What's he doing this for? As long as it pleases him and it gets me out of here, I'll do it.* I thought.

Once Dr. Keogan was finished, Dr. Kamari had me sign some papers. I had no idea what I was signing. When this was completed, Eileen and Connie left and Dr. Keogan said he would escort me to my room. We walked silently down a long empty corridor, at the end of which we turned right into a hall which was guarded by a heavy metal door with a tiny window in it. My heart sank.

"What's behind there? Why are they putting me in there?" I asked miserably.

Dr. Keogan unlocked the door, allowing me to enter. Right inside the door stood a grotesque creature, an old man, eyes bloodshot and bulging right out of their sockets. *Oh my God! Is this what's going to happen to me?* My heart throbbed. Within seconds of this shock, a middle-aged, bored-looking nurse came walking up to me.

"I'll show you to your room," she said.

We walked past three other rooms before stopping at one. Once inside, I stood horrified at my surroundings. There were two single beds, one stripped bare to the mattress, the other with a fluorescent blue rag used as a bedspread. The walls were block cement in dire need of a paint job. The haphazardly-hung curtains matched perfectly with the uneven, unmatched, and dented dressers.

I went to see what the bathroom was like. There was no mirror but there were spots of dried glue where a mirror once hung. I went back and sat on the bed, afraid to touch anything in fear of contracting something. A strange aroma filled the air. I sat there inhaling until I was able to make it out. It was urine! I was disgusted. *I gotta get out.*

The nurse snatched my purse, saying she had to search it before she could allow me to keep it. She tore through everything. My anger grew as I stood there watching. Then she started to go through my wallet. She pulled as hard on it as one would pull at a stubborn jackass.

"Hey, take it easy," I objected. "That's a brand new wallet and it isn't exactly cheap."

"You're in a mental institution," she said, "and shouldn't expect better."

I shook my head, tears spilling from my eyes. I backed away silently in fear of what lay ahead. Her search over, she strewed most of my things on the bed. She kept my nailfile and mirror saying, "You aren't allowed to have those things."

"Why not? I've always had them," I asked.

She disappeared without replying. Left to myself, I began thinking. *I gotta get out of here. I don't belong here. But no one believes me. Even my family thinks I'm crazy. How am I ever going to get out?*

The entire area I was boxed into was no more than a hallway thirty feet long with a room here and there. I went and found the middle-aged nurse who had been in my room. I pleaded with her hysterically, "Please call the doctor for me."

"I will," she said, "if you go back to your room."

I complied, and not long after, Dr. Kamari walked in. He looked different than he had at our earlier meeting. He didn't have those funny little glasses at the end of his nose. He sat down on my bed.

"What can I do for you?" he asked quietly.

"I want out of this place," I yelled. "How can you be

so calm?" I began pacing from wall to wall, kicking the wall at one point.

"Won't you let me go home? I don't belong here!" I kicked the wall and stopped.

"I understand," he commented as cool as he could be. "We'll talk more about it tomorrow," he added as he got up to leave.

"I want to leave now. Christmas is coming," I cried.

He nodded without replying.

After Dr. Kamari had gone, I went into the television room. I sat there facing the television, but staring into space. My nerves were frazzled. I was trapped with no way out and no one to listen to me. I chain smoked.

Not long after, a strange boyish face appeared. The person it belonged to was making all sorts of racket, causing mayhem by kicking over ashtrays and other items. I never heard anyone talk so fast or so much in one breath. He sat down on a couch across from me and started telling me, as though no one else was present, about an accident he was in.

"I'm going to become rich by it," he said drawing out the last word and winking.

"What's that supposed to mean?" I asked innocently.

As he continued to talk, he started to practice karate moves while sitting on the couch. Flinging his arms and legs wildly, he came close to hitting me a few times. He scared me. He was talking but not making sense. I got up and ran out. Hurrying back to my room, I fell asleep.

The next morning I got up to take a shower; however, I had not even the basic necessities. I went to the nurse on duty, a short paunchy redhead, to ask for some.

"I can give you everything except a razor," she said with a half-smile. "You aren't allowed one."

I asked her why. She made no reply and went back to what she was doing. I was sorry I even asked and even more sorry after I took the shower. It was ice cold. I wandered around after I was finished until I ran straight into the middle-aged nurse who had searched my purse. She was very friendly as she greeted me, asking me if there was anything she could do for me.

"Can you get me out of here?" I asked.

Her friendliness paled, her tone became more icy. So I asked if there was anything to do.

"I have to check to see if you have floor privileges first," she said.

"What are those?" I asked naively.

In a minute she returned, "You don't have any, so you have to stay in ICU until you're granted them."

"Granted? ICU what?" I said, but she walked away.

I headed back to the television room and whiled away a few hours in there. I was watching reruns, when a woman dressed in a navy blue suit came over to talk with me. She started asking questions about how much I smoked, how much I slept, if I did drugs, and if everything with my family was all right. She wrote all my answers down.

I didn't like this; *it was none of her business*. I lied left and right. Everything was going fine, I smoked moderately, and slept like a log. She asked questions regarding hearing voices or if there was ever any ringing in my head. All of which I replied honestly to with a no. When she was done, another woman came in, this one with a starched white coat.

"I need to draw some blood and to examine you," she said.

We went to my room. She had me kneel on the edge of a chair and then ran her fingers up and down my spine. I didn't know why and never asked. She checked every part of me and left, without giving me so much as the time of day.

As soon as she was done with me, a nurse came in carrying a tray, announcing it was lunch. I squatted Indian style in the middle of my bed and had her place the tray in front of me. As she was doing this, an attractive dark-haired woman walked in.

"You're beautiful," I said admiringly. "I like your out-fit."

She smiled, "I'm Dr. Michele Lee. I'll be your psycho-therapist," she announced as she pulled a chair up to sit in front of me.

"Why don't you tell me what's been going on?" she suggested quietly.

Having begun to twist my spaghetti around the fork, I looked up and asked, "Do you know what kind of cheese this is?"

She leaned over and said, "It looks like parmesan to me." I toyed with it.

Once again she asked, "What's been going on, Fran?"

I sighed, "I don't really know. I think I was at First Memorial after I got in a car accident. Then somehow, I got here."

She looked down at the folder she was carrying and said, "You certainly were at First Memorial. From what I understand, they did a pretty good job on you."

"Was I hurt?" I asked.

"No physical injuries. It says so right here," was her response.

"If I wasn't hurt, what am I still doing in a hospital?" I felt confused. "And why do I feel so sick? I don't under-stand."

"This is enough for right now," she smiled again. "Why don't you finish your lunch? We'll be meeting on Wednesdays and Saturdays. This isn't to say you can't talk to me any time you need to," and she patted my shoulder and left.

I sat there waiting for someone else to come in. It was around three o'clock before anyone else came into my room. A fortyish woman in a blue dress with white collar and cuffs came in to announce the Fact Group was starting in a minute and I was more than welcome to join.

Another group. I got up and went. This one wasn't as bad as the one at First Memorial. I spent a half hour in

Group and then stayed behind to waste some time watching television. The rest of the day and evening was uneventful and dragged by slowly, each minute feeling like an hour.

The next morning finally arrived. I was told I was granted floor privileges. I was excited, even though I didn't know what "privileges" meant to their way of thinking. I soon found out. They unlocked the door for me and let me step onto the other section of the floor.

This area was much larger and there were a lot more activities. I went to the lounge, and a dozen or so people were there. I made several friends immediately. As we talked, the subject came up about being able to write a letter asking to be released. Within three days you had to be released if you were voluntary.

"What's that?" I asked. No one seemed to really know what it meant but writing a letter and being released sounded good to me. I tried to get more information about it. However, the subject had changed to the lunch menu. I expected trays to be brought in, but not so. I walked downstairs with everyone else to the dining room. Even this temporary freedom seemed wonderful and I sat cherishing it.

At my table were three new-found friends, Dave, Jeremy, and Nancy. They seemed pretty normal to me. Nancy offered one of her cigarettes.

"She smokes the cowboy killers. How can she stand them?" Dave said.

I declined her offer saying I had my own, and dug deep into my pocket to retrieve them. I had the cigarettes but no matches. I asked no one in particular for a light. All three stared back with expressions which said, "You gotta be kidding."

"You have to kiss the wall," Dave said.

"What?" I asked back.

He pointed to a little metal box bolted to the wall, saying, "There's your light, sweetheart. You'll get used to it."

I got up, went over to the box, and pressed a button on

its front. A red glow appeared and I pressed my cigarette against it.

"This is unbelievable," I said slowly. "I'm not even allowed matches."

I went back and sat down, "At least I'll get some exercise around here."

This caused Nancy to laugh, it was no ordinary laugh. It came from deep inside and was loud enough that several people at neighboring tables turned to stare our way. I was embarrassed. She was in tears, almost hysterical, practically rolling on the floor.

"I like you. What did you say your name was?" she asked in between gasps.

"Fran," I timidly admitted.

"I don't know about you anymore," she said, growing angry. "That's my mother's name."

"What a coincidence," I replied.

"I hate my mother," she said almost menacingly.

I gulped as my eyes widened. *What does all this mean*, I asked myself, feeling scared. *Is she crazy?* I started a conversation with Dave and Jeremy, ignoring Nancy completely.

Back upstairs, we went into the lounge. Dave, Jeremy, and I sat at a table. Nancy went to the television and turned on MTV at high volume. Trying to be heard over the noise, we started talking about karate. I was trying to get Dave and Jeremy to teach me some self-defense moves.

Finally, they agreed and we stood a while flexing our muscles and laughing. Nancy came up behind me and flung her foot directly at my head, missing only by inches. Without saying a word, I ran out of the room, Dave and Jeremy followed.

Once outside, Jeremy said to me, "Too bad your name is Fran."

I didn't understand his reasoning but I let it pass.

"We'll finish our lesson in the Quiet Lounge," Jeremy said.

This room turned out to be impressive. It looked like a

formal living room. On the wall hung a gorgeous pastel blue and gray picture of a woman. We made ourselves comfortable and started talking. Talking about why we were there. Dave said he was there for trying to kill his wife. Jeremy, for doing too much heroin.

I gasped. These types of experiences were completely foreign to my world. I thought they were making it up, but soon found out they were very serious when Jeremy showed me his "tracks." When my turn to explain came, I was speechless. I had no idea why I was there. Eventually, I talked about the car accident and told them that was my reason. They seemed not to believe me and began talking about their own lives again. Sitting there listening to them increased my anxiety.

I had to get out of there. I didn't belong with those people. But how was I to do it? There was no way out. I decided I'd have to make the best of it even though it would be the hardest thing I'd ever done.

"I have a headache," I said slowly. "I have to lie down." Banging on the ICU door, I waited for the nurse to unlock it. Then I headed for the television room.

As I sat there, the young man who had been in the car accident came stumbling in and sat down. He began to talk wildly about the accident, his wife, and what he was going to do about this, all the while banging his fist on the table.

My anxiety exploded. This was the last straw. I felt I couldn't handle Brookhollow for another minute. I got up and headed for the door, banging on it once again for my release.

I went directly to the phone and called my sister Eileen. "You have to get me out of here! These people are crazy! I don't feel safe in here!" I cried out the instant I heard her voice.

"Hold on a minute. What's going on?" she asked in total confusion.

I explained to her about everyone and everything. She replied that she would talk to the nurse and see if I was safe and call me back. I waited at the phone for her call. When it came, I wasn't told what I wanted to hear. The nurse had told Eileen that nothing could possibly happen to me and she herself would look after me. Eileen said she couldn't get me out, but would call and check on me.

I felt terrified, my heart beat fiercely. "Why isn't anyone listening to me?" I cried out.

A suddenly tapping on my shoulder broke my reverie. I turned to discover Dr. Kamari standing right behind me.

"Would you like to come talk to me?" he asked with his quaint accent.

"I've been waiting all day to talk to you," I said and got up to go with him. We walked side by side in silence down an empty hall, stopping at the very end in front of a locked door. Dr. Kamari unlocked it and held it open for me to enter first. *Is he going to lock it behind me?* I wondered. He followed closely.

When the door was closed and both of us seated, directly in front of each other, I asked, "Am I voluntary or involuntary?"

"Voluntary," he replied. "How are things going?" he asked.

"Fine. How are things with you," I responded. I had no idea what we were supposed to be talking about. My pulse was still beating fast, and as I sat there trying to decipher the purpose of our meeting, it began to beat even faster—causing me to feel more confused.

I was growing restless when he asked, "What happened during the past few days?"

I don't remember much, I thought. *What I do remember, I'm certainly not going to tell him about. I'll never get out of here. He'd never believe it.*

"I got into a car accident," I told him.

"What happened after the car accident?" he asked as if he already knew.

My pulse and heartbeat accelerated. I felt out of control. I drew my feet underneath me and sat on them, exclaiming, "My thoughts are going so fast. They always do. I'm always ahead of myself."

He interrupted with, "You have supersensitive antennas."

"What?" I quickly said.

"Supersensitive antennas," he once again said.

"What's that?" I asked.

I couldn't understand his explanation and was afraid
to ask. *He might think I'm crazy.* My whole body was trembling as more thoughts flashed through my mind. I started
running my fingers across the side of my head. *Supersensitive antennas?*

Dr. Kamari interrupted once again, "I'm going to start
you on Trivel tonight. The nurse will be around at bed-
time."

"I don't want any tranquilizers. There's nothing
wrong with my mind, I won't take it," I said in an all-
knowing pose.

Dr. Kamari stood up and said, "I'll see you tomorrow," and was gone.

I went back to the lounge and asked one of the nurses
for a pen and paper. She returned and sat down right next
to me as she handed me the pen and paper.

I turned to her and said, "Do you mind, I'd like some
privacy here."

"I have to stay with you as long as you have the pen,"
she responded.

"Fine!" I said in total disgust.

I began to write my letter for discharge but had to stop
and ask the nurse what to say. She told me, I finished it,
and I handed both the letter and pen back to her. She left
with letter in hand and I turned to the television, *I'm out of
here in three days!*

EIGHT

Dave walked in and sat at the table with me. We started telling jokes and in no time at all we were laughing. We were joined by Jeremy. Our gathering was getting louder.

Nancy walked in and wanted to join us. I hesitated but ended up letting her pull up a chair. *I'm going home. What do I care.* Her laugh alone had all three of us in tears. In the middle of our conversation a fire alarm started going off. Not caring in that moment that the last fire alarm I had fled from had ended in my incarceration, I jumped up.

"I'm out of here," I said heading for the door.

Everyone evacuated to the top of a rear roof. It was freezing. None of us had coats so the four of us huddled in a group. Nancy began talking about the ins and outs of Brookhollow. I was all ears.

"This is my eighth admission here. I know the place and everybody in it. You want to get in good with the nurses like Sue, Linda, Tom, and, of course, Alf."

I interrupted with, "Who's Alf?"

"That's one of the male nurses. Alf is his nickname," she answered. She continued, "Stay away from Fran."

I interrupted, "That's me. What are you talking about?"

"There are four Franceses on the Adult floor, including you," she replied very irritably. "Stay away, and I mean away from Mrs. Shulz and Mrs. Clancy. They'd think nothing of stabbing you in the back. And make sure you're careful about everything you say and do, they have spies everywhere. They write down everything."

Before she had a chance to finish, we were called back inside. As we walked along I thought, *Nancy isn't so bad after all.*

Once back in the lounge, we resumed our joking as if no mention of the evils lurking at Brookhollow had ever been made. An attractive dark-haired nurse walked in pushing a huge cart, saying, "Time for medicine." She stopped in front of me, "Who are you," she asked quizzically.

"Frances. Frances Deitrick," I told her and she explained I'd have to go back to ICU for my medicine. I didn't bother, I had no interest in medicine.

Ten minutes after she left, in walked another nurse. This one was also dark, but older and pinch-faced. She walked right up to me, "I'm Sam," she said, "I'd like you to go back to ICU with me."

"I don't want to be locked away," I said refusing her request.

Without a word she took hold of my arm, pulled me up, and led me back.

The heavy metal door slammed closed behind us. As its echo traveled the hall, another nurse approached us.

"Why don't you want to take your medicine, dear?" she asked.

"There's nothing wrong with my mind," I insisted. "I don't need that Trivel medicine," I explained.

"Your doctor doesn't think that or he wouldn't have ordered medicine for you," she replied in a condescending tone.

"I'm not taking that medicine," I told her, pronouncing every syllable. I walked away. "I'm leaving in three days and everyone who did this to me will be sorry!"

I went and lay on my bed. My thoughts were on Steve. *I wish he was here right now. He'd get me out of this place.*

He'd believe me. Then the fights Steve and I had that summer began to enter my thoughts. We were constantly fighting. What brought about this change? I couldn't figure it out. And, even though these thoughts angered me, I had an overwhelming urge to talk with him.

I got off the bed, walked over and banged on the door. Outside, I went to the phone and placed a collect call. Steve's roommate answered and refused the charges. I called right back and said he had to accept the charges. I left a message with him for Steve. I wanted Steve to call. I desperately needed to hear his voice. It would make me feel normal, alive.

After my unsuccessful attempt at trying to reach Steve, I withdrew into myself as I headed back to bed. *I can't handle all of this. I'm confused. I might as well give up. What is everyone else seeing about me that I'm not seeing that makes them think I'm crazy?*

After breakfast, I went to the ICU lounge. It was quieter than the main lounge and I needed to think. Think about my life and what had happened to it, what I could do to help myself. No sooner had I sat down, when I was interrupted by a young blond male nurse. He wanted me to take my medicine. *They haven't learned by now?*

I responded, "I won't take that medicine. There's nothing wrong with my mind." I pointed to my own head in approval and told the nurse to get lost. I returned to thinking. Arms crossed in front of me, legs resting on a chair, I felt total despair, and I lost myself to a world of thoughts.

What's wrong with me. Why has this happened to me? What do Dr. Kamari and Dr. Keogan really think? What are they really planning on doing to me?

My thoughts were interrupted once more, this time by Dr. Keogan.

"I want to talk to you in your room," he said in a serious tone.

We walked there together. I sat down on the bed, he sat in a nearby chair.

"From what I hear, you've written a letter of discharge. Is that right Fran?" he asked me.

"You heard right," I replied.

"Why do you want to leave us? Are we that bad?" he said laughing.

"I don't belong here. There's nothing wrong with my mind. It's my body that's a mess and you're not doing a damn thing to help."

"I wish you wouldn't leave us. You haven't even given the place a chance," he responded.

"If I stay here, I'll miss Christmas. So I have to go," I said as if I were pleading. "I have to get out of here. I'm not crazy."

"I'll make a deal with you," he said in a patient but firm tone. "You rescind your letter of discharge and I'll make sure you get help and make it home for Christmas," he finagled.

"I don't know," I said, beginning to back down, but he kept on prodding.

"All right, I'll rescind," I said finally and got up, more confused than ever.

Dr. Keogan got up right behind me and put his arm around my shoulder as he said, "You won't be sorry."

I was dazed. I felt as if I had been manipulated but I felt so sick and so miserable I thought, *maybe he's right. Maybe they can help me. Maybe he knows something he's not telling me, after all he's the doctor.*

We stopped at the nurses' station and Dr. Keogan handed me pen and paper. When I handed it back he said, "Thank you," in a condescending tone. Tears came to my eyes.

"I've made a mistake," I said.

"No you haven't Frances," he said firmly. "You've done the right thing. Now be a good girl."

I understood then that I had trapped myself. In front of me was the heavy metal door. I banged on it nonstop until it opened.

I went to the Main Lounge. Nancy was there listening

to MTV and smoking what was now only a filter. I plopped myself next to her on the couch.

"This place rots," I said loudly.

My eyes were piercing as she turned to my saying, "What's wrong Fran?" She placed her arm around my shoulder.

"Dr. Keogan got me to rescind my letter. I don't know how he did it," I replied.

"You fell for that!" she said laughing. "They intimidate everyone who writes letters. It's a game they play," she added.

I was steaming mad. *How dare he.* Immediately I was up and heading for the nurses' station in that section.

"I'm looking for Dr. Keogan," I said. "Where is he?" My heart pounded, my head ached. One of the nurses told me he would not be back before that night. "It's lucky for him," I said.

There was nothing to do but return to the lounge.

As we both sat there, a man in a navy pin-striped suit came walking in. He had every touch of class about him. And the well-groomed beard on his face pegged him right away as a doctor. The moment he walked in Nancy yelled to him, "Hi, Dr. Lee." *I was right, he was a doctor.*

"Wait a minute, Dr. Lee is a woman," I said to Nancy.

"That's his wife," she replied.

Dr. Lee started to move the furniture around. As he did, he was declaring, "Time for Group." I wanted to find out what Group was like so I decided to hang around for it. Every seat in the room was filled.

Dr. Lee started off with, "Welcome to Group. For those of you who are new, I'm Dr. Lee. Now, let us all introduce ourselves to the rest of the group. Who wants to start?" he said in a monotone.

I started with, "Hi, my name is Fran." Then one by one, the rest of the group introduced themselves. There were so many of them I forgot everyone's name by the time the introductions were made.

I sat there listening. I couldn't believe my ears. One

guy had drunk Draino in an attempt to end his life. He had destroyed his whole insides. He spent weeks in the hospital and all because of Christmas. He couldn't stand the thought of Christmas coming.

A girl with long blonde hair described how she had taken so much LSD that she now had recurrent hallucinations without even taking the drug.

An emaciated-looking woman with dark hair fashioned in braids described how they weighed her morning and night because she would only eat lettuce.

There came a point in the group discussion where I stopped listening, putting my hands up to my ears to close them off. I was so alarmed by what was being discussed. All these morbid thoughts were too much for me.

I had to change the subject and piped up with, "Did anyone watch "Frosty the Snowman" the other night?" Everyone roared in laughter except Dr. Lee. He gave me one of those raised eyebrow looks. I returned a meek smile. He didn't say anything, only continued on with the group. When Dr. Lee closed the discussion, I was the first one out the door.

I ran into Dave and Jeremy. I told them about my latest experience in Group. They offered to teach me more karate to take my mind off it. I refused, saying I needed some time alone. They went into the Quiet Lounge. I turned and headed to my room.

On my way, I was sidetracked by the new faces I noticed in the ICU lounge. I went in and introduced myself. As I began to sit on the couch, I noticed Cecilia, a new patient. Her wrists were wrapped in heavy bandages, and there were spots of dried blood showing. I knew what it meant: she had attempted suicide.

She started to tell me how the bandages came about. I sat there yessing her, fearful of saying something that would upset her. One small comment made in jest seemed to push her over the edge. For some reason, she clung right to me. I was sympathetic to her story and sat there for the next half hour listening to her, never once saying a word. It lifted her spirits, temporarily anyway.

The instant I left Cecilia's side, my attention was drawn to an eccentric-looking young man sitting in the corner, playing solitaire. He looked so pathetic, as if he needed a friend. I went over and started talking to him. He grunted and groaned back at me. I tried again. I got the same response. I wouldn't let up on him. *I'm going to get him to say something to me.*

As I prodded, I noticed a set of checkers nearby. I asked him if he wanted to play. This got a response out of him. He had the board in front of him in no time flat. I sat down, chattering. He responded to every question. We played several games. He creamed me at every one. As I was about to give up, I noticed the tattoos going up his arm. The symbols and words were unknown to me. They scared me. *What kind of a person did I make friends with?* I told him I had enough and went to the other side of the room to safety.

Nancy came walking in with Jill, one of the nurses.

"It's time for ICU Group," Jill said.

They like talk around this place, don't they. By this time, I had completely forgotten about the experiences in the earlier Group and decided to stay for this one. There were fewer people in this Group. A half dozen or so. And I was doing all the talking. I was bullshitting about everything from Christmas to life experiences. Whenever there was silence for more than a minute, words popped out of my mouth. Toward the end of the group, I realized Jill and I had done all the talking.

Finally, Nancy piped up with, "What is Frances doing here? There's nothing wrong with her."

"Finally, someone has realized I'm not crazy," I said. *How strange that it's Nancy.* I got up and hugged her.

After Group, I went and took a nap before dinner. I was rudely awakened by Dave, Jeremy, and Nancy. They scared the living daylights out of me by jumping on me and screaming, "Wake up." We went to dinner. The food was incredibly delicious. Craving cigarettes afterward, both Nancy and I got up to "kiss the wall."

When we returned to the table, Joe, the man from the other night, the one who was in the car accident, was sitting at my place. He had a collar wrapped around his neck. Visions of the collars wrapped around my neck after my car accident started going through my head. I stood there staring at him.

"Fran, I'll go get you another chair," someone said.

I just stood there making no reply, my mind playing tricks on me, my head aching.

"Fran! Fran!" someone shouted.

I jerked my head around saying, "What?" I went over and got a chair and sat down, feeling better again.

Now there were five of us talking nonstop and laughing periodically. Thoughts of my accident had completely disappeared. We were on our way back to the unit when Dave and Jeremy stopped to talk to Nancy. I paid no attention and kept going. Joe followed, lagging far behind. As I was making my way up the stairs, Joe came running out of nowhere, leaping the stairs two at a time. I had to look twice at this one. I didn't understand.

"I thought he was in such pain and could hardly move," I murmured. "How could he be going up stairs like that?"

After Joe disappeared, I started walking again. *Did I really see him* I thought, frightened. *Was I hallucinating?* I shook the thought off.

At the top of the stairs, I had to decide what lounge should I go to: the Main, the Quiet, or the ICU. I chose the Main. I got involved in a card game, and afterwards I went back to my room.

It wasn't long before someone began knocking at my door. It was Peggy, an ICU nurse. She told me there was a phone call for me on the main floor. It was my sister Eileen. She was calling to find out how everything was going, if I had calmed down any. Then she started give me a pep talk to help me survive my new surroundings.

"You have what it takes. Don't let anyone intimidate you. You'll make a lot of friends. You have a great personality. And, before you know it you'll be home. Remember who you are and what you've done in your life," she said, sounding loving and sincere.

I believed it while she was saying it. However, once we were off the phone the belief vanished. *How could they make me stay here? Even my family thought I was mentally ill. My life was in the pits and there were no two ways about it.*

Dr. Kamari showed up as I was about to bang on the metal door once again. I followed him to the same room as the night before. Our conversation started normally enough, but soon evolved into sheer chaos.

I was screaming and yelling at him, "I want to get out of here. You don't understand how sick I am and you never will."

"Oh, but I do," he said.

I began crying hysterically.

He said calmly, "You can write a letter. We won't take you to court," he said abruptly.

I got up and walked out the door. "I'll write my letter," I said quietly fuming.

As I walked back to the lounge my anger grew immense. My arms flung wildly at my side, my pace was fast and long, and my heartbeat was rapid. The door to the lounge was half closed. I kicked it square in its center to move it out of the way. It flew back against the wall, making a horrible crashing noise as it went. The door continued to swing slightly back and forth as a portly nurse with a pig-like nose came running in.

"What's going on here?" she demanded as she placed her hands on her tubby hips. No one said anything.

"What caused that noise like thunder?" she angrily asked.

Dave piped up with, "Oh! Sorry about that. I stumbled into the door accidentally."

This didn't quite satisfy her, but she let it go for she

knew no one was going to say anything more. She left and we all burst out laughing.

"Thanks guys," I said.

"What's wrong, Fran?" Dave asked as soon as she left.

"Everything!" I snapped back. "I don't want to talk about it. Let's have some fun," I said.

"There's a movie downstairs in the dining room," Nancy said.

In a flash, we were on our way. It was a horror film, the worst movie I had ever seen. It must have been one of the first ever made. Halfway into it, I grabbed Dave and pulled him to the other side of the room.

"I can't handle the movie. Let's talk instead," I said as I motioned Dave to sit down.

Dave began clowning. In no time at all we were both laughing nonstop, banging our fists on the table in approval. Our laughter halted abruptly with the appearance of Jack, the activities director.

"You guys have to hold it down," he commanded.

"Sorry about that. We will," Dave replied.

Jack turned and left. Dave moved his face close to mine and whispered, "He's such a puny little sucker, what's he going to do to us."

I burst out laughing and in no time at all we were back at our original antics. And, in no time at all, Jack was back. He kicked us out.

On our walk back, Dave and I started fooling around with karate moves. Then, Dave grabbed me and flung me over his back, head first. Then suddenly, Dave lost his grip. Screaming, I crashed to the floor. Instantly, my head started ringing. I felt dazed, nauseated.

Dave stood over me, "Are you all right?" he questioned.

"I will be in a minute," I wept.

He helped me up and said he'd get a nurse.

"You can't do that!" I told him.

With a confused expression he asked, "Why not?"

"Because they'll never let me out of this place. You can't tell anyone, you have to promise," I replied.

He promised and helped me back to ICU.

"Hi, Fran, are you okay?" the sympathetic motherly nurse exclaimed as I made my way through the ICU door. Her voice sounded as if it were ten octaves higher than a normal voice.

"Hiiii," I said back with a painful grin. The echo of her voice remained in my head even as I crawled under the covers. The pain was unbelievable. I cradled my head in my arm and fell asleep.

I never moved a muscle until the next morning when I was awakened by Alice, the sober-faced floor nurse.

"Fran, you get a new room this morning," she said cheerfully.

I pulled the covers over my head and moaned.

"I want you to gather your things and meet me at the nurses' station," she continued as she pulled the curtains open, letting in the sunshine.

My head didn't hurt as much; however, the echo was still present. I didn't feel like getting out of bed, much less moving to another room.

"Your room is going to be in the main section," she happily reported.

I'm getting out of ICU. Although I was thrilled with this idea, I felt so weak that I remained lying on the bed. After the nurse left, I fought with myself to sit up. This feat accomplished, I bent over to pick up my sweatsuit. My whole body quivered. I maneuvered myself very slowly while I gathered the rest of my belongings. *You have to keep going, Fran. Forget about the pain.*

With belongings in hand, I headed for the nurses' station. Halfway there, I was stopped by a disturbance in the hallway. Joe was battling it out with a male nurse.

"I don't need this. I don't need this at all," I murmured.

I practically attached myself to the wall and slithered past. At the nurses' station, I decided a few aspirin would help. *A headache is a headache,* I thought. *They'll never know why.* The nurse gave me a few aspirin and we headed out the door.

My new room wasn't very different from the one in ICU, except this one had a mirror in the bathroom. Once the nurse left, I dropped everything at the foot of my bed and sprawled on top. There I slept for the next several hours. I was awakened by Liz, one of the activities directors.

"Do you want to go for a ride with us? We're going to stop and shop a bit," she said.

A chance to get out of here. "I'd love to go," I replied.

I sat up slowly. My head almost felt normal.

"Give me a minute and I'll be right out," I said and didn't even bother to comb my hair.

There were six of us going. We were a motley crew, to say the least. I looked as though I was still in bed. Others were unshaven, hair strewn everywhere, and a few were wearing their breakfast. One had a wool hat pulled way down on his head. Another had her coat buttoned the wrong way, leaving one side higher than the other. *If this was any other time, I would not be seen with these people,* I thought. But I wanted to go out so badly, I didn't care who it was with.

I sat with my nose pressed against the glass, staring out the window as we drove.

"What a beautiful day," I said to no one in particular. *I wish I were out in the middle of that field right now.* We passed a huge white colonial with a pastel-colored rose garden. *I wonder what the people in that house are doing?* I thought, fantasizing. The van stopped. We all shuffled out.

"Let's go for a walk instead of shopping," I suggested. My idea was unanimously approved.

We straggled as we walked. I began to move faster until I was several blocks ahead of the others. I was taking in as much as I possibly could. I want to save these memories for later, when I was locked away.

As I passed people, I received the strangest stares. *I*

now know what it feels like to be one of those people I myself used to stare at. I'll never do it again, I promised myself, and waited for the others to catch up. We had walked for nearly a mile when we turned and headed back to the van. I was walking much slower on this route, trying to delay the inevitable.

Before I knew it, we were back at Brookhollow. And I was back, bored and miserable, smoking cigarettes in the lounge. After every cigarette, I would go to the refrigerator, or go bother the nurses, or go to the Quiet lounge.

On one of my jaunts, I noticed two tissue-paper thin old women, holding onto the railing which ran along the middle of every wall, walking and walking. I stood there watching them. When they got to the exit door they turned and walked back to the exit door on the other side.

They never stopped, they simply kept walking. They never said anything to me even though I tried to talk to them, remembering my promise to myself not to judge others by their appearance. Finally, I threw my arms up in exasperation and walked away, determined to get them to talk to me sooner or later.

Back in my room, I discovered a roommate. She was old and haggard-looking. I said, "Hello" trying to be friendly. She refused to say anything to me, she only stared. Finally, I walked out, scared by her lack of communication.

I went to the nurses' station to complain. I told them very calmly what was going on and that I wanted a new roommate. They denied my request, saying there were no other rooms. I didn't believe them.

I flew off the handle, screaming and yelling at the top of my voice, "You're going to do something about it and *now!* I'm not spending a night in that room with her." I began pacing in and out of the nurses' station door. As I did, the male Dr. Lee came walking up to me.

"What's the problem?" he asked.

"I have a roommate who won't speak, she's frightening. I want a new room. They won't let me have it," I said back to him. He turned to the nurses and asked,

"Is this true?"

One of the nurses replied back, "Yes, and there are no other rooms."

Dr. Lee then turned to me and said, "I'm sorry, but you'll have to stay where you are."

"Like hell I'm staying where I am. She gives me the creeps. You have to do something about it. Who knows what she's capable of doing to me," I yelled at him hysterically.

In the tumult, the two little old ladies I had watched earlier approached the door where I stood. Others gathered as well.

Dr. Lee announced, "I've told everyone to stand up for themselves; however, Fran's behavior is ridiculous. But we'll see what we can do for you, Fran," and he placed an arm around my shoulder. Within the hour, I had a new room.

My new roommate was older also; however, she was a motherly type and we hit it off instantly.

Satisfied with my new sleeping arrangements, I went back to the lounge. It was after nine o'clock and not many people were there. *What am I going to do now?* I thought. *I'm not tired.*

Dave walked in and we started talking. We came up with a brilliant plan to occupy us. We would make a collage. A collage which represented us, the people of the world, but especially those at Brookhollow.

I went to the nurses' station and requested pencils, paper, tape, and a pair of scissors. They gave me everything except the scissors. Before they had a chance, I piped up with, "I know, I'm not allowed to have them."

The nurses laughed at this saying, "You're getting used to things around here aren't you Fran."

Very sarcastically, I replied while pointing my finger at no one in particular, "Unfortunately, I am."

Dave and I set to work on the collage immediately. We went from room to room collecting everything we could think of. We ended up with cigarette butts, packets of mustard and ketchup, pop can tabs, swizzle sticks, barrettes, globs of peanut butter and jelly, and last but not least, the pictures and words we tore from magazines.

When our masterpiece was finished, we taped it to the wall. Underneath it we taped a picture of a lovely, decorated Christmas tree; we had an arrow pointing from it to our collage. On the bottom of the arrow we wrote, "This is Christmas"; at the top, "This is us."

We decided something more should be added, and that our Christmas wishes would be appropriate. I started tearing off pieces of masking tape, writing on each one what I desired. At the top of my list was "freedom." As I was taping this wish to the wall, Nancy walked in. She joined us.

We began taping wishes to the wall one right after the other, laughing as we did. We were coming up with some pretty wild desires. Then we began writing anything someone said and taped it to the wall. We plastered every inch of the wall with tape.

Then all three of us stood back to admire our creation. I wasn't satisfied, it still needed something. On a long strip of tape I wrote, "Philosophy of the Mind 101" and taped it to the very top of our collage.

I couldn't stop there, I started going wild with ideas, writing them all down and taping them anywhere I could find a place. I wrote notes to the doctors, I wrote reasons as to why anyone in their right mind would do something like this, and I wrote, "I'm not crazy." This, I placed right under "Philosophy of the Mind 101."

The next thing we knew it was one o'clock in the morning and Alf appeared telling us we had to leave and the lounge had to be locked. Before we were out the door, Alf called us back to tell us what a wonderful job we had done. He said it was cute.

"I don't want it to be cute," I insisted seriously. "There's a message there, I want to go home," I said definitively. We left and went to bed.

The next day was Sunday. At breakfast, Jeremy explained to me there was nothing to do on a Sunday. No groups, no doctors, no activities.

I decided I'd go exploring, find out what this whole place was about and formulate a plan to get out of it. First, I had to get dressed. On my way back to my room I noticed a bulletin board hanging on the wall directly opposite the nurses' station. It was cluttered with papers. This intrigued me.

"My first task is to locate everything," I murmured. I started sorting through the papers. The first few I looked at weren't of any importance, a menu and a calendar. The next one I began reading threw me for a loop. It read, "Weekly support groups for Bipolar, Manic Depressives, Alcoholics and Children of Alcoholics. St. Luke's Church, 141 Daryll Lane."

"What's bipolar?" I murmured. "A bear." I grew solemn. It had finally sunk into my head, *I was in a mental institution. It was time to stop trying to adjust to an impossible situation. I had to get myself out. But how?* That was the real question. I sat meditating on it for a long while but got nowhere.

Then I noticed an activities sheet. It listed day by day, hour by hour, what there was to do. There were all kinds of Groups: The Body Image, the Anger, the Life Experiences, the Men's, the Women's, the Assertive, the Community Hour; the list went on and on.

I was fascinated by the fact that people actually had to take lessons for some of these things. They had a time set aside for a walk, arts and crafts, and swimming. I was shuffled away from the board by a group of patients who were looking to see what the menu read. I didn't mind, I had my fill. I went to my room to get dressed.

As I headed back to the lounge to see if anyone wanted to go with me, I noticed those two little old ladies back at their posts. I chuckled to myself. *Quite the characters.* Then, I saw a vision of myself twenty years from now doing the exact same thing. I shivered in disgust. *I'm not going to let that happen to me. I'm going to find a way out of here.*

I went to find Nancy. She didn't want to go, so I made my way down the stairs by myself. At the bottom of the stairs was the reception area. Making myself comfortable on the couch, I lit a cigarette. There was no hurry. I had all day to waste. Suddenly, I noticed several closed doors with tiny windows.

Looks as good a place as any to start my exploring. I got up and went to one of the doors. It was locked. Peeking through the window to see what mystery lay behind this locked door, the only thing I could see was a set of stairs going down. *I wonder what they keep down there? Patients?*

I went to the next door. It was locked also. I peeked through the window blinds. It was an arts and crafts room. I went to the next door. It was open.

The entire room was little bigger than a closet. There was a small desk and two chairs in it. I decided this had to be an interrogation room, it looked spooky. I got away from that one fast and headed for the hall which I knew led to the cafeteria.

I wanted to see what all the offices were and where the hallways off them led. Most of the doors were locked. But some had windows for me to peer through. Several were patients' rooms and one I noticed had vending machines. There was nothing of great interest so far.

I turned the corner into a short hall. At the end, a set of double doors stood wide open. Inside there were pool tables, ping-pong tables, televisions, a stereo, and several card tables. As I stood there examining the room, a husky man bearing a pool cue approached me. His eyes were narrowed almost shut, his lips clenched.

"What unit are you from?" he asked intimidatingly.

"My room is upstairs," I replied.

"Sorry, you can't come in here then. This room is only for the patients down here. I suggest you go back to where you belong."

"Why?" I said. "It looks like fun. Can't I stay for a little while?" I pleaded.

"Get out of here before I call a nurse," he threatened.

That was all I needed to hear and I was gone. I headed for the cafeteria. I went in and kissed the wall, lighting up a cigarette. I was the only one there. I enjoyed my moment alone.

Halfway into my cigarette, I noticed a bowl of fruit sitting on the buffet table. *Looks good. I wonder if I dare. Go ahead Fran, there's no one here.* I went and took the biggest, reddest, red delicious apple there was. Along with it I took a banana, an orange, and some grapes. I ate everything except the apple. *I'll save it for my walk back upstairs.*

With my stomach full, I made my way back to the door. I opened it smack dab into the swollen face of Lydia, one of the nurses.

"We've been looking for you, Frances," she scolded.

"Well, you found me," I said, smirking.

I hated Lydia. She always had a scowl on her face.

"Don't be smart. You're not allowed down here alone," she hollered back at me. Then, without so much as a chance to explain, she forcefully took me by the arm and pulled me toward the elevator.

She never let go until we were standing in front of the Main lounge where she said, "Don't let me catch you down there again or you'll be sorry," and she pushed me into the lounge.

"You bitch," I said in a tone half muffled by tears. "I wasn't doing anything. It's not like I was going to torch the place. I smoked a cigarette and got an apple. Big deal."

I walked over and joined an ongoing card game with Dave, Jeremy, and Nancy.

"What was that all about?" Nancy asked.

"Nothing. Forget it. She's a bitch," I replied.

The card game went on and on. Luckily, I was winning. It made me feel as though I was in control of my life again instead of locked away. I soon was reminded by Lydia returning.

She walked in and pulled several items off our collage, saying, "I don't know where you people get these things but you're not allowed to have them." She walked out, her big fat ass jiggling the entire time.

Then Nancy and I simultaneously said to each other, "Who does she think she is?" We shrugged our shoulders, laughed a bit, and went back to the card game. *What do they think I'm going to do with all these things they won't let me have? What kind of a person do they think I am? No one answers.*

Having had enough of the card game, I decided to take a shower. First stopping at the nurses' station, I asked for some of the things I needed but wasn't allowed to keep in my room.

Actually, they had three-fourths of my belongings stored away in a box in one of their cabinets. I wasn't very happy about having to ask every time I wanted to floss my teeth, shave my underarms, put makeup on, or if I wanted two dollars for cigarettes. It was degrading and made me feel like an incompetent nitwit.

Standing first on one foot, then on the other, I waited at the nurses' station to gain one of the two nurses' attention. Lydia was the first one to look my way. I ignored her and looked over to Mary. As I bided my time, I tapped my foot continuously and kept my arms folded against my chest. *They keep me waiting on purpose,* I thought. *They like to see me beg.*

Finally, Mary looked my way and very sarcastically, while batting my eyelashes, I said, "May I please have my little razor and some dental floss? I want to take a shower." She handed me my razor and tore off a piece of dental floss. *She touched my dental floss, how disgusting,* I thought.

Then she followed me to my room to wait for me to finish with the razor and give it back. She came right into the bathroom with me and stood there while I showered. I started to shave my legs as well, knowing she was anxious to leave.

After ten minutes in the shower I heard, "Frances, what are you doing? Is everything all right?"

"I'm committing suicide," I replied very seriously. She flung open the shower curtain. We stood staring at each other. "I'm only kidding," I said with a smile. She was steaming, took my razor and left. I finished my shower in peace.

NINE

At six the next morning, I jumped out of bed. I felt better than I had in weeks. My mind was fresh and alert. I hopped into the shower singing Christmas carols. I continued singing as I made my way to the lounge.

The dawn light streamed through the grated windows. The lounge was still locked when I got there. I headed to the nurses' station to ask Alf if he'd unlock it for me. Sitting right outside the door was Cecilia. She was wet with perspiration and shaking like a leaf. I knelt down in front of her, took hold of her hand, and asked what was wrong.

"I haven't been able to sleep all night," she said trembling. "My bed is an old iron cot. It's hard and dirty." I felt sorry for her.

"Cecilia, you can sleep in my bed if you want," I said softly.

She hugged me. "You're so sweet," she said and began to cry. While I was helping her to her feet, Alf appeared.

"Where do you think you're going with Cecilia?" he inquired.

"To my room, she can't sleep in her bed."

"Oh no you're not," he said.

Alf and I started arguing and, of course, he won. It was again evidence of my lack of rights in this place. I had to deny Cecilia my previous offer. I felt awful about it.

"Where does this place get some of its rules and why am I here?" I asked tearfully.

Even though we had been battling, Alf shook his head and agreed to unlock the lounge door for me, earlier than the rules allowed.

As we headed toward the door Alf put his arm around my shoulder and said, "That was a nice offer, but the hospital doesn't like items being interchanged between patients like that. You can understand that, can't you?"

I felt about an inch tall. He was doing his job and nothing more. It wasn't his fault I was here. In fact, I didn't really know whose fault it was. The whole thing was unreal like some nightmare from which I couldn't wake. I apologized and we stood talking a while.

Not long after I entered the lounge, Nancy walked in and the music from MTV filled the air. She sat down next to me on the couch. In her husky voice she started to tell me about her family history. I didn't understand her.

She was babbling, skipping from subject to subject without making any connections, although I did gather she was proud of who she was. Then she started explaining about all the gold jewelry she had displayed on her arms and hands. They were her prize possessions. Her father had given them to her before he had passed away. That's really all she had to her name, but the way she talked you would have thought she was a millionaire.

I sat there concerned about her. *Why would she be telling me such intimate details? I was a stranger.* I watched her more intently. She continued on with her stories, seeming to have forgotten I was even there. *Maybe she's not telling me but trying to figure it all out.*

She shook her head violently as she began arguing with someone. Obviously, it wasn't me, I wasn't saying anything and no one else was in the room. So I figured it was "someone." She was trying to get her gold jewelry back from the person who stole it. This was confusing me—all her gold jewelry was on her.

Then suddenly, she changed the subject. She wanted

me to go to breakfast with her. I was leery, but I went, why not?

On our way down to the dining room we ran into the two little old ladies walking their way to nowhere. I smiled at them and said, "Keep it up, it's good for the circulation." I got no response from them but it didn't deter me, I was going to keep trying to make contact anyway.

We walked into the dining room. Dave and Jeremy were already seated at our table. Before we joined them we stopped and kissed the wall. While everyone else ordered breakfast I went over and got two glasses of cranberry juice. That's all I intended to have for breakfast, no more pigging out.

When I sat back down with them Dave asked, "Do you have a problem with cranberry juice or something? All you do is drink it."

"Do you mind, I happen to like it," I said prudishly.

Right then, a vision passed quickly through my mind, one of me lying on a table with no clothes on. I jerked my head in response. I didn't understand where a vision like this came from. As quickly as I began thinking about it, I stopped. I didn't mention my vision to anyone I knew. I sipped my juice and quickly involved myself in the conversation, trying to forget it ever happened.

After breakfast, I called Steve. I wanted to talk to someone who would make me feel real, normal. In my lonely state, he seemed the perfect candidate to reverse what Brookhollow had done to me. A girl answered the phone. My heart sank as I slammed the receiver down. I sat at the phone dumbfounded, my body trembled. I sat sulking.

Then I looked around me at where I was. Being at Brookhollow added to my misery and confusion too. Being locked behind closed doors made me feel like a caged animal. I felt trapped.

More than anything right now, I needed some fresh air. I tried everything I could think of, asking the nurses to let me go outside, but no one would let me out, even for a little while.

As I retreated to my room, I bumped into Dave; he had his coat and hat on. "Where are you going?" I questioned.

"Burt, one of the counselors, and I are going to the bookstore downtown," he said.

"Can I go along?" I pleaded.

"It's all right with me if it's all right with Burt," he said.

I ran out to find Burt. "Can I please go downtown with you?" I asked.

"Do you have supervised privileges?" he asked.

I didn't know what they were, much less if I had them. "I don't know, how do I find out?" I asked.

"They'll tell you at the nurses' station," he said.

I flew to the nurses' station, "Do I have supervised group privileges?" I asked.

"Not any more," was the response.

I didn't even stop to ask how I could have lost what I never knew I had. "How can I get them?" I asked.

"Your doctor has to grant them," Ann, the brisk, businesslike nurse on duty, said.

"Well where's my doctor?" I asked.

"He's not here, he won't be here until tonight," she said.

"Will you call him for me and ask him if I can go out? Please."

"He doesn't like to be bothered like this," she responded. As Ann said this, I noticed Dave and Burt standing in the middle of the hall, pacing.

"Please! Call him!" I said to her. Then I quickly turned toward Dave and said, "Hold on for five minutes, please."

"You'll have to tell me why you want to go out," she said.

"The bitch," I murmured.

"What!" she snapped.

"I'm claustrophobic, I want to go to the bookstore with Dave and Burt. Please call him," I pleaded. She picked up the phone and slowly started to dial. I looked behind me, Dave and Burt were still pacing. I looked back at Ann, she was still dialing. My adrenaline started flowing. "Hurry up."

Finally, Ann was off the phone, "Dr. Kamari said it would be all right . . ."

Before she was even finished I was on my way to get my coat. I flew to my room, grabbed my coat, and ran back to Dave and Burt.

"Let's go," I said with a smile. "Freedom."

I pulled my coat on as we walked down the hall. The horrendous buzzing noise of the outside door opening once again filled the air as we made our way out.

Letting the wind riffle my hair, I walked as slowly as I could, drinking in the crisp air. I started thinking about Steve, then I stopped myself, not wanting to ruin this rare opportunity. We walked for seven or eight blocks before we were at the bookstore. I wanted to stay outside and wait for them but Burt insisted I go in.

Once inside, even though I was told not to, I strayed from them both. I grabbed any old book, acting as though I was reviewing it, and leaned against the shelf, contemplating a way to escape. Before my thoughts were complete, Burt was at my side.

He took hold of my arm and asked, "Are you interested in the Women's Movement?"

"What?" I looked down and noticed the book in my hand, "Women in History." "Very," I replied.

"Are you going to buy the book?" he asked.

"No, I forgot my money," I said.

"I have some you can borrow," he offered.

I smiled at him—"the kindness of strangers", where did that line come from? "Great," I said. "When we get back to Brookhollow, I'll pay you back. Thanks." Both Dave and I waited in line and made our purchases.

The walk back went too fast for me. Before I knew it we were headed to the lounge. I only stayed for one cigarette, I still felt restless. Getting up, I walked to my room, shuffled the items around on my dresser, decided there was nothing else to do there, and left.

I strolled to the nurses' station, hoping to bother them, but they were too busy. I left and walked to the ICU door and peered in. Nothing was happening. I walked to the other end of the hall. Nothing was happening.

I went back to where I started. I grew bored. I got up and walked back to my room, turned and walked to the end of the other hall, turned, and walked back to my room.

I kept this up until Dr. Keogan stopped me with, "Out for your morning constitutional?"

I laughed and replied, "Gotta get some sort of exercise around this place; besides, it's good for the circulation." I went back to walking.

Once again I was interrupted, this time by Cecilia. She wanted to know if I'd help her into the kitchenette for coffee. I took hold of her bandaged arm, supporting her against me, and led the way. I didn't have the heart to make her go in with all those people, so I made the coffee and delivered it.

Cecilia was appreciative; however, Fran (not me—one of the other patients) let me know in no uncertain terms, that Cecilia would have to fend for herself from now on. I didn't understand. *It must be part of her treatment? Why else would they make a rule such as that? Or, are they against me?*

I went and helped myself to some cranberry juice. As I leaned on the door and reached for the juice, Fran popped her head over the door.

"Hi, Fran," she said.

"Hi, Fran!" I replied. The other Fran came walking in.

Both of us said, "Hi Fran!" We all began laughing, deeming ourselves the Fran Club. *This place has its moments.* We hung around in the kitchenette, gossiping.

Then the bigger Fran asked, "Why are you here?"

"You got me," I replied.

"You got me too!" she said. "See, no one thinks you belong here."

"Thanks," I said. "I'm glad for any reinforcement I can get."

After lunch, Jeremy and I sat down to a serious discussion about our presence at Brookhollow. He explained the attacks he had when he went out in public, when he panicked and lost control. He had been at Brookhollow for almost two months and planned to stay until he was over this fear which controlled his life.

I told him I had been feeling very ill and how I had been in a car accident. In the hospital, they hadn't believed how sick I really was and had thought it was all emotional. Now even my family had started to believe them but there wasn't anything wrong with my mind and I was going to get out of here somehow.

From here our conversation shifted to other aspects of our lives. Jeremy had some quite interesting ones. He was from a very wealthy family; however, he would have nothing to do with their money. He had been practically all over the world. He had a Master's degree in computer technology. The more he talked, the more I liked him. He reminded me of my brother Vince—he always wore only Wrangler jeans, like Vince. I felt secure with him, he wasn't like the others.

In comparison, my life was boring. I explained that I'd spent most of my life in the small town I grew up in. I had almost been married to someone named Steve but we had broken up and I was still missing him. I was the last in line of eight children. And I too had a degree, in Business.

As we shared confidences, we related well to each other. He, and our conversation, made me feel as if I was "out there" instead of "in here."

Dinner time was approaching and we went to the dining room, where we met up with Dave and Nancy. I wasn't even hungry, but going to dinner gave me something to do. It was a highlight of the day, a way to escape "the floor."

After everyone finished eating, we sat talking until a waitress kicked us out. We were the last to leave. Dr.

Kamari was striding up the hall as we headed for the lounge.

"How are you tonight?" I asked.

"I should ask you this," he replied.

"I'm fine, thank you," I said.

"Would you like to come talk to me?" he asked.

"Yes, I would," I replied. Seriously, I had to start making him believe me. We headed for our usual meeting place.

He started right off with, "Why don't you want to take your medicine?"

"That again!" I said exasperated. "I've explained several times Dr. Kamari. Do you really want me to go through it again?" I said.

The loudspeaker boomed, "Dr. Kamari, Dr. Kamari, please answer the hall phone." He walked toward the phone.

I sighed with relief when he returned and said, "I have to leave." There was little use trying to talk about my real problems when all they wanted to do here was sedate me.

Brookhollow was a timeless prison sentence. I had finally begun to realize that I wasn't going to get out of it by pleading or explaining. Everyone was fixated on my being mentally ill. No matter how hard or long I tried to show them that wasn't the real problem, they couldn't or didn't want to understand.

Even my family had turned against me. These doctors had convinced them that my problems were emotional and now they believed them. There was no one I could turn to, I thought desperately, no one. *Except,* a voice within me said, *yourself.*

At first, I tried not to hear it. *How was I going to do it all by myself? With no one believing me. Even if I found a way they'd all still think I was crazy.* Still, it was the only way out. Deep down I knew it, even as I continued to search for help. My resolve hardened as I returned to my bedroom and slept.

However, when another morning dawned, I decided to try a new tactic. Practically flying to the nurses' station, I figured out the day and time I should be released. I wouldn't make Christmas Eve. I was pissed. When I got to the office I asked for pen and paper, wrote a letter asking for my release, and handed it in.

Then I went to the phone and called home to let them know when they should pick me up. My sister Jackie answered.

"I'm being released Friday morning at nine," I said.

"They're discharging you already?" she asked. "Are you sure? They've been saying you're too confused to go, Fran."

"No, I wrote a letter. Now they have to discharge me," I replied.

"I want to talk to your doctor," she stated. "We're worried about you, Fran."

"You don't have to talk to him. I'm telling you what you need to know," I said.

"We won't pick you up until we talk to your doctor," she said.

"He's here at night, you can call him tonight," I said.

"We will," she said right before she hung up.

The thought of going home thrilled me. I walked around the rest of the morning singing and acting like a total fool, laughing at everything. I participated in all the Groups that day, and in each, I shared my enthusiasm for life. Even in the "How to deal with loss" Group I was able to uplift spirits.

By mid-afternoon, my gallivanting caught up with me. My head was aching again. I went to my room to rest. Dr. Kamari walked in as I lounged on my bed.

"Would you mind coming to the Quiet Lounge with me?" he asked.

"No," I replied.

He led the way. Once inside, he closed the door and grew very serious.

"I hear you wrote a letter asking for discharge," he said.

"I did and I'm leaving this time. You can't stop me."

"I'm not going to stop you," he said gruffly.

"Good!" I answered firmly. "By the way, I need to know my diagnosis for my insurance papers."

"Schizophrenia form disorder," he said in a monotone.

"Whaaat! What is that?"

"A nervous breakdown."

"You're kidding," I was shocked, "I don't feel as if I had a nervous breakdown."

He looked into my eyes, his own steely blue and icy, "I'm not kidding. If you leave now, you'll be sorry. You'll be leaving AMA."

"What's AMA?"

"Against medical advice."

Nancy warned me about this. This was their intimidation. "Will my insurance pay for everything even though I leave AMA?"

"I don't really know. But I should think it would."

"Then I'm leaving." I got up and walked out.

I spent the rest of the day ignoring all staff members. Then at three, Sam, a counselor who had become sort of a buddy, asked me if I wanted to go to the mall later.

"Of course I want to go," I said. "I'll be out of here."

He nodded, "We're going to leave at six. Fran, why don't you find out who else wants to go."

I agreed and made my way from room to room doing this. I was told there was a phone call for me. It was my brother Tony, he wanted to tell me they were coming over tonight to visit and talk to the doctor.

"He's already home for Christmas," I said, "but if you want to come, I'll cancel my trip to the mall." I felt upset at cancelling out on my friends but didn't say anything to him, because I also didn't like to disappoint my family. I had always been a "pleaser"—it was a hard habit to break.

After I hung up I went and told Nancy about the change in plans and why. She told me I shouldn't let my family run my life, I should call them and tell them they shouldn't come. I had to think about this. I did, for more than an hour. I decided I would do it even though the advice had come from Nancy. After all, I really wanted to go to the mall and have some fun.

I went to the phone, dialed, and waited. My mother answered. I took a deep breath and said, "Can you bring my black and blue flannel shirt with you tonight?"

"Fine," she replied. We hung up.

"You chicken, Fran," I murmured. I picked up the receiver again, dialed a few numbers and hung up. *Do it Fran*, I prodded myself. On the third ring Tony answered.

"I hate to tell you this but you can't come over tonight. I forgot about plans I made previously, I'm going out," I said.

"But you said earlier it was all right. What's going on?" he replied.

"Nothing. I gotta go, 'bye," I said and quickly hung up. The guilt was tremendous!

The trip to the mall was well worth the guilt. I had fun until we lost Nancy. We split up searching for her. A half hour passed before I found her in a jewelry store. Sam had told me to tell him if I found her and not approach her myself. I did just that and reported to him.

Sam was steaming by this time and he went to get Nancy. When they returned, Sam was propelling Nancy by the arm. We immediately went back to Brookhollow.

As I headed to my room, Jess stopped me. "You had visitors while you were gone." My family had left some things for me in my room. I ran there and saw the clothes I had asked for, neatly piled on top of my bed. Then I noticed a note lying on top of the pile. It read: "Came over for a visit. Sorry to have missed you. Love, Jackie, Connie, Tony, Eileen, and Mom."

The guilt I felt at disappointing them returned. I began to think now, *they're not going to let me come home for Christmas! I'm going to have to stay here!* I sank to the floor sobbing. The adrenalin flowed. I picked myself up and began pacing. *What am I going to do?*

I stopped at the window, leaned against it, and peered through the iron grates at the shadows and lights of the real world. Tears streaked my face. I felt alone, deserted. I went back to the bed, reread the note and crumpled it. As I finished, my head began throbbing.

I sat down in the corner next to the bed, curled my legs to my chest, and lowered my arms and head on top. *What's wrong with me?* I sobbed. I stayed in this position for almost an hour, alone and in utter despair.

My roommate walked in. I told her, "Please don't let anyone know about this, I don't want any questions." I excused myself and left, heading to the reception area so I could be alone. At the top of the stairs I ran into Sam. He wouldn't allow me to go down and walked me back to the lounge.

As we headed in, there was Dr. Kamari. He asked, "Would you like to come talk to me?" I followed. Halfway to our usual room he said, "I just got off the phone with your brother Vince."

"What did he want?" I asked shivering.

"He wanted me to give him some background information," he replied.

What did Vince say to him? "What kind of information?" I asked.

"Oh, just information," he replied.

I shook my head wearily, the conversation was going nowhere as usual. We weren't in the room long before I grew bored with the nonsense I didn't need, and left. Dr. Kamari followed without saying a word.

I wanted to find out what Vince had said and why he called. I went to the phone and called home. Vince wasn't there he wasn't expected until tomorrow. *He called from Chicago to ask about me,* I thought, *more guilt.*

Then I asked about my Visa bill and care insurance, I wanted to know if the bills for them had arrived yet. Eileen told me Dad had paid all my bills and had taken care of everything with the insurance. By now the guilt was overwhelming. I was bound and determined to make it up to him, especially now. I'd take care of my own business.

The phone conversation had left me frustrated, too tense to relax and too tired not to. My heart beat faster and faster, which caused my entire body to quiver. I went to the lounge, for a cigarette.

Holding my cigarette between two fingers, I tapped the other digits on the arm of the chair. My legs were crossed, however, my one foot followed the rhythm of my fingers. *What a mess,* I thought. *Everyone is worried about me. They think I can't handle my life.* I sat there staring.

Dr. Keogan walked in and said to me, "Hi, Fran. How are you doing?"

"Go to hell!" I said back.

He kept right on walking. I didn't want to deal with anything, so I stood up and went to bed.

At breakfast the next morning, I stayed alone, then sat through Dr. Lee's Group silently. I refused an offer to go outside for a walk. I even refused my karate lesson. All I wanted was to get out of there.

My first noticeable response that entire day, which one had to look hard to notice—very hard—came when Nancy started acting up in the lounge. She began pacing back and forth while talking and cursing out loud. Then she began kicking walls, hitting window grates, and pushing furniture.

"Why don't you grow up." I blurted out as I got up from the chair. As I walked away, I could feel her moving right behind me. I quickly turned and there she was, lunging toward me. I moved out of her path as fast as I could.

I stayed in my room until Dr. Lee stopped by. "I'd like to meet with you in a room down the hall," she said.

"Why not?" I answered. "Something to do." Sitting down next to her, I waited.

"Why have you written a letter of discharge?"

I gave her the usual answer, "There's nothing wrong with me. I don't belong here. Besides, Christmas is here, and afterwards I have a lot of business to take care of."

Then she suggested I go home only for a day and if everything went all right I would be discharged later. "I won't even consider it. That's your intimidation again."

I wanted to know something about her so I asked several questions. She declined answering any of them by saying she never talked about herself. It was the usual reaction.

"I should at least know something about the person I'm talking with," I insisted, then gave up. *It really didn't matter, this would be our last meeting.* This thought instantly lifted my spirits. We closed our meeting and I went to the lounge.

Dave and Jeremy were there. An older lady I had never seen before was with them. I joined all three at the table where they sat. They gave me the latest news about Nancy. She had been put into ICU for acting up. The new woman, Gert, said she was scared to death of Nancy, after only a short time with her in ICU. I felt sorry that Nancy was locked away in that tiny area, but I was glad she was away from me.

"She'll be back to normal soon," Dave said.

I grimaced and told Gert there was no reason to be afraid of Nancy. They continued gossiping about her, so I excused myself and left. *Nancy has a problem they don't understand,* I thought. *Even though she tried to attack me, I don't want to gossip about her.*

I went to the Quiet Lounge and joined Sam and Marty. They were two of the best counselors. They didn't treat me as some of the others did. I was a real person to them, and a mental case to others. We talked openly about many different subjects. As we talked, I forgot about my surroundings, my problems. I was enjoying myself—it was as if I was at home with my family.

Later, needing a cigarette, I headed to the Main

Lounge. Dave was there, so I sat with him. I always knew I could depend on Dave for a laugh. This time was an exception, he was quiet, serious.

I waited for him to speak before I said anything. I needed to know how he felt, what was on his mind, before I proceeded with my thoughts. He came right out and told me what his problem was: he wanted to be home for Christmas. I could relate to that, I wanted the same thing.

Still, talking about it didn't help. I changed the subject as fast as I could. Assuming the part of a clown, I nagged and played around. For a short while, I had his mind off Christmas. Then his cheerfulness faded, and once again he was serious.

"Fran, I want to thank you," he said, "you don't know how much you've done for me."

I tried to change the subject but he stayed on the same track. He told me I had brought him out of his shell, helped him to relax.

"Could we go somewhere more private where you can help me sort out things?" he asked. I nodded. We walked to the end of the corridor and sat in a corner. Our in-depth conversation concentrated on him. I refused to talk about myself except for a few sketchy comments. So far, no one knew what I really thought. I intended to keep it that way; it was safer.

Dr. Keogan and Jeremy strolled our way, interrupting our conversation. They asked if we wanted to go to Captain Quick's for a bite to eat.

"Just give me a minute to get my coat," I smiled. In no time, the four of us were walking out the door. *Fresh air and freedom.* I felt as if I was a new person every time I walked out the door.

Inside Captain Quick's I saw a new side of Dr. Keogan. He was all right. He had a quick wit and gentle air. I wondered if he could understand, *Can he help find out what is really wrong with me?* For a moment I wanted to try, but the moment passed and we went back to Brookhollow to endure the present and make time pass.

TEN

Tinsel and barred windows—Christmas Eve at Brookhollow. *One day left until I could sign out.* I sat in the Quiet Lounge, staring at my surroundings, wishing it were tomorrow. I was interrupted by a phone call, it was my sister Eileen.

"What time will you be discharged?" she asked softly.

"Nine," I said, savoring the sound.

"We'll be there," she said.

Inside I cheered. It was my first confirmation that I would really be home tomorrow. Obviously, my family's qualms had been alleviated by the doctors. That must mean people were beginning to believe me.

Right after I got off the phone, Dr. Kamari approached me. *What's he doing here during the day?* I wondered.

"I'd like to talk to you in your room," he said in that half polite, half commanding way. We walked down the hall together. Inside, I plopped myself on my bed. He sat stiffly on the other one.

Before he had a chance to say anything I asked, "Am I crazy?"

"Just a little bit crazy," he replied as he spread his thumb and forefinger an inch wide, demonstrating the little bit.

"A little bit," I said quietly. *What does that mean? What did he see,* I wondered, *that would even suggest this?* I didn't pursue it. I knew this was wrong.

He continued with, "Since it's Christmas, how would you like to go home today instead of tomorrow?" he asked shyly. His eyes narrowed to slits. I didn't care about the whys.

"You mean leave today? Yes! When can I go?" I asked.

"Three o'clock this afternoon, I'll be back to discharge you," he said quietly as he got up to leave.

"I don't know how to thank you," I smiled. I was right behind him.

I began singing on the way to the phone. Tony answered.

"I get to come home today!" I said.

"Fantastic! When?" he responded enthusiastically.

"Three o'clock, can someone come pick me up at three?" I said.

"Someone will be there. Fran, your doctors do think everything is all right then?" he asked.

"My doctors don't have anything to do with it, they say it's AMA. I'm discharging myself, I don't belong here," I replied.

"What do you mean," Tony's voice had begun to take on an anxious tone, "you discharged yourself? What's AMA?" he said.

"It's against medical advice. But Tony, these guys don't know what they're talking about. They said I had a nervous breakdown but there's nothing wrong with me," I replied.

"Someone will be there at three," he said grimly as he hung up. *I knew I shouldn't have told him so much. Why did I open my big mouth?*

Even though it was four hours before I would leave, I went to my room and packed. "I can't wait to get out of here!" I said to my roommate.

When I finished packing I went to the lounge where I

met up with Dave and Jeremy. They told me about a Christmas party in the dining room later that afternoon. I was in the mood for a party. I was going home!

I was so excited, I couldn't sit still, I began to pace the hallways. As I paced I greeted everyone with a smile and a Merry Christmas. Everyone noticed my spritely walking and asked if I was nervous. I didn't pay any attention. My only reply was that walking was good for your circulation and they should try it.

I didn't care what anyone thought, I was going home! I even pounded on the ICU door in order to walk through there. I noted that, John, the first person I had seen when I was first locked in ICU, was still there.

A lot of people at Brookhollow were afraid of him or made fun of his mental disability. But I liked him and he liked me. It wasn't his fault he was born mentally retarded, he was still a person. I treated him gently as I wished some of the people there would treat me.

"Come on to the Christmas party," I said. "You'll be my guest." He was thrilled. In the lounge, we listened to music. As I sat there, I said, pulling on his arm, "This will be a good Christmas after all."

Dave, Jeremy, and Timmy, a psychiatric aide, joined us. Timmy was a hunk, and likeable too. It was too bad I was a patient. We joked for a while and then we headed to the party.

In the dining room, a long table had been covered with a green and red holiday cloth. On it were all kinds of cheese spreads and tiny tea sandwiches. In the corner, Jess was ladling out cherry fruit punch.

All the patients from every wing were there so the room was crowded with people I didn't know. Dr. Keogan and a few others were acting as D.J.'s, playing Christmas music. I settled John in a chair and left him.

Then I went to the lounge to wait out my last hour at Brookhollow. Not long after, Dr. Keogan and several others declared it was now time to sing Christmas carols.

Someone began playing the guitar and "Silent Night" filled the air.

Tears filled my eyes, I missed Steve, my ex-fiancé. *How many Christmas's did we cuddle in a room lit only by the lights of the tree and listen to this very song?* I pulled myself together when "Mrs." Dr. Lee, as I called her, began to motion me from the room.

"How do you feel about going home Fran?" she said a bit ominously.

"Are you kidding?" I asked. "I'm thrilled, I can't wait to get out," I exclaimed and began walking away.

"Well then, I'm happy for you," she said, obviously having hoped I would give her an opening; I didn't.

Our meeting ended—the last thing I was going to do was sit around and answer questions when I was about to go home. There was only a half hour left before I became a free person. I went to my room to make sure I had packed everything. Then I headed back to the lounge to kiss the wall for my very last cigarette at Brookhollow.

The closer it got to three o'clock, the faster my pulse raced. Finally, the clock struck three. Neither Dr. Kamari nor my family were there.

"What's going on? Everyone in my family is punctual if not early," I said to no one in particular.

I went to the nurses' station to see if anyone had called. No one had. I went back to the lounge. It was three-fifteen and still no one was there. *Am I going to have to stay here?* I wondered.

Three-thirty rolled around and still no one. I went to the nurses' station to see if they would call Dr. Kamari. They wouldn't. I went back to the lounge for a cigarette. Three-forty-five, and no one. *They never intended to let me go home. They're playing games.*

I grew more aggravated than ever, my hands and feet twitched. *Where are they?* I went to the nurses' station once more to see if they would call my house. They wouldn't.

As I turned to head back to the lounge I saw my mother and Vince walking up the hall with worried looks

on their faces. I headed toward them. As I got closer I
noticed each one was carrying something. My mother had
a tray wrapped in aluminum foil with a red bow in its center. Vince had a bag.

*They're not letting me go home. Oh God! They're bring-
ing Christmas to me.* We were inches from each other,
when Vince spoke, "We've been waiting downstairs an
hour for the doctor, where is he?" *I didn't understand why
they were waiting for the doctor, but I figured I'd better get
him.*

"I don't know. I'll go find out though," I said and
turned toward the nurses' station. When I got there I was
told Dr. Kamari had just called and said he was on his way.
I relayed this message.

Vince held the bag up and said, "Merry Christmas
Fran."

"If I'm going home, shouldn't I open my present
there?" I asked quizzically.

Then my mother said, "Fran have the nurses put these
on another tray, I need this one back!"

"What are they?"

"Cookies."

"This is in case you need to pack anything." Vince
brandished the bag.

I breathed a sign of relief realizing the package they'd
brought contained presents for the nurses and other patients. I headed back to the nurses' station, Vince and my
mother followed. After stopping at the nurses' station, we
went to my room to wait for Dr. Kamari. We all sat on my
bed silently.

A half hour passed, then an hour. I was beginning to
be afraid I'd never get out.

"Maybe we'd better ask the nurses for an update,"
Vince said. My mother and I nodded almost together and
we rushed out.

As we approached the nurses' station, Dr. Kamari
walked through.

"Where have you been? You said three o'clock!" I said

frantically. He ignored my comment and directed his attention to my mother and brother.

"We can meet in a room down the hall," he said ominously.

"You don't have to meet with them. You only have to discharge me," I objected. "You said you were going to discharge me," I said. I was ignored once again.

"Fran, let us talk to him. It's for your own good," Vince said.

"You'll have to meet without me," I yelled.

He walked down the hall without replying. Vince and my mother followed. They disappeared into a room. *What are they doing in there? What are they talking about?* I wondered fearfully. A nurse interrupted my thoughts.

"Fran, do you want to take these to the lounge?"

I snatched the goddamn cookies away. I ran smack dab into Jeremy.

"Here, have some cookies!" I said as I thrust the tray toward him. Instantly I turned and headed for the room where Dr. Kamari was holding his meeting. *I'll find out what's going on and stop it.*

I walked right past the room, looking right and left to see if I could discover anything before entering. The door was wide open, but, I couldn't hear what they were saying. I passed by several times, trying to decide what I should do.

Finally, I stopped, leaned against the wall, and cocked my head to the side in order to hear better. My hands and feet had begun twitching, my heart pounded. My head throbbed. "He has no right to do this," I said half to myself. The longer I stood there, the angrier I got.

Finally, I turned and walked in yelling, "You have no right to be here talking to *my* doctor. It's none of your business. I don't talk to your doctor, do I?"

Instantly, my focus switched to Dr. Kamari with, "All you have to do is discharge me. So, why don't you do it?" I left and went back to leaning against the wall.

They went on talking. I went back in and demanded, "Why aren't you stopping?"

Vince shook his head, "You're being irrational, Frances."

"I am not. I want this meeting over."

"You're spoiled rotten," Dr. Kamari said.

I looked him straight in the eye, "And you're incompetent. Something's wrong with me. You can't find out what so you've labeled me crazy."

Dr. Kamari interrupted me, turning toward Vince and my mother. "Frances won't be discharged until tomorrow."

"What!" I screamed.

He ignored me and continued to talk with Vince and my mother. "Frances won't be discharged until tomorrow. You can come back tomorrow and pick her up." He got up, said goodbye, and left. Shaken but obedient, Vince and my mother did the same.

I followed Dr. Kamari. I found him at the nurses' station. "Do you know what you just did? You made me miss Christmas. I hope you're happy. I hope you have a nice Christmas because some of us won't. *Merry Christmas!"* I screamed sarcastically.

"You could have gone home if you'd been more obedient in front of your family. I told you this earlier," he said.

"Who do you think you are?" I said. "You're not my father and I'm not a child," I cried frustratedly.

I walked away and then returned to ask the nurse for my medicine. The medicine I had been refusing since I came here. *Something has to calm me down. I'll try it once anyway.*

After she gave me the medicine I went to the desk where Dr. Kamari sat. My eyes filled with fire as I leaned over the top of the desk, placed my hands firmly on top of it, put my face directly in front of his, and very sternly said, "Merry Christmas."

I went to my room, kicked the door open, sat in the corner, and stared into space. Tears began flowing down my face. "The bastard," I cried. "I'm not crazy. Now he's made me act like I am." I sat in the dark for almost fifteen minutes before my roommate came in.

I got up and left right away. I went to the lounge and stood off in the corner, not speaking. My body was trembling. I popped cookies in my mouth left and right. *These might calm me down. The room started closing in on me, it was getting tough to breathe.*

"I have to get out of there," I murmured. I went to my room, grabbed my coat. "I have to get out of here," I said blurrily. "I'll make it home for Christmas Eve somehow."

I went to the lounge to see who would take me for a walk, I could escape then. No one would. Walking out into the hall, I bumped into Jerry, a counselor. I couldn't control the tears running down my cheeks as I asked, "Will you please go for a walk with me, I gotta get out of here."

"I can't do that," he answered.

"Then will you just walk outside with me for a second? Just outside the door, that's all. I gotta get out of here. Please! Please!" I begged.

"I can't do that either," he replied once again and walked away.

I followed him to the office. At the door I began pleading, "Please, I have to get out of here."

My foot began to stamp the floor. Jerry turned and stood against the door which exposed Dr. Keogan at the desk. As Dr. Keogan looked toward me with deep concern in his eyes I began ranting, "I gotta get out of here! I'm claustrophobic. I gotta get out of here!" And my foot stamped, tears flowed, and my body bent in two.

"Please!" I said.

Then a prickly feeling began to flow through my body. It made me feel as if I were disappearing. "I gotta get out of here."

"I feel the same way," Dr. Keogan said. "This is Christmas Eve, I have four children."

I stopped dead in my tracks. I felt guilty as I stood straight. Dr. Keogan walked over and hugged me, "Sorry kid, I can't let you go out there. Everything will be all right." He patted my back several times.

"You don't understand. There's nothing wrong with me. I don't want to be here. I need some fresh air. Will you please go outside with me? I'm claustrophobic," I said.

"If you're claustrophobic in this big building, then I'm claustrophobic too. I can't let you go out, it's dark out there. How about if I open a window for you," he replied. He led me over to a window and opened it. The cold air came rushing in. I put my face against the metal grates and took deep breaths.

"I'm stuck in here forever," I cried out.

Finally, Dr. Keogan closed the window. As he did he said firmly, "I'll be in tomorrow morning at nine to discharge you. Dr. Kamari wanted me to make sure everything was all right before you left. I'll see you then." He left. I tried to believe him. I went back to the lounge feeling miserable, my head aching.

Everyone was singing Christmas carols when I arrived. I was in no mood to join. As I sat there silently, I noticed the food everywhere. I took some of everything and began shoveling it into my mouth. It was as if I hadn't eaten in days. I was hoping the food would stop my insides from shaking. But it didn't. I continued to be filled with anxiety.

Jeremy made his way over to me. He sat next to me and put his arm around my shoulder and began singing. Neither one of us said anything, however, we both knew what the other was thinking, feeling. *Betrayed and lonesome.* When the song was over, we hugged and left for our rooms without a word.

I was up at five, showered and dressed, and waiting to go home. It seemed as though days passed before nine came. When the hour came, there was no Dr. Keogan, no family. My heart beat fiercely. Fear filled me.

I went to the nurses' station to ask where Dr. Keogan was, but they had no idea. I had started back to the lounge when the nurse called out to me that she had just hung up with Dr. Keogan and he was on his way.

"Thank God!" I said, "I'm going finally and this time no one can stop me, no matter what." Forty-five minutes later, Dr. Keogan showed up but there was still no one from my family.

"Maybe they're not coming to pick me up," I said.

He smiled, "Maybe they're just late, traffic or something."

"I might have to take a bus."

Dr. Keogan led me to the conference room. His tall and husky physique shadowed my view. Silently he leafed through my file. *I wonder what this man thinks of me, especially after last night.* Running a hand through his hair, he looked up and at me intently.

"Fran, can you tell me what happened that sent you to Brookhollow?" he asked.

"I got in a car accident," I replied.

"Where are you going once you leave?" he asked.

"To my family's home," I said.

"Where do they live?" he asked.

I gave my own address, "19 Marbleview Drive."

"You can't leave until your family comes," he said.

"They're late—I'm worried," I said.

"Do you want me to call them?" he asked agreeably.

I nodded. He left and came back a few minutes later. "A misunderstanding, they'll be here about 3 P.M."

As I sat there while he wrote, I grew weaker and weaker, my head was becoming fuzzy, pulsing. I had a hard time concentrating, and my stomach started churning as though I was about to throw up.

I wanted to tell him about how I was feeling but I thought fearfully to myself, *Don't say anything Fran, you'll never get out of here. It's your nerves, that's all.*

Finally he stopped writing and asked me to sign some papers. I couldn't see, everything was dancing around. I acted as though there was nothing going on and blindly signed my name close to where he originally had the pen pointed. *I'm free.*

I went back to the lounge to wait. Nancy came walking in as I sat there. Her strong voice instantly filled the air with, "I'm going home for Christmas. My mother is coming this afternoon. We're going to my uncle's house. You big shit."

She began to monopolize the entire lounge with her loud motions and voice. She was on the move constantly, going from one person to the next, intimidating them. No one was brave enough to say anything to her. She made her way over to where I was.

I stopped her midway, "Don't you even think about coming another step closer. You don't scare me." She turned and headed away to bother someone else.

A new face burst into the lounge. It was a woman, covered with the ugliest black cape I ever saw. Her hair was solid white and she walked with a cane. She looked like a witch! Soon enough, Nancy was all over the woman saying, "Merry Christmas, Mom."

"Like mother, like daughter," I murmured.

Suddenly, and without any warning, their friendly greeting turned into an all-out war. I couldn't make heads or tails out of what they were arguing about. When I had enough of them, I got up to get some cranberry juice.

In the middle of the hall I stopped. An eerie feeling swept through me. I could barely keep my balance. The entire floor was deserted except for a single nurse who was deep in thought at her desk. I wasn't going to tell her how I felt. I might not get released.

As I headed back to the lounge, I saw my mother and Vince coming down the corridor. The closer they got the more nervous I became. We stood solemnly in the middle of the corridor.

"Fran, please get your things right now," my mother said. I did what I was told without saying a word. When I had everything together I walked down the hall. It seemed longer than ever. My mother and Vince were at the nurses' station when I returned. I stopped where they were and plunked my things down.

"You have to sign out and get a pass before you can leave," my mother said. I did this and began collecting my things. This time, both my mother and Vince assisted me. As we made our way to the door, the buzzing noise from the lock began. I looked up, then back down, closed my eyes, and sighed gratefully. *It didn't matter who believed me, I was out.*

ELEVEN

When the car stopped in the driveway, my brother Vince pulled the lever to release the trunk. I got out, retrieved my things, and headed to the door.

Once inside I took a step back. *It doesn't seem like home.* It was as if I was in a dream, the house full of a mist. The kitchen door was closed as I approached. Before opening it I took a deep breath.

My parents, brother Tony and sisters Eileen and Jackie were waiting for me. The anguished looks on their faces as I walked in made me take a second deep breath to prepare for what lay ahead.

"Merry Christmas to you," I said slowly. They all returned perfunctory greetings but kept staring intently at me. Always in the past, they had always greeted me with hugs and kisses. This time, no one moved to embrace me. It was almost as if they were afraid to touch me.

"Why is everyone acting this way?" I cried out. Suddenly I felt I had to get out of there. I started to make my way to the bedroom, lugging my things along. I headed up the stairs.

Tony came and stopped me, "Mom and I want you to open your presents first," he said. I followed Tony to a pile of presents. He was the only one there as I opened them.

My mother and sisters were in the kitchen, my father and Vince sat solemnly in the living room.

Tony handed me a small gift from him to open. It was an envelope full of pictures of me from Thanksgiving, each done with some photographic magic. In one, I was posed in several different positions, and on another, my name was written across in lights as I stood alongside.

I remembered him taking these pictures. He made me feel special when he took them. I had sent him a thank-you note filled with love because his gesture had touched me. I thanked him over and over again for making me feel so good.

"I hope you like the results, Fran. I got your note," Tony said.

I turned, hugged and kissed him. "I'll treasure them," I said.

As I went on opening other gifts, Eileen sat down alongside of me saying, "There's one from each one of us. We all love you Fran."

Then my mother walked in, carrying a bag, "This is for you," she said handing the bag to me. It was a new winter jacket.

I had quite a collection of gifts by the time I finished; however, the gift I wanted the most—one from Steve— wasn't there. Thanking everyone, I gathered up my gifts and made my way upstairs.

My room was spotless, not at all as I had left it. Everything was in its place, the bed was made, and not an article of clothing was on the floor. It didn't seem like my room, I got an eerie feeling being there. I dropped my things where I stood and sprawled across the bed. Exhausted I fell fast asleep.

I slept until the next morning. Dressed, I went to the kitchen for some coffee. My head got light and I grew weaker and weaker. Every once in a while I felt twinges throughout my body, especially at my joints. "Great, all I need now is to be sick," I mumbled.

"Sick?" my mother, who had come into the room, asked agitatedly. "Frances, what's wrong with you?"

"Nothing," I murmured desperately. "Nothing, I'm just tired."

"But you've just slept for twelve hours," she said, her forehead wrinkling. "How can you still be tired?"

"Mom, please, I can handle everything. Just give me some space," I interjected.

She sighed, "You're all dressed to go out," she said, questionably.

"I'm going to see my lawyer."

"Lawyer," she said, echoing me. "Why?"

"I want to see what he has to say about both the accident and the commitment."

She looked shocked, but said nothing. I headed out the door and to my car. Later, while waiting in my lawyer's office, the light-headed feeling returned. I hoped I could make sense when I spoke to him.

Once inside his office, I began to explain about the accident and how I discharged myself from the hospital I was put in. I had a tough time following his reply even though it was brief. All I wanted to do was lie down. Next, we started talking about how he'd have to set up a meeting with another lawyer in order to deal with the commitment. We closed the meeting and I flew to my car. I had to get home and lie down.

At home I called Dr. Kamari and asked for a prescription for the tranquilizer he wanted me to take, figuring this might help me. He was pleased with the idea of my submission and offered to call it into my drug store. Dr. Kamari then set up an appointment for me to come in the next Monday.

The next day I felt a little better and talked my sister Eileen into giving me a perm. She wasn't the one who usually gave me perms, my sister Molly was; however, Molly wasn't there. Eileen wasn't as good as Molly. As she rolled each rod my head tingled in pain. *I know she's not this bad,* I thought. *It's my head.* I never mentioned anything to her, I wanted my perm no matter what.

When all the perm rods were out, she massaged my head under warm running water. The ringing sensation from the other night began again. I still remained silent. The longer she massaged, the more it hurt and the dizzier I felt. Still I said nothing.

When I stood up, after leaning over the sink, my head felt ten times lighter than before. It was as if the top and back weren't even there. It scared me! I still wouldn't say anything though. I didn't want anyone thinking I belonged in a hospital, a mental hospital.

As soon as the perm was done I went back to the couch. I couldn't lift myself off the couch no matter how hard I tried. Again I stayed there for the rest of the day.

The next morning, still feeling awful, it was back to the couch again. I didn't even have the energy to get dressed. As I lay there, pictures of the morning after the accident began flashing through my head.

Did this happen or didn't it? Should I ask someone or will they put me back in the hospital if I do? The picture of me stopping my friend Liz in the hall, asking her what year it was, appeared. It should be easy enough for me to find out if it really happened or not, I mused. *I'll call her and ask.* I persuaded myself to get off the couch and called her.

She laughed hysterically at my question and replied, "You did Fran, you did! And, I'm sorry I wasn't able to stop and talk, but I was late for work. I knew something had happened to you when you stopped me. Do you remember being in the emergency room?"

"Thanks Liz, give me a call later," I said and hung up. I went back to the couch to think about what I should do.

Every once in a while I got up from the couch to get something to drink. Other than that I didn't move for the rest of the afternoon. My thoughts remained tangled. I could not come up with an answer for my constant question of, "Why?" Finally, starving, I went into the kitchen for something to eat. I hadn't eaten all day.

When I showed my face in the kitchen, my mother started asking again, "What's wrong Fran? What's wrong?"

Tears began pouring down my face. "Are you trying to drive me crazy?" I asked and I went back to the couch. Right before I was about to doze a horrendous ringing noise started.

Where's it coming from? Why? Should I say something to someone? No you can't Fran. They'll think you're crazy, they'll put you back in the hospital. I couldn't figure out where it was coming from, then it hit me, it was in my head. I closed my eyes tight and waited for sleep.

A few hours later I sat up startled. Suddenly my body started falling. I screamed. Grasping at the couch, I wildly attempted to secure my trembling body. It felt as if there was nothing there to support me. Nothing to hold onto. Finally, I got hold of myself. "It must have been a nightmare," I murmured.

I looked around realizing I had been reaching over the edge of the couch and that's why I couldn't grasp onto anything. I settled myself back down, relieved to know I wasn't having a fit or being possessed. "Thank God no one heard this or I would have been a goner for sure," I murmured.

Then my mother coughed and, raising my head, I looked right into her eyes. After that my parents began questioning me incessantly. I tried not to answer. I didn't want to make them more fearful than they already were.

Each day I forced myself to go on. I tried everything I could think of to make me feel better. I took aspirin, Dr. Kamari's medicine, and I even went to the store for antacid. Nothing worked. I spent most days on the couch. *Maybe it's Dr. Kamari's medicine which is making me feel this way?*

On Saturday I called the hospital. He wasn't there on

Saturdays. I left a message. During the next few days, I didn't move off the couch except when Dr. Kamari called. I explained to him some of what I felt, though I still had to be careful what I said. He told me it was the medicine and not to worry about it.

Back on the couch, my stomach started cramping up and I doubled over in pain. My head started pounding. *This can't be the medicine.* I laid there for hours waiting for the pain to cease.

Finally, I was able to get up and went to the bathroom. There, I discovered my period had started. *This is all happening because of my period and Dr. Kamari's medicine.* I laughed. *You stupid jerk, Fran. Nothing like being paranoid.*

Even though I was now less concerned, I still watched what I said and did. *There's always that chance.* I spent the rest of the week acting as the best little girl there ever was. Being committed had destroyed my confidence and it showed.

Then, on Saturday, it started getting tough to move even an inch. My back hurt, my feet hurt, even my arms ached when I moved them. I called Dr. Kamari, but he wasn't there. I panicked. *Did this happen in the accident? When Dave dropped me?*

I began to envision spending the rest of my life in a wheelchair. I was horrified and retreated to the couch. I didn't move until hours later; Eileen and Connie wanted me to go sledding with them. I was tempted to tell them I thought I was becoming paralyzed; however, I avoided the issue and refused their invitation, saying it was too cold. I spent the rest of the night on the couch afraid to move, afraid of the pain.

I had to inch my way out of bed the next morning. Even the slightest movements were agonizing. Making my way down the stairs was a feat in itself. I went right to the couch, never moving until Thursday, when I felt better. That day I walked from room to room and enjoyed the movement.

Suddenly, in the middle of my jaunt my bones stiffened. I felt as if I were enclosed in a body cast. I slowly headed back to the couch. Even at a slow pace, I began to feel lightheaded. I lowered myself to the couch. Nothing was standing still or distinguishable. Tears formed. *Maybe Steve had something to do with this?* This thought was unbearable.

I cradled my head in my hands as I tried to figure out what was happening to me. As I stared blankly at the floor the back of my head seemed to be moving in and out and the floor beneath me began moving about. "What is *happening!*" I cried out. I leaned against the pillow hoping to stop it all and afraid to say anything, for fear of being sent back to Brookhollow.

Several hours later, the phone began ringing nonstop. Although I was scared to death of moving from the couch, I maneuvered myself up and into the other room to answer it. It was Missy, an old friend I hadn't talked to since being hospitalized.

I explained to her what was happening and asked for help. She asked me how many tranquilizers I was taking. "Five a day," I said slowly. As soon as I told her, she told me to cut down the dose. I did, but I seemed to worsen. My parents' constant carping at me continued.

I sat at the dining room table one night, almost two weeks later, and couldn't keep silent any longer. I didn't explode. I seethed, "Why don't you get off my case? Stop trying to control me. You don't understand, why don't you butt out."

Moments later, my sister Jackie grabbed my wrist. I told her to let go, she wouldn't. Instead, her grip got tighter and she began to lecture me, "Why don't you get a job, do something with your life. You're an inconsiderate, spoiled rotten snot."

Frantically, I tried to free myself, my wrist turning bright red. All I was accomplishing was to twist her hand around, thereby strengthening her grip. My wrist stung. Tony came to my rescue and pulled her off.

Within seconds, Vince was standing in front of me saying, "You are going back to the hospital."

"I'm not. You can't make me. You can't recommit me," I said.

"If you don't get hold of yourself, we can and we will," he replied.

I pushed the table out away and began to walk away. Vince followed. I tried to escape through the hallway; however, my father blocked that exit. I was trapped!

Then, my father raised his hand to his temples, his eyes filling with tears, "I don't know what's wrong with you, Frances."

Vince stepped in front of him as he said, "I'll handle this Dad, go back into the living room." As he talked he stepped away from me. I took the opportunity to flee.

Running to the front door, I unlocked it, flung it open, and was on the porch in seconds. I took the stairs two at a time. At the bottom I realized Vince was right behind me. I ran as fast as I could up the street yelling back, "Leave me alone! Please!" Vince pursued relentlessly.

A block and a half past, I lost him. I kept running. I had no idea where I was going. Finally, satisfied no one was around, I slowed to a fast walk. *I'll call Dr. Keogan, see if he'll help me. Maybe he'll talk some sense into them.*

At the nearest phone booth, I stopped. After dialing the number, I realized I had no money. I hung up and tried calling collect. The line was busy. *Now what? I can't stay here, they might be out looking for me.*

I began walking to where I knew another phone booth was, keeping to side streets to elude followers. I tried the number, my collect call was refused. *Whose phone can I use?*

I decided to go to the church, they were sure to help me. I walked another five blocks to get there. The doors were locked so I tried the rectory, no one answered. I sat on the steps in front of the church holding my head in my hands, crying. *Please God, help me!*

It was freezing sitting there. I had to keep walking,

keep warm. *I'll try Missy, she'll let me use her phone.* I began walking in the direction of her house, stopping a quarter of the way there. *It's too long a walk. Now what? I have no money, nowhere to go.*

I kept walking, my head bowed down low. I stopped in a park and huddled among the trees. *Fran, you have no alternative. Go home, get money, call Dr. Keogan, and later tonight leave.* I walked to the main street and began walking on the sidewalk with my head held up high. *No one will conquer me!*

I was almost home when a police car pulled up alongside of me. My eyes began to move rapidly. The officer popped his head out the window, "Can we talk a second," he said.

I kept walking as I replied, "I don't have time right now, I'm on my way to use the phone." My pace quickened. Another police car stopped in front of me. I stopped. The officer got out of the car and walked right up to me. *Play it cool, Fran,* I said to myself. *He can't do anything to you unless you ask for it.*

"Your family is worried about you, Fran," he said.

I stared at him, pictures flashing through my mind. *Maybe he's the doctor who drove me to the hospital.* The other officer approached. My heart raced. *What are they going to do?*

"I was just about to call my doctor. You can talk to him if you'd like. I'm perfectly normal," I said.

"You seem to be," was his reply. They both left.

I started back home. I got into the house with no problem. In my room I tried to call Dr. Keogan. He wasn't there. I went back downstairs, prepared to leave once again.

When I got into the kitchen Jackie was on the phone. She noticed me and instantly held out the receiver saying, "Someone wants to talk to you, Fran."

"I don't want to," I replied as I continued to the door.

At the cellar entrance stood Vince, "You're going back to the hospital," he said.

"No I'm not and you can't make me," I said turning and heading toward the front door. Tony blocked the front door, "You're going back, Fran," he said.

I began running around like someone demented trying to flee from captivity. I was back in the kitchen—now Vince and Tony both started to move closer. I began screeching, "Leave me alone! Leave me alone!"

Vince grabbed me around the waist, I grabbed on to the door frame. Tony pried my fingers free. I made myself become dead weight. Vince yanked me back, resuming his grip.

"Let go of me! I'm not going anywhere. I can't breathe," I told him. He wouldn't let go.

"She can't get out of here Vince, let go of her," Tony said. Vince let go. My arms were like spaghetti, they hung loosely at my sides trembling.

"Frances, we have to get you some help."

"I know," I said slowly. "Look, just let me call my doctor."

"Let her," Tony said firmly. "All of us need help," he said.

I called Dr. Kamari's office. He told me to come right over.

Halfway there my back began to move up and down with the motion of the car. It was as if my spine were floating loosely through my body. I had them drop me off in front of Dr. Kamari's office. Staggering into his office, I confronted his secretary, "I need to see Dr. Kamari right away."

"He's with a patient right now, but they should be though in a minute," was her reply. I stood at his door waiting. The moment it cracked open I flew in, "You said you played games. Why are you giving me these drugs? What game are you playing?" I said.

"No, *you* said you played games," Dr. Kamari replied.

I sat down in the chair in front of his desk, "I don't feel good. My bones are stiff, my head aches."

"You don't look good," he replied.

"Taking tranquilizers five times a day is a lot," I objected. "Why do you have me taking so many?"

"Maybe you needed that much," he replied.

"I can't walk. I'm all sore," I added.

"It's just the medicine," he replied.

"My head is moving in and out. My back is moving, and the floor is dancing. How do you think I'm doing?"

"That's not the medicine," he stated abruptly.

"Would you like to go talk to Dr. Keogan?" He stood up. I nodded my head yes and Dr. Kamari said, "He's at the hospital. I'll call and let him know you're coming."

We headed toward Brookhollow. It was freezing out. I shivered standing outside. Finally, the buzzer rang and I entered Brookhollow. The receptionist smiled, "Dr. Keogan will be with you in a moment. Make yourself comfortable."

I went to the couch and waited. Fifteen minutes passed and no Dr. Keogan. Tears flowed down my face. *I'll have to go back home without anyone even helping me.* I was about to give up on Dr. Keogan when he walked through the door.

The instant he saw me he extended his hand and said, "Fran, how nice to see you again." I got off the couch, sobbing out of control, to greet Dr. Keogan. When I was face to face with him I tried to stop my tears, but they only flowed harder.

"Let's go talk over there," he said pointing to the room I knew as the interrogation room. I tried once more to stop crying as he placed his arm around my shoulder and led me to the room.

For a few moments they stopped, but when I sat down next to Dr. Keogan, my tears returned in full force and I sobbed hysterically, "Dr. Keogan, I don't feel good." Without saying anything he reached out to take my wrist. Automatically I yanked it back.

"I want to get your pulse, that's all," he said. Timidly, I placed my wrist near him.

He took my pulse and said, "You should be dead."

"What do you mean, I don't understand," I replied.

"I think you should stay here for a few days Fran," he replied, watching me intently.

"I can't, my family is waiting for me," I said as I trying to gain control of my emotions. I was calm only for a moment before my tears returned.

"I don't understand. I'm so confused," I said.

"Don't go anywhere, I'll be back in a minute," Dr. Keogan replied. When he returned he was carrying a folder full of papers.

"I think you should stay with us Fran. We all like you here," he said as he spewed the papers across the desk.

"But it's not mental, I don't feel good physically," I said trying once more to get someone to understand. Just then Dr. Kamari walked in.

"Dr. Keogan wants me to stay, I don't feel good," I said to him between sobs.

"I think that's a good idea," he replied.

"I'm not going to stay," I said.

"We can make you stay," Dr. Kamari said.

When I heard this, I grabbed a pen and cried, "I'll stay, I'll stay. Please help me. Where do I sign?"

"Settle down Fran, Dr. Keogan and I will be right back," Dr. Kamari said. And they both walked away.

At the door Dr. Kamari turned and smiled, while he fiddled with the doorknob, "Sorry I forgot."

What is he talking about? What does he know I don't know? My head throbbed more after they were gone. Running to the door, I jiggled the doorknob to see if they had locked me in. They hadn't. I returned to my chair and waited.

A few minutes later they walked in, accompanied by another man. After introducing him, they left us alone.

"Why don't you tell me what happened Fran?" he asked.

"I was in a car accident."

"When?"

"December twelfth." My hands began to tremble. My

cigarette dangled between my fingers. I was unable to grasp it, and I knew he was watching this.

"Can you tell me what happened in the accident? Did you hit your head at all?"

"I don't remember hitting my head. I remember my car spinning around." Just then Dr. Kamari and Dr. Keogan returned.

"I think you should stay Fran," Dr. Kamari said.

"But I don't feel good," I replied. Both Dr. Kamari and the other man, Dr. Hander, replied simultaneously, "You belong in the hospital."

"I don't understand," I replied as all three doctors made their way out. In a few minutes Dr. Kamari returned, "Your mother has arrived. I don't want to keep you here against your will, why don't you sign the papers? If you don't, I will keep you here anyway."

"I'll sign, I'll sign," I replied. I really didn't understand what I was signing or why. I only knew I felt too terrible to fight anymore. When I handed the pen back to Dr. Kamari, tears flowed as I said, "I don't understand. But, please help me." He didn't say anything in return, he simply walked out the door.

Sitting by myself, motionless, in the room, I had no idea what I was doing. I got up and went to sit with my mother, brothers, and sisters in the reception area. None of us spoke. We sat there solemnly until Dr. Keogan came walking toward us, grinning from ear to ear. He plopped himself next to me on the couch and put his arm around my shoulder.

"I'm so glad you're going to stay, Fran. However, Dr. Hander, Dr. Kamari, and myself have decided that it would be better if you were considered involuntary instead of as a voluntary patient.

"I don't want that. I don't want to stay anymore," I replied. "I made a mistake."

"It's too late. We're only going to keep you here until you feel better," he said.

"I feel better already," I replied, glancing at Dr.

Kamari walking toward me. My brothers, sisters, and mother looked stunned. They said nothing.

"Come on Fran, I'll show you your room," Dr. Keogan said. I didn't want to go. I couldn't. I stood there in a daze, my body numb, and I felt lightheaded again. But Dr. Keogan took hold of my arm and led me out of the room and down the hall.

"Where are we going?" I asked.

"To the elevator," he replied. I had been on the elevator more than a dozen times before; however, it looked different this time. It was smaller, full of haze. I squinted. Losing control, I turned wildly about. Dr. Keogan grabbed my shoulders and stopped me in the right direction to get off the elevator. When the door opened, the area it exposed looked different as if we were in a completely new building.

"Dr. Keogan," I said slowly, "is this the same floor as I was on before?" He nodded and led me straight to ICU. As I stood waiting for him to unlock the door I began to panic, "I don't want to go in there. Please don't make me go in there." My pleas fell on deaf ears. Unlocking the door, he half-led, half-pushed me in.

TWELVE

I looked around at my surroundings. Locked doors, barred windows, interrogation rooms; I was back in the hospital from which I'd escaped. Was I trapped in a situation from which I would never be able to free myself?

In my hand I still clutched the pen I'd been given to sign myself in. I threw it across the room and screamed, "You've tricked me again." The pen whizzed past Dr. Keogan's head. He said nothing and didn't move an inch, he only stared at me.

Dr. "Mrs." Lee appeared with one of the nurses, Sue, at that instant. "I never expected to see you here again," she said slowly. There was silence for several minutes, then she continued, "I know, Fran, you've been through the mill."

Dr. Lee was standing directly in front of me now. "But, Fran it's better we solve things now then wait till later."

She thinks I'm crazy. I realized my depression was increasing.

"I don't feel good physically," I said.

She patted me on the shoulder and said, "Okay, Fran."

She doesn't believe me, I thought, *what's the use.* Dr. Lee and Dr. Keogan left, Sue walked over to me. She took my purse and began searching through it, and said, "You know the routine, Fran."

After she handed me back my purse she led me down the corridor. As we walked she said, "You know the room. It's the one with no mirror."

I nodded miserably and walked in. I had a roommate this time. Her name was Sam. She looked strange to me, as though she had had a lobotomy; the front of her shiny forehead was huge and protruded. Her eyes were wild and unfocused. She scared me, but there was no alternative, I had to sleep there.

I lay down on the bed feeling dirty and tired. I couldn't even shower. I had nothing with me except the clothes on my back. I began thinking. *This is all because of the accident. It has to be. I should call my lawyer, maybe if he tells the doctors about it, they'd believe me.* With this thought, I got out of bed and went to the nurses' station, asking for my doctor.

The nurse on duty called him, "He says he'll be more than happy to come and talk to you," she said. "Why don't you wait in your room." Fifteen minutes later he still wasn't there. Impatient, I called home to see if they could have my lawyer call me the next day.

As I was about to hang up, Dr. Kamari peeked his head around the corner, "Oh sorry, you're on the phone. I'll come back later," he said.

"No. Wait!" I said, "I'll hang up." Dr. Keogan joined us. "Look, I don't feel good," I said.

"I know," he replied glancing at me strangely. "We're going to work on that," Dr. Kamari said.

"But . . ." Before I had a chance to finish Dr. Kamari and Dr. Keogan began walking away.

"My head is moving in and out," I called out.

"I never heard that one, Fran," Dr. Kamari exclaimed as the door was closing.

They're not listening to me, I thought desperately.

I went back to my room and lay down. There was a hospital gown on my bed, and I changed into it. In no time,

I was fast asleep. I awoke in the middle of the night with the feeling my body was about to explode. The pressure inside me was was building, I couldn't stand it. I crawled out of bed screaming, "The pressure. The pressure."

I ran into Sue, "The pressure. You have to stop the pressure."

She grabbed me by my arms and sat me down, "You have to calm down, Fran. You have to tell me more about this pressure before we can help," she said.

"It's in my whole body. It hurts. It feels as if I'm on a rack being stretched." She disappeared, leaving me sitting in the middle of the hall alone. The huge hospital gown I was covered in flowed to the floor. My head toppled low into my chest and my body began trembling all over.

When Sue returned she knelt down in front of me, "My friend, I promise you, you will walk out of this door a free person; feeling one hundred percent better than you do right now," she whispered. I hardly heard her, my mind was in the past.

"The collar they had around my neck was too tight," I mumbled. "It still hurts," I screeched. "They put a catheter in my bladder. It hurts," I added. With this last comment Sue disappeared again.

When she returned she said, "Fran, Dr. Keogan wants you to take this medicine. It'll make you feel better. I promise," she said handing me a few pills and a cup of orange juice. I swallowed the medicine and Sue assisted me back to bed. I was already fading into unconsciousness.

The pressure was still present the next morning; however, not as strong. Now my head was throbbing. I thought a shower might make me feel better. Borrowing my roommate's shampoo and soap, I headed to the shower. The streams of water caressed my body; I felt normal.

Suddenly, as I washed my hair, I experienced excruciating pain on my head. I stopped shampooing and allowed the shower to soothe me. The back of my head felt like it was growing. I placed my hand over the sore area and a sharp pain soared throughout my head.

Automatically, I pulled my hand away. Then I turned the hot water spigot up hoping this would be the cure-all I was seeking. It relieved the pain until I was out of the shower. Then it returned full force.

Slipping into the same clothes as I had on the day before, I went into the lounge. I tried to sit motionless in front of the television. Each movement aggravated the pain.

As I watched the talk show I was interrupted by a little old man and lady who sat opposite me. He was tiny and covered with wrinkles. She was just as small, but younger. He began a commotion over his pipe—it wasn't lighting properly.

She turned toward me. "His name is Fred," she said apologizing for his actions. Then she began to tell me why he was in Brookhollow. He had been in a car accident in a New York ghetto.

Before any help could arrive, he was attacked by a maniac with an ax. His entire skull was split and he was never the same person. Sometimes, when his headaches grew worse, he would be sent to Brookhollow. There was nothing anybody could do to help him.

Is this what's going to happen to me? I'm going to spend the rest of my life floating in and out of mental institutions? I couldn't handle being near them anymore. Excusing myself, I got up and went back to my room.

Dr. Keogan appeared while I was staring at the walls. His face was grim as he studied me.

"How are you doing this morning?" he asked.

"Not good. My head, back, and neck hurt," I replied.

His strong gray-green eyes met mine, "I want to order some tests for you," he said biting his lip. "I don't know if I have enough time before Dr. Kamari gets here, but I'm going to try to set them up."

"Tests," I echoed. The word intimidated me.

"I had them scheduled the last time you were here, but you left."

"Where's Dr. Kamari?" I asked.

He flashed a strange look at me and said, "I know he's the senior physician on the case, but he's out of town for a few days. I'm your doctor until he returns," his voice hardened.

"Can I get out of here?" I implored him. "ICU gives me the creeps."

"I've already given you floor privileges," he answered, and slowly walked away.

My head was throbbing as I looked at the clock on the wall. The black numbers jumbled as I read them. Knowing it was almost time for Dr. Lee's Group, I decided to go. First, I stopped at the nurses' station and asked for some aspirin.

My head began to feel better as I waited for Group to begin; however, suddenly my body began to grow weaker. My head felt lighter and lighter. Dr. Lee opened the group with hardly a glance at who was there.

When he noticed me he said, "Well Fran, it's good to see you again." I didn't have the energy to reply. Instead, I let my head drop forward. The person next to me introduced herself to the group and this went on until my turn was next. I didn't say anything.

"Fran, aren't you going to introduce yourself?" Dr. Lee asked. My mouth was dry; my throat hoarse, but I began to speak anyway, to please Dr. Lee.

"Hii-ii," I said slurring my words. Pause. "My name." Pause. "Is Fran." Pause. I tried to pull myself together and continued. "I don't feel good. I just want to feel better." Another pause. "But I'm not crazy."

At the end of my introduction a girl walked up to me with a box of tissues and said, "We're all with you, Fran." Then she hugged me. I remained silent and motionless.

The Group continued loudly. After a short while I couldn't handle the noise. My body began to twitch as I grew more and more disoriented. The noise was confusing me. I had to get out. When Dr. Lee stopped the Group for a break, I headed back to ICU.

Waiting for someone to unlock the door, I began to

move involuntarily to the corner of the hall. My hand ran clumsily down the side of my twitching face. The ICU door opened and the nurse called me in. In the lounge I lay down on the couch, covering my aching head with my arm. The silence calmed me.

The girl who had handed me the tissues in Group walked in. "I'm Cindy," she said cheerfully. Then she began preaching. "Jehovah would heal you," she said rapturously. "Jehovah will draw the evil from your body." As she spoke, her eyes glazed over. She seemed to be in a kind of trance.

I questioned her, but she ignored me and kept right on preaching. I couldn't handle this either; getting up, I went to my room. My roommate was there, crying.

"What's wrong?" I asked.

"I'm scared about going home for the weekend," she replied.

"There's no reason for that," I said trying to ignore the whole issue in order to rest. But she kept talking. I walked back out and went right to the main door. "Maybe I can get some quiet in the Quiet Lounge," I murmured. I lay on the couch and fell asleep.

Jeremy awoke me and asked if I wanted to join him for dinner. Getting off the couch, I hugged him, "It's been so long." On the walk to dinner he explained that Dave had gone home a few days after I left. So Jeremy and I were the only two left to sit at our table.

After dinner, I started pouring myself a cup of coffee. My hands became uncoordinated, I missed the cup entirely, and spilled hot liquid over my hand and leg. I couldn't feel it and wasn't bothered; however, Jeremy screamed.

"You better go to the ladies room and run cold water over your hand," he said. "You might get a bad burn."

In the bathroom, I kept my hand under water until it felt almost frozen. Returning to the table, I told Jeremy, "It's weird. I finally felt the cold but I couldn't feel the hot." He shook his head questioningly but didn't comment. I continued our conversation.

"You know Jeremy, I'm embarrassed about being here. If anyone ever finds out I'll die. I keep trying to tell these people there's nothing wrong with me, but they don't listen. You know what I mean."

"I know what you mean," he squeezed my hand. "But this time you can't write a letter to get out. Try to think of it as being for the best. It'll help to think this way," he said. When he was finished talking we both got up and headed back upstairs.

The medicine cart was waiting for me at the entrance to ICU. This time I took my medicine without arguing, even though I had no idea what it was or what it was supposed for me. I was too sick to care.

After that I went to my room to rest. I was interrupted by a phone call from my lawyer. It was an extremely short conversation. He said he knew I was in the hospital again and tests were going to be performed. He would keep in touch with my family.

As I was hanging up the phone Sue came in. "I want you to go to the office to have your blood pressure checked," she said. I started walking toward the office when a sharp pain shot through the soles of both my feet, making walking difficult.

"Sue," I screamed out, "it hurts to walk, you'll have to take my blood pressure here."

"Fran, I don't know what's wrong with you," she shook her head and walked over to me. When the blood pressure cuff was secured in place, Sue began to increase the pressure. The cuff wasn't even half inflated when the circulation of blood to my arm was cut off.

I screamed in agony, wildly attempting to loosen the cuff. Once I was free, Sue immediately wanted to try again. I told her there was no way and scurried off to my room.

Changing into the hospital gown, I made myself comfortable in bed. The gown was the only other clothing I had. I was determined to make do with these two outfits—I refused to call my family. This time I was going to get better alone.

Besides, all I wanted was my head to stop throbbing. I didn't care about my things. All the events since the accident flashed through my mind as I lay in bed. My cheeks moistened with tears, my breathing became erratic, and my heart pounded. *I'm nothing. I'm caged like a wild animal. What am I going to do?* I felt as if I were alone in the world, not a soul cared or understood.

Sue walked in and told me I had a phone call. I crawled out of bed and wrapped the blanket around me as a robe. I headed to the phone barefooted and hair amiss. With each step, the bones in my feet and knees crackled; pain traveled through my body.

It was Steve, he was worried about me. He explained how much he hated to see me at Brookhollow and offered to kidnap me if I wasn't out soon. Then he told me he would be coming to visit tomorrow. I was elated.

Before he hung up he asked what the doctors thought the problem was. I told him I couldn't remember, although I knew they were planning to do some tests on my brain. His voice grew more concerned as he told me to call him collect, anytime. Instantly, I regretted telling him about the tests. I didn't want him to care only because he felt sorry for me.

Hobbling back to my room, my head started to throb again. Nothing I did relieved the pain. I stayed motionless, waiting for sleep, for relief. Every time I moved, pain shot up my spine and vibrated throughout my head. The pain extended to my shoulder and infiltrated my back.

I tried to keep my body immobile. That didn't help so I curled my pillow up and let my head hang over it by an inch or two. The pain diminished.

Dr. Keogan came in with concern on his face. He sat down in the chair next to my bed. Without saying a word he held my wrist. I yanked it under my pillow. Then the pain returned, so I stretched my arm back to its original position. The pain eased. Again, Dr. Keogan reached for my wrist. He patted it gently and sent a message of caring as he did.

"Why do my back and neck hurt so much?"

"I don't know," was his reply. "Fran, we're trying to find out. I know it's hard but try to be patient. Has Steve come for a visit yet?" he asked.

"He's coming tomorrow. He thinks . . . ," I said.

Before I was able to finish Dr. Keogan interrupted, "I don't think you're up to a visit. Why don't you call him and tell him you're not up to it."

What does he know about Steve? Dr. Keogan stroked my hand tenderly and left. Minutes later I wasn't even sure if he'd really been there or if I had been dreaming. Everything was a blur.

Confused, I tried to puzzle things out. My life and thoughts were in Brookhollow's hands, where I didn't want them. But, maybe I was wrong and they were right. I knew during my first stay I had neglected to mention how badly Steve treated me, what I was really thinking, and many other details of the events I experienced.

I had thought all this would only hinder my ability to leave. *Perhaps telling might help Dr. Keogan treat me; to find out what really is wrong.* An overwhelming urge came over me to talk to Dr. Keogan now; not to waste any time and wait until tomorrow.

I decided that writing my thoughts would be less embarrassing and less confusing. Immediately I jumped out of bed, ignoring the pain, and searched through my dresser for pen and paper. *Maybe if I repented I would be saved.* My thoughts were out of control.

Suddenly, with pen and paper in hand, thoughts of being dragged to Ward Nine flashed through my mind. I screamed in horror, fell to my knees in the corner of the room, and began writing. *I lied last time I was here. This is what happened. I'm sorry.*

Then more thoughts flashed through my mind, of Steve, of arguments, of my lies; and I let out a horrible shriek of remembrance. Writing wildly, I tried to capture each thought. Sue came flying through the door, "What's wrong?"

"Leave me alone. Leave me alone!" I replied.

She continued into the room, "Are you all right Fran?"

"Leave me alone!" I screamed.

"All right, all right," she said as she closed the door.

I continued writing, moaning as my aching hand grasped the pen. When I was satisfied that my story would help me be released, I stopped, went back to bed, and slept.

But despite my attempt to cleanse myself by disclosing my inner-most feelings, my head felt no better. If anything, it was worse the next morning.

Without even asking, I took my roommate's shampoo, conditioner, and soap. Then I drew a hot shower, the bathroom steamed up in minutes. The streams of water relaxed me, relief came immediately. Once again I tried to wash my hair. My scalp was numb and the back of my head seemed huge. It throbbed and I was unable to touch it.

Then, as I bent over for the soap the shower stall seemed to turn and twist. I panicked and hugged the wall in an attempt to stop the motion. *You're not losing your mind Fran,* I told myself. *Something is wrong with you.*

As soon as I felt steady enough I flung the shower curtain wide open and stood there trembling. I risked the few steps and got out of the shower. Once I was out, I stayed behind the closed bathroom door, hoping to calm down and not draw any attention to myself.

In my room, I began massaging myself with my roommate's body lotion to try and unknot my muscles. *I can't let anyone know about this. Dr. Keogan was right, Steve shouldn't come today. Besides, what would I do with him?*

I put on the same clothes I had been wearing for the last two days and went to the phone. My conversation with Steve was brief and to the point. Immediately after, I hung up; if I had talked any longer I would have changed my mind. Back in my room, I tried to rest.

By midmorning I was almost feeling normal. I wanted

desperately to go outside for a walk and went to the nurses' station to make this request.

"You'll have to ask Dr. Keogan," the nurse on duty said, so I hunted him down. He was in the empty room directly across from mine, on his hands and knees, poking at a radiator. A nurse was leaning over watching. I slouched against the door frame and watched too.

"Hi Fran," Dr. Keogan said, looking up toward me. "This is Jane, a new nurse. Is Steve coming today?"

"No . . . ," I said. He interrupted, "You called him?"

I nodded.

"Good."

"But I do want to go outside Dr. Keogan. For a short little walk that's all," I said.

"I don't think so Fran," he replied.

I gave him a foul look, and he returned to what he was doing. Turning to leave I heard Jane, the nurse, saying, "What we need here is a carpenter." *That's what Steve is*, I thought. *They're bringing Steve here, that's why they don't want me to go out.* I was much happier now.

I went to the lounge and saw that nothing was happening. I made myself comfortable in front of the television and sat for hours, mindlessly watching Saturday morning cartoons. I didn't have the energy to do anything else, I felt lifeless. Then Jane came in and joined me by the T.V.

"Why is that room always empty?" I asked.

"That's where we put patients we can't control. They can't hurt themselves or anyone else in there. They don't stay in there long, just until they've calmed down," she replied.

My eyes widened. *Are they going to put me in there?* I changed the subject quickly before she got any ideas. "I wrote down some of my thoughts. Do you think Dr. Keogan would read it?" I asked.

"You can ask him," was her reply.

Suddenly trying to get up, I became dizzy and stumbled out of my chair, almost falling head over heels into Jane's lap. I steadied myself cautiously and made my way to the nurses' station. Several times, I lost my balance and crashed into the wall.

In the nurses' station, I stopped in front of Dr. Keogan's desk. "This is for you," I said, shakily handing him a wad of papers.

"Thank you," he replied.

I headed back out. Right before the door I stopped and went back to Dr. Keogan, "You know what? I poured hot coffee all over myself and couldn't even feel it," I said.

"I know," he said, his brow creased, "they told me."

Then I headed back to the door, back to my room.

My body was loose and limber, and everything seemed dream-like. I convinced myself this was because of the atmosphere of the ICU unit itself. Stale air stagnated. Dim lights abounded. Lying on my bed, I stared at the ceiling lights. *Why are they keeping me here? They must want to do something to me.*

My eyes open wider as I continued to stare at the lights. They seemed to hold a mystical power over me. My eyes wouldn't budge from their glowing bulbs. *It's the lights! They're hypnotizing me with the lights. This way they can control me. Soon enough I'll be like those old ladies who walk with that empty stare.* I pulled my eyes away; however, they floated back. I tried again. Still they floated back. I got up off the bed, yet my eyes stayed fixed on the lights.

When I left my room, my eyes soon affixed themselves to the hall lights. I began walking down the hall, my eyes staying with the lights. I was getting nervous: *what is happening to me?*

"You're just the person I was looking for, Fran," a voice rang out of nowhere said.

I stopped walking. *Is this part of the hypnosis?* I flinched when Jane came walking out of the lounge. *It was her talking. Thank God,* I thought.

"Dr. Keogan said you and I could go for a walk. Only to Captain Quick's and back, though. Go get your coat and meet me at the office," she said.

My pace quickened as I walked back to my room;

however, my eyes still flirted with the lights. Exhausted, I made my way to the office. There was no way I was going to give up this opportunity to get out in the fresh air. I stood in the doorway, waiting for Dr. Keogan and Jane to finish talking. I couldn't keep my body straight. My head ached; soon I leaned my shoulder on the door frame and bent my head.

"Will you pick up a soda and some onion rings, when you go to the store, Fran?" Dr. Keogan asked.

"No, I don't want anything, thanks anyway," I replied.

Dr. Keogan responded, "I want the food."

I laughed. Jane moved closer to me, took hold of my arm and we made our way out the ICU door. I felt like a toddler with Jane holding onto me.

"Please," I said, shaking myself free. Jane didn't argue.

We headed down the stairs to the main floor. As we turned the corner to the next flight of stairs, I abruptly stopped. My mouth dropped and I stood staring into the reception area.

My mother and sisters, Eileen and Connie, stood in the middle of the reception area among a pile of suitcases and bags. They looked agonized with their arms folded in front of them. I didn't move an inch, and I remained expressionless. We stared at each other.

"We thought you might like some things," Eileen called.

I didn't say anything in return, wanting to go back upstairs. Jane nudged me down the remaining stairs. I was now standing in front of them with a bleak expression on my face.

"Where are you going?" Eileen asked, obviously trying to be cheerful.

"For a walk," I replied.

"We just called upstairs and they said that you were in ICU and weren't allowed to go out or to have any visitors," Eileen said.

"I don't know," I replied. Then I took a suitcase and a

few bags. Jane took the rest, and we headed back upstairs. I didn't look back.

In the corridor near ICU, my upper arms began to throb, I stooped over as pain shot through my arms and shoulder blades. "It hurts," I screamed dropping everything.

"Why don't you rest a minute," Jane said.

We stopped, then I picked up the bags back up and continued walking. The pain returned and I felt as if my arms were stretching to the floor and swelling. Again dropping everything, I cried, "It hurts!"

"All right, Fran, I'll come back in a few minutes and get the rest," Jane said. We both went in to ICU.

Ignoring everyone and everything, I went to my room. My family had brought my mail. I threw myself into bed and tore at the envelopes.

As soon as I started reading Jane came in. "Don't you want to come check your things in?" she asked.

"I don't care about my things," I replied.

She left and in a few minutes returned with another nurse. Each was carrying some of my luggage. They began unpacking, showing me what there was, item by item. I paid no attention.

After they finished and left I studied my mail. There was a card from Steve. "God, how I miss him," I murmured. I buried my face in my pillow to muffle my sobs. *If he were only here. I know he'd fix this mess I'm in. He'd make them understand. I certainly can't.* I lay there for hours remembering the times I shared with Steve: how good we were together, how much fun we use to have. Then my thoughts floated back to the present, to my nightmare of a life. Chills ran up and down my spine.

Getting up, I rushed out of the room and went to the lounge for a cigarette. I stopped for my medicine at the nurses' station on my way, and saw Dr. Keogan.

"Am I voluntary yet?" I asked. "I can write my letter if I am."

"No," was his only reply. He left before I had a chance to ask him why.

Reaching the lounge, I started watching T.V., then noticed a guy sitting nearby. He was about thirty, with dark thick hair. The top of his head was square, he had a beer belly, smoked a pipe, and mumbled and grumbled to himself.

I soon discovered his name was Henry. He moved closer to me, acting friendly. I quickly moved to another seat. He moved with me. I moved back. This game continued until several others walked in the room, including Dan, the man who had his skull split, his wife, and Cindy. *At least they'll get me away from him.*

I sat down next to Cindy. In her arms she cuddled a stuffed white cat with a red bow. I leaned over to touch it and she yanked it closer to her. "I'm sorry," I said and went back to watching T.V. The smoke from Henry's pipe and Dan's cigar waffed through the room. Unable to breathe, I went back to my room for the night.

My roommate was already asleep. I put on the nightgown my family had brought, crawled into bed, and was asleep in no time.

The next morning, I awoke to the sound of my breakfast tray being shuffled about. Pulling myself up in bed, I asked the nurse to place the tray on my lap. It didn't look very appetizing so all I had was the coffee. "This can't be real coffee," I mumbled.

After I had choked the metallic beverage down, I went to the bathroom and showered. This time I didn't try to wash my hair, even though my aching head didn't throb too much. Afterward, I put fresh clothes on. This made me feel a little better.

Walking down the corridor, my eyes affixed themselves to the lights once again. *I can't have this happening to me. I gotta get out of here.* I went to the door and started banging on it. Sue came to my assistance. However, before she would unlock the door she had me take my medicine.

Once I was free of ICU I went to the Main Lounge. Jeremy was there.

"I'm going home tomorrow," he said.

"I'm really happy for you," I said. "But what am I going to do?"

"Nancy will have to be your partner in crime."

I shook my head, "Not a chance," then I kidded him.

"How can you abandon me like this?" As I said it, I realized I was only half kidding. I felt suddenly angry and left.

Stopping at the nurses' station, I asked to see the other things my family had dropped off. When they brought my box, anger filled me. All my jewelry, perfume, and toiletries were strewn inside. My good pearls, gold, and perfume were just dumped there. I sorted through everything, growing madder. *How could my family bring these things here! Did they think I'd be here forever?*

I handed the box back and flew to the phone to find out who was behind this. My mother answered. "What's going on here?" I screamed at her.

"Please calm down, Fran."

When I kept yelling she said, "Talk to Connie." Then she hung up.

I called Connie, but she hung up as soon as I started accusing her. Suddenly, I was not only angry but completely frustrated. Flying from one end of the hall to the other, I yelled, "I hate Connie." I even kicked the wall a few times. *How can they hang up like that?*

Sue rushed over to my side, "What's wrong Fran?"

I didn't reply and rushed over to the front of the glass door. I bit my lips and mumbled, my eyes tinged with anger. Sue began interrogating me. Instantly, I changed the subject, my anger receded, and I actually began to enjoy our conversation.

We were interrupted by Dr. Keogan, "I want to see you privately," he said.

We walked together to an empty room. It was exactly like the one Dr. Kamari always used. I was just starting to make myself comfortable on the couch when the phone rang. "Sorry, I have to leave," Dr. Keogan said distractedly. Stopping at the door, he opened my file, took out a form, and said, "Here Fran, fill out your admission forms."

I took the paper and went back to my room. Sprawling on the bed, I started reading the questions. The words were complex and my head tingled, so I changed my position, flipped over on my back, and held the form directly over my eyes.

As I held the form close, the words started scrambling together; an instant later they unscrambled. Then they changed size, becoming bigger and smaller. At times I couldn't see the form, then I could. I wondered what was happening to me and felt totally confused. But then the words returned to normal and I forgot about the whole occurrence.

"I can see!" I yelled out. Sue and another nurse rushed in.

Sue took a hold of my hand and asked, "What's wrong, Fran?"

"I can see," I said.

"That's good, isn't it?" she asked.

"I'm not sure. I usually need glasses," I replied.

Suddenly, my body seemed to grow smaller, my bones stiffened. "It feels like I'm hung up on the board in the hospital," I cried.

"Calm down, Fran," Sue said patting my hand.

The other nurse added, "You haven't been feeling good for a long time, Fran. That's why it feels strange, but there's nothing to worry about."

"Dr. Keogan wants to see you now, downstairs," Sue interrupted.

They both had to help me out of bed. Unsteady on my feet, I wobbled to the hall. Sue attempted to assist me by holding my arm, but I was determined to stand by myself and pushed her away.

They made me take the elevator to the first floor even

though I begged to walk. Once I was in the room with Dr. Keogan they both left. I sat in the chair right next to Dr. Keogan and gave him the form.

"You filled this out?" he asked.

"Yes," I replied.

"I should give you a job," he said jokingly.

"Dr. Keogan, you know what I've been thinking. When I was little, I smashed my head on a huge tree. The bump on my forehead was as big as a mountain. And, I never had it examined by a doctor. Maybe that's what's causing some of these problems," I said.

"I don't think so," he replied shaking his head.

Then he finished the form. I was angry that he wouldn't even consider thinking about my idea, but I kept quiet.

The longer I sat there the more lightheaded I became. After a while, I couldn't understand his questions, "Please," I kept saying, "could you say that again, I'm mixed up."

Then he started asking me about the accident. The mention of it made me feel as if I back were back there. I panicked at the thought that the officer had smelled gas on my car and threw my arm wildly in front of Dr. Keogan. "Save me," I cried.

He stared at me for a few moments and changed the subject. When the forms were complete, we walked back to ICU.

Henry, one of the more frenzied patients, was right inside the door. He was jumping up and down, screaming for Valium. I ran by him and went into the lounge. Cindy and Dan were there. Dan was talking nonstop. Cindy was preaching the word of Jehovah. The whole scene was driving me crazy. Slipping out the back, I left.

Right outside the door was Nancy. She had a red flower in her hand, "This is for you, Fran," she said softly. "It smells beautiful, as beautiful as you are."

I took the flower and sniffed it. "That's really nice of

you Nancy," I said. It was one of the few times I saw her gentle smile instead of those laughing hysterics.

As I strolled to the Main Lounge, Nancy followed. Two grizzled, unkempt men were sitting at the table with sulking expressions. "They don't look too inviting," I whispered. Three others were playing cards. *I've never seen any of them before.* Jeremy was nowhere to be seen.

I left to try the Quiet Lounge and Nancy followed. Outside, the two little old ladies marched back and forth. Ignoring them I looked up at the lights, trying to decide if the same hypnotic process was working on the women. *Why else would they be walking around like that?*

Jeremy wasn't in the Quiet Lounge either; however, a girl I remembered from the Christmas party was there. I sat down next to her, "I'm Angela," she said slurring the words."

Thorazine, I concluded.

"I've attempted suicide several times. That's how I got committed to Brookhollow." At that moment she was as white as a ghost. Her eyes had an eerie emptiness to them. Her petite body was listless as she slouched in the corner of the couch. She spoke softly as though every word haunted her. Yet there was something about her that intrigued me, I wanted to know more about her. We began talking intensely.

Angela was only twenty-years-old and thought of life as being a tremendous burden, one which got heavier as the years passed. She had been brought up by very strict Baptist parents and hated every moment of it. But in a way I envied her. She was beautiful, patient, open-hearted, and extremely intelligent. How could someone like that try to kill herself so many times? I knew her reasons must lie on a level too deep for me to understand.

My friendship was all I could offer to express how much compassion I felt for her. As the hour grew later, we both felt exhausted, hugged, and said good night, vowing our friendship.

It was eleven P.M. and ICU was humming with activity.

There seemed to be a hot debate going on. Walking over to investigate, I lit my last cigarette of the day. Henry and one of the male nurses, Dutch, were quarreling heavily and loudly. "I'll be damned if I cooperate with anyone," Henry yelled and threw a few garbage cans to punctuate his position.

Dutch, who weighed well over three hundred pounds and looked very intimidating, had always seemed like he'd never have a problem getting a patient to comply but he was having more than his share of problems with Henry. Suddenly Henry swung wildly at Dutch, missing only by inches. Dutch grabbed him and swung him high in the air.

I took this as my cue to get lost and headed out the door. As soon as I was safe in my bed, I fell asleep.

THIRTEEN

Morning seeped, dark and dreary, through the blinds of my room. Sue woke me and asked me to take my medicine. Sitting up, my head swayed with heaviness and my vision blurred as I reached for the cup. *Don't say anything. The more you say the longer you'll have to stay here.* I swallowed my medicine and laid back down hoping to sleep longer.

As soon as my eyes closed, my roommate Sarah bounced into the room, "I feel wonderful," she exclaimed. She began singing as she dressed. I buried my head under the pillow. Her singing soared louder and louder. A dreadful ringing began in my head.

I pulled myself up on my elbow, "Please, can't you see I'm trying to sleep?" In a huff she walked out.

It was another hour before I was able to reopen my eyes. When I got out of bed I checked to make sure she was really gone. Then I went into the bathroom to dress; however, I didn't want to start the day yet. I felt exhausted, sluggish.

Instead, I took a blanket, wrapped it around my shoulders, and went to the lounge. My feet ached as I walked, and my body was in agony. It was a relief to sit down once I got there. Moving a chair directly in front of me, I placed my feet up on it.

My head was still felt fuzzy. I flipped on the T.V. but

had a tough time—even the cartoon, "Tom and Jerry," was hard to follow. The show was soon interrupted anyway when Alf came striding in. This was the first time I had seen him since my return. He greeted me with vigor, but I hardly had the energy to say hello.

"Fran, I've never seen you so pooped," he said. "Come with me to the nurses' station to have your blood pressure checked."

I nodded, limping slowly to the nurses' station alongside him. As soon as we got there, I scrunched into the chair outside the door. While I waited for Alf to return with the cuff, Tom walked in.

"Hi, Fran," he said walking over and patting me on my shoulder.

I sighed trying to smile, "Well Thomas, it's about time you showed up."

"What are you doing sitting out here?" he asked.

"Waiting for Alf," I replied.

"I hear you don't feel good physically," he said emphasizing the word "physically."

Slowly I nodded my head yes, my head felt wobbly. I placed my hand against the back of my neck and began to massage it. My neck felt strange to my touch. Never had I felt so terrible. Alf returned and Tom left, waving as he went.

"He doesn't believe me. He thinks I'm crazy too," I mumbled.

"What?" Alf inquired. I didn't answer.

As Alf was taking my blood pressure he said, "Well, sleeping beauty, do you think you'll be able to get dressed today, maybe even in time for Dr. Lee's group?"

"I don't know," I murmured listlessly. "What's so important about Group anyway?" I asked.

"Oh, lots of things," he replied and began to unwrap the cuff from my arm.

Slowly I headed back to the lounge. Sitting on the table in the lounge was a dish heaped high with honey-roasted peanuts. I loved them, and since no one else was around, I decided to help myself. My mouth had been bone dry for the last few days. The salt from the peanuts brought the saliva back.

The more peanuts I ate, the better my mouth felt; so I continued to eat them until the dish was almost empty. Then I decided to eat the last few very slowly in order to savor them, but I wasn't able to get them down my throat. Yellow bile rose in my throat. I spit the peanuts back up and headed to my room for water. "My throat is narrowing, it's going to close on me," I mumbled.

I guzzled cup after cup of water. Then suddenly I tasted the rest of the peanuts coming back up my throat and headed for the commode. Here I stayed until every last peanut was out. As I picked up my head, the walls began moving as if they were breathing heavily. They moved back and forth before my eyes and then swirled back.

Covering my eyes with my hands, I prayed, *God, please don't let me go crazy. Please,* I pleaded with him. My prayers were interrupted by a knock on the door.

Alf called in, "Are you all right Fran?" I inched off the floor and stood hunched over in front of the sink.

"Alf, I'm just getting ready for Group."

He replied, "Well it's about to begin, so hurry," he said, and left.

I threw some water on my face, brushed my teeth, slowly strolled to my room and put on my sweatsuit. Then, limping along, I headed for Group. Everyone and everything floated by me as I walked. I seemed to be soaring overhead, not walking. Several times, without warning, I bumped into the wall as I inched forward.

Finally, I made it to Group and took a seat next to the window. Leaning back in the chair, I let my feet dangle, not touching the floor. My arms and legs twitched, and I constantly wiped the side of my nose with my finger.

I sat there and watched as the others shuffled in. Cindy, Henry, Nancy, Dan, the counselor Marty, Angela, the two little old ladies who walked the corridor, and a dozen others I didn't know.

After our introductions Cindy began preaching the word of Jehovah directly to me. I grew more fidgety the longer she preached. Finally, I exploded, "Stop the lecturing." Dr. Lee quickly took control of the situation.

"Cindy, I think Fran is right. We shouldn't discuss religion."

Then he turned to me and asked, "What happened during the time you weren't here Fran?" *Should I tell him?* I wondered. *Maybe just a little bit.*

"My family tried to re-commit me but my brother Tony put his arm around my shoulder and saved me," I said.

"How do you feel toward your family now?" he asked.

I didn't reply, I was interrupted by Henry. He began talking about all his problems with his wife. Then another guy on the other side of me joined him. Their voices got louder and louder until the noise from both directions was unbearable.

I began shaking and shot a glance at Dr. Lee, begging for help. He wasn't paying attention to me. Then I tried to get Marty's (the attendant) attention, but he was busy listening to Henry. I closed my eyes and covered my ears in an attempt to block out the noise.

Suddenly I lost control and began to fall. I gripped the arms of the chair to try to keep seated. "I wish they'd stop," I murmured. I glanced at Dr. Lee again. He slouched relaxedly with his arm resting on the back of the couch and wasn't looking my way. *He reminds me of Tony in the car. Tony had his arm on the back of the seat around me.* Then I glanced at Marty. He was still inclining his head toward Henry.

They're trying to tell me something. Tell me everything will be all right. I relaxed a little. But Henry's and the other man's voice swelled, drilling into my head and soon I was twitching, moving all over my chair again. I gripped the arms of the chair tighter. "I gotta get out of here," I murmured.

Suddenly, Henry upset an ashtray. I leaped from my chair and words came pouring out of my mouth, "Leave me alone! Leave me alone!" My back felt like rubber and I bent over, hysterical, and continued to scream, "Leave me alone!"

In this bent-over position I made my way to the door. "Leave me alone!" I repeated over and over. The room was silent and all eyes were on me as I opened the door and made my way through it. In the hall, I managed to straighten up and stumbled to ICU. I beat on the door and started down the corridor to my room.

Marty's voice called, "Fran."

Turning, I called back to him, "I'm a mess, I need a hug badly."

He came over and wrapped his arms around me. As my head lay on his shoulder, he repeated over and over, "Everything is all right. You'll be fine." Too agonized to be comforted, I freed myself from his embrace and headed to the window in my room. As I stood there desperately staring through the grates, I felt something on my shoulder.

Startled, I jerked my head sidewards and screamed. Marty was standing there. "Fran," he said. I was too upset to listen.

Interrupting, I yelled, "Just leave me alone! Leave me alone!" For a minute he stood there bewildered, then he left. I went back to staring, crying. I still didn't understand what had happened or why I was here. "You're losing it, Fran. You're losing it." I kept repeating over and over.

After nearly a half hour, I calmed down, gathered my strength, and I went back to Group. I sat down between Dr. Lee and Marty. They welcomed me back and told me how proud they were I was able to return. For the remainder of the session I sat silently. Eventually, everyone left except for Marty and me.

He asked, "Can I talk to you for a little while?" Miserable, I nodded. Marty was a caring person. I felt horrible because I had screamed at him and more than willingly accepted his offer. But as I leaned on the edge of the couch listening to him, my entire body suddenly spasmed wildly.

"Fran, what is it?" He yelled, "Are you all right?" The spasm ended as quickly as it had come.

I nodded. "Marty, if you wouldn't mind, I think we better cut our conversation short. Could you help me back to my room?" I asked.

"Of course I will, Fran."

Sleep came and hours passed. When I woke up and ambled back to the lounge, no one said anything about what had happened during Group and I wasn't about to bring it up. I sat there sheepishly, hoping no one was laughing at me. Since it was still painful to move, I sat with my legs resting on a chair, right next to the T.V. My vision was blurry.

Dan and his wife joined me. Dan started talking nonsense as he puffed on his cigar. Watching him, I shivered, scared to death I would end up like him. I stayed in the lounge until I couldn't listen for another minute and then got up and wandered back to my room.

My solitude ended when Dr. Keogan walked into my room carrying a folder. He sat on the other bed and opened the folder on his lap so that I would be able to read it.

"Fran," he looked puzzled. "Your blood pressure is fine. Your iron is fine. Your bladder is fine . . . ," he said.

I pulled myself up and interrupted with, "I don't care about that. My eyes are moving, my head throbs; am I crazy, is that what you're saying?"

"Look Fran, my eyes move too," he said as he shifted his eyes back and forth.

"Am I crazy?" I asked once again.

He replied with, "I thought you'd be interested in seeing this but I guess not." He closed the folder, got up, and left.

I was more confused than ever before. Obviously, Dr. Keogan, the only doctor who seemed to be taking my complaints seriously, was now beginning to think I was as crazy as all the rest. I buried my head in my pillow in total frustration.

I lay there pondering on the past, trying to make sense

out of everything. All I knew was that I had gotten in an accident. I couldn't figure out what everyone saw that made them think I was insane.

I decided to give up trying to find causes and concentrate on getting out of Brookhollow. I knew I didn't belong there. I didn't care what anyone else thought. But how was I going to accomplish it? After all, I was an involuntary patient (2 P'CD) and couldn't just write a letter this time.

The longer I lay there the more my head ached and the more tired of thinking I got. Finally, I got up to change into my nightgown. While I was dressing, I remembered that when I was admitted Dr. Keogan had said that I would only be involuntary a few days and then I'd be classified voluntary.

I threw on my robe and headed to the nurses' station. If Dr. Keogan was still around I'd be able to find out if I was voluntary.

As I walked down the corridor I noticed Cindy following me. It was eerie and I asked her to go away. The instant I stopped, she stopped. As I faced her, she was staring into space and holding her tattered nightgown by both sides so that it would flow like my housecoat. "She's imitating me," I mumbled. *Is that the way I looked?*

Her trance-like appearance momentarily stopped me from objecting. I was afraid of what she might do. I simply turned and continued strolling toward my original destination. She followed right behind me. I walked faster and faster to escape her, but her pace matched mine. Why is she doing this?

Finally, I stopped and leaned against the nurses' station door trying to get someone's attention. She stopped right behind me and leaned against the wall just as I did. I turned to face her once again and she was still imitating me. "Stop it!" I yelled. She didn't blink.

"Stop it," she yelled back. I didn't dare risk an open confrontation. The nurses would surely discipline me. Leaning over the nurses' station, I questioned Sue on Dr.

Keogan's whereabouts. Cindy remained in the background, staring.

"Dr. Keogan has left for the night," Sue said. Ignoring Cindy (though it wasn't easy), I turned and headed for the lounge to smoke a cigarette. Within seconds she followed. I looked away and entered the lounge.

Cindy stayed outside. Alone, I enjoyed my cigarette and then started for my room. Cindy stood in front of my door, twirling from side to side, over and over. She spread the bottom of her gown with her hands and turned up the collar of her nightgown so that it was the same as the collar on my housecoat. In awe, I watched her motions.

Then as if she were a bride walking down the aisle, she began slowly walking toward me. Her blank stare was centered on my housecoat. I stood motionless, not knowing what to do. Right before I was about to run away, Cindy silently walked into her own room. "My God, she is strange," I murmured.

I hurried to my room and closed the door behind me, even though I knew closing the door was against the rules. She wasn't going to sneak in here in the middle of the night. Hours passed before I relaxed enough to sleep. Throughout the night I kept searching my room.

To get away from Cindy the next morning, I left ICU as soon as I was dressed. This was the first morning I would be allowed to eat in the dining room. Strolling there, I sat at my old table, the one nearest the cigarette lighter on the wall.

I was the only one in the entire dining room. Enjoying the solitude, I helped myself to coffee. As I poured my second cup, Angela joined me. I was more than happy to have the company and we sat there gossiping about Brookhollow.

Remembering the names of the nurses Nancy had told me to avoid, I asked Angela what she thought about the women, since I had not had any real run-ins with any of them.

"I have no complaints about them," she said. "As a

matter of fact they all seem okay." I realized that I'd have to make up my own mind about them and should never have paid attention to Nancy's complaints.

Dr. Keogan walked past as I sipped my coffee. I waved to him to stop.

"Good morning, Fran," he said.

"Good morning Dr. Keogan. I have a favor to ask. Can you tell me if I'm voluntary yet?" I said.

He laughed as he was walking away, "Not yet, Fran."

"Damn," I murmured. As soon as he was gone, Jess, one of the nurses, came walking up to the table, her hands on her hips.

"Fran, we have been looking all over for you. You're not allowed down here unless you're accompanied by someone from ICU. Now get back upstairs immediately," she said.

"Can I finish my coffee first?" I asked.

"No, upstairs now," she spat out.

"It looks like Nancy may be right after all," I murmured. I got up from the table and started upstairs. Jess followed me.

As we approached the elevator, Jess said, "You'll have to go with me on the elevator."

I was about to give her an argument but decided it was better to keep my mouth shut. We both got on the elevator. When the doors opened I could see Nancy standing in front of the bulletin board. I slipped silently out of the elevator and around the corner to ICU. Jess followed. Once inside I stopped at the nurses' station for a pack of cigarettes.

"You don't have any left," the nurse on duty said.

I could see several packs of my brand on the shelf. "Harriet, look over there," I said.

She went over to check and called back, "They have Cindy's name on them."

"I'm positive they're mine," I objected. I knew Cindy didn't smoke that brand. "Tell Cindy to give them back to me."

"But they have Cindy's name on them," she objected. I was pissed and stormed away, looking for Cindy.

She was sitting in the lounge stroking her stuffed cat. This time she had on a different nightgown, a longer pink one. The collar was still turned up like mine.

"Cindy, you have my cigarettes. I want them back!" I said. She didn't make any sort of a reply. I screamed at her, "I want them back now!" She still remained motionless and silent.

"Cindy, I want them back," I screamed right into her face. There was no response from her; however, Jess and another nurse came flying into the lounge.

"What's going on here? What are you screaming about Fran?" Jess asked.

"She has my cigarettes and I want them back," I replied.

"Now Fran, you're not certain they're your cigarettes so stop accusing her," Jess said.

"I am too certain," I said.

"Alright we'll handle it from here," Jess said. "Cindy, will you come to the office with us for a minute?" Jess asked as I stood looking on.

"Yes," Cindy said staring off into space.

We all headed for the nurses' station. On the way we passed Cindy's room and I noticed my bottle of conditioner sitting on the edge of her tub.

"She has my conditioner too!" I screamed as I pointed toward her tub. "She's driving me nuts, stealing my things, imitating me."

"Fran, you don't know that for certain," Jess said.

"Oh, give me a break," I interrupted. "She's always taking things—especially mine, anyway. It is my conditioner. What would a Jehovah Witness be doing with something like that, they're supposed to be 'non-materialistic,'" I said. I was steaming hot. "First she imitates every move I make. Now she's trying to steal all my things."

At the nurses' station Jess held a pack of cigarettes in

front of Cindy's face, "Are these yours," she asked, "and if so, where did you get them?"

"They are my cigarettes. Fran gave them to me this morning," Cindy slowly replied.

"I did not!" I said.

"All right Fran," the nurse sighed, "a mistake was made." They are your cigarettes and you can have them back," Jess added.

"Now get my conditioner back," I said to Jess. Then I turned to Cindy and screamed, "I think someone has brainwashed you."

"Stop it Fran. We'll handle her," Jess said.

"Now Cindy, is that your conditioner in your room?" Jess asked.

"Yes, Fran gave me that also," Cindy replied.

"I didn't give it to her. Now Jess, will you go get it back for me? And while you're there, see what else she has of mine. If you don't, I will," I said.

In no time, I had my hair conditioner in hand and returned it to my room triumphantly, as if I had won the ultimate victory. I knew I was being petty, but at that moment I didn't care.

I stayed in my room to talk with my roommate, Sam, who was going home for good that day. How I envied her. My prospects of leaving were little or none. I had been condemned here. I had completely forgotten what life was like in the real world, what it was like to be treated as a real person. More than anything, I wanted to light my own cigarette and take a shower; even to shave my underarms in peace.

The more I talked to Sam, the more I convinced myself it was Brookhollow that was driving me insane; the people here were rubbing off on me. I was acting crazy to cope with crazy people. Realizing that my jealousy was irrational, I excused myself, saying that Dr. Lee's Group was about to begin and I couldn't miss it.

As I stood banging on the door, Jess reminded me that I had forgotten to take my medicine. Again, I still didn't know what it was or what it was supposed to do. I gulped down the pill. I wanted out of Brookhollow, any way I could get out, and if taking medicine assisted my cause, so be it.

No one else was at Group, so I made myself comfortable, lit a cigarette, and waited. Burt was the next person to come into the lounge. He sat on the couch next to me and shook his head, giving me a pathetic look.

Then he asked, "Now Fran, just how are you doing today?"

The condescending tone which he used to ticked me off.

"Who do you think you're talking to, a mental case?" I looked him square in the eyes and said, "Go to hell."

This set him back for a minute and then he said, "Now, now Fran, you know I'm concerned about you, especially after what happened in Group yesterday. Won't you talk to me?"

"I know how concerned you are. Just go to hell," I replied. This time he got up and walked to another chair.

At least he got the message, I thought angrily. *I don't need anyone treating me like I'm a nutcase or trying to talk to me about something that is none of their business.* The rest of the group started coming in, and I was relieved that Burt wouldn't have another opportunity to talk down to me. Henry was one of the last to enter. His loud voice and jerky gestures scared me.

Plopping down in the chair next to me, he said, "Hi Fran."

I nodded but didn't say a word. Instead, I got up and went to the other side of the room to sit next to Dr. Lee. Henry sat there with a bewildered look. Henry started the Group, yelling and gyrating for the entire hour.

My head ached. When the session ended, I started back to ICU. Right in front of the door, I heard a horrendous buzzing noise coming from inside. Peeking through the window, I discovered two construction workers with electric drills working in the corridor. That made me more uncomfortable; the noise would only intensify my headache. On the other hand, I didn't feel like being alone, so I went in, hoping they wouldn't be there too long.

Cindy stood in front of the lounge twirling her hair. As soon as the door was closed I realized the banging noise was too horrendous. "I gotta get out of here. I can't handle it," I murmured while waiting for the door to open.

Cindy walked over to me and said, "I know why." She squinted her eyes, contorted her face, and made her voice gruff and satanic. "I know why and so does he," she said once again, walking away.

"What in the world are you talking about?" I asked. At the entrance of the lounge she stopped, flashed me a wicked smile, rolled back her eyes, and said, "It won't be long."

"Holy shit," I said, "this place is the pits."

I banged furiously on the door. Jess finally arrived to unlock it, "Impatient aren't we." I didn't reply as I slipped out the door.

My headache was worse now than ever. The pain slowed me down, seemed to infiltrate my whole system. My body was heavy and listless as I maneuvered down the corridor bumping into everyone. Several times I slammed into the wall. "Damn, I can't even walk straight," I cried and stumbled through the Quiet Lounge door.

Suddenly, I ricocheted off the door frame. My only thought was to lie down. Seeing the empty couch, I sprawled on it. I never wanted to move again. Sleep came easily as the pain subsided.

Dr. Kamari was the first person I saw when I opened my eyes. "Would you like to come talk to me?" he asked. It took several tries to get to my feet, wobbling back and forth as I tried to move forward. Dr. Kamari waited patiently.

As I stumbled toward our meeting room, Dr. Kamari stayed several paces ahead. I felt like a dog being dragged by his leash. We began a conversation, at least going through the motions; however, I had a lot of difficulty following anything he said and found it even tougher to speak intelligibly. Dr. Kamari, taking this as an affront, cut our meeting short.

On the way out, I remembered this was the first time Dr. Kamari had been at the hospital in days. I realized that whatever tests Dr. Keogan had been talking about had probably been scrapped. Most likely he had been talked out of them by Kamari. I shook my head dispiritedly and let Dr. Kamari lead me back to ICU.

My eyes were drawn to the lights, the dim lights. *You shouldn't watch them Fran. They're making you dizzy in the head. Take your eyes away before they gain control of you.* I knew all this was true, yet I couldn't stop watching them. It was as if they had some kind of power over me. No matter how hard I tried to keep my eyes away they were drawn back. *What did they do to make the lights attract me?* I wondered.

Cindy was nowhere to be seen so I headed straight to my room. A half hour later Sue came in. "Fran, would you mind going into the lounge for awhile? You're getting a new roommate and they want to use your room."

I threw on my housecoat and headed for the lounge. Out of the corner of my eye I saw Cindy imitating me, dancing circles in her new nightgown, the stuffed cat cradled in her arms. *This has got to stop. I'm having enough trouble sorting things. I don't need to try and figure out what and why she's doing this.*

"Cindy, get away from this room," I growled. "Sue, you have to stop whatever she's doing or I'm going to raise hell," I said.

"What do you mean?" Sue asked.

"She's copying me. I can't handle the mirror image. Make her stop," I said.

"I think you're imagining things Fran," she said.

"I am not!" I replied.

"We'll look into it for you," she stated, flashing me a puzzled look. I wasn't satisfied with this appeasement, I wanted Cindy stopped immediately; however, Sue was gone before I had a chance to say more.

As I sat in the lounge smoking, waiting to go back to my room, I saw a State Trooper and another lady carrying someone down the hall.

The person was crying and calling out, "Stop! Let me go," in a little girl's voice. I ran out the door to see where they were taking her. They headed straight to my room. *What kind of roommate am I getting?*

I went to the nurses' station to ask them what was happening and to object. Of course, no one paid attention. I decided to go to my room to check the girl out. My eyes opened wide, my heart raced as I saw her sitting on the bed.

She was only twenty or so. Her head bent low to her chest, her knees curled up in a fetal position, a long plastic tube hung from her nose, as she moaned and groaned. In the corner of the room sat the State Trooper staring at her.

"Am I," she gasped out the words, "in your way?"

I told her absolutely not, picked up a pen and paper, and left the room. At the nurses' station I asked, "What's wrong with my roommate? Why does she have a State Trooper with her?"

"That's not for you to worry about, Fran. Nothing is going to happen to you, now settle down," Sue said.

"I don't want her to be my roommate if she's committed a crime," I objected.

"There's going to be a twenty-four hour guard outside your door until we can get you a room on the other floor. There's nothing to worry about," Sue reassured me.

Nothing to worry about? I flinched, thinking about having to spend the night in that room. Finally, knowing my efforts were useless, I turned and headed back to the lounge.

I started writing a letter to Steve to pass the time. As I laid my pen down, intending to have a cigarette, I noticed Cindy floating past the door in her nightgown, imitating me again. This time I had had it.

Jumping out of the chair, I went after her. She ran out and I followed right after her into the corridor. She sprawled in a chair pretending to write a letter.

It blew my mind, "What are you doing?" I said. She continued writing, ignoring me.

"You're not cute," I screamed. Sue and two other nurses came running toward us.

"Fran, leave Cindy alone and go back to the lounge," Sue said.

"I didn't do anything, it's her," I said. "She keeps imitating me."

"I don't care, go back to the lounge, now," Sue said. Steaming mad, I walked away.

Back in the lounge, I sat tapping my fingers and feet. I hated the whole idea of being locked away and having my every move, my every word monitored. I hated the staff, I hated the patients. The hatred grew inside me until I began pacing, slamming anything in my way. *Why is this happening to me? Why is this happening to me?* I kept repeating.

Lydia, one of the nurses, came striding into the lounge, her excessive mounds of blubber jiggling. As she stopped near me an ashtray banged on the floor.

"Just what do you think you're doing, Ms. Von Bueren?" I hated Lydia. She was a combination of circus bearded lady and a hell's angel with zero personality. Every time I saw her I wondered when she was going to expose a tattoo.

"I'm getting some exercise before I go to bed. Do you mind?" I said.

"There's to be no exercising in here. Put out that cigarette and go to your room right now," she ordered.

I sat down, picked up my cigarette, and started smoking.

"Did you hear what I said?" she stuck her face next to mine.

"I'm not going to my room. I want to watch T.V. and finish my letter," I replied.

She grabbed the cigarette from my hand and butted it out. "To your room, now," she yelled.

"I'm not going anywhere. I didn't do anything," I said. Lydia was about to grab my arm when Sue appeared.

"What's going on Fran?" she asked.

"I accidentally knocked over an ashtray while I was stretching my legs. Ms. Lydia thinks I should be banished to my room. I think differently," I said.

"Can I talk to you for a second, Lydia?" Sue asked. They both turned and left.

A couple of minutes later Sue returned. "The lounge closes at eleven and you're to be in your room by then. And leave Lydia alone, will you," she said.

"No problem," I replied chuckling.

Actually I wanted to go to my room, my head throbbed. But now there was no way I would go until it was absolutely necessary. Instead, I lay down on the couch and rested my head on my arm. I stayed like that until eleven, when Alf came in to lock the lounge.

He didn't even have to say anything, I started heading to my room before he had the T.V. turned off. A nurse was sitting outside my door reading when I got there. The sight of her didn't make me feel any safer, she was a puny little thing hardly qualifying as a guard.

Before crawling into bed, I checked my new room-mate to make sure she was asleep. The tube still hung from her nose and her breathing was labored. Hesitantly, I went to bed.

Hours passed before I could fall asleep. Up at five-thirty the next morning, I wrapped myself in a blanket and went to the lounge. It was still locked.

Walking back to my room, I sat down in the hallway, on the floor next to the nurse. Her name was Patty. I was astonished when she showed me the muscles in her arms. While we got to know each other, Alf came striding by.

"I want to take your blood pressure and give you your medicine," he said.

"Look, I'll make a deal with you," I countered, "you

can take my blood pressure and I'll take my medicine if you unlock the lounge and let me have a cigarette."

In no time I was in the lounge. Thoughts of Steve filled my mind. In one flashback, I was in love with him. In another, I hated him. I was totally confused. What did life hold without him? Tears flowed as my whirling thoughts continued. I wished we were together so that I would know for sure.

Then Alf appeared. He sensed how upset I was. I longed to tell him what I was feeling and thinking; however, I held my tongue, fearful of what he might think of me.

"What's wrong Fran, you can tell me," he said gently.

I replied with a half lie, "I'm tired of feeling as sick as I do."

I hated myself for lying to him, but I was convinced it was better this way. What hurt the most was when he responded to my feelings with genuine concern.

He replied to the real Fran, not the crazy Fran, with a few simple words, "You're a beautiful person and don't ever forget that." These words penetrated and for the moment raised my spirits, responding to my need.

Alf disappeared after a quick hug. Once again alone, I drifted into another, more peaceful world; thinking not a thought, moving not a muscle. Dan's shambling appearance crashing into the room crumbled my euphoria. The reality of Brookhollow came back with a thud. Dan reminded me what my destiny might hold. I slipped out of the lounge without a word.

In the corridor, I tried to decide where my next resting place should be. As I stood there I saw my roommate leaving the room. I decided to seize this opportunity to shower and dress.

But as I walked toward the room, my eyes caught sight of the hypnotizing lights. *They're going to control you soon. Look at what they've already done. Take your eyes away Fran.*

Still my eyes stayed fixed on the lights even as I undressed to shower. In that instant I was convinced the lights were the reason it was becoming harder and harder for me to concentrate, to rid myself of the cloudiness that filled my head.

The shower brought temporary relief to the constant pain I had grown accustomed to. A sigh of relief echoed through the bathroom as the hot water caressed my body. My skin was beet red before I stepped from behind the curtain.

I put on the same outfit I had been wearing for days, my sweatsuit. My appearance meant nothing anymore. Not long after I was dressed, the relaxation brought by the shower disappeared and I floated back to a hypnotic state. *Stop looking at those lights, Fran.*

As I bent to put on my sneakers, I wasn't able to fit my feet in them. I had no idea why and told myself not to say anything to anyone for fear of what they might think. My slippers would make a viable alternative. I retrieved them from the corner of the room.

With each step pain shot through my feet; it felt as if I were walking on bare bones. "What is happening?" I mumbled. The comfort of the slippers soothed the pain as I hobbled to the door.

Making my way to breakfast, I stopped at the nurses' station to ask if I could go there alone. "We're all busy," the nurse snapped, "You'll have to wait for an escort."

As I stood leaning against the wall, trying to gather my strength, an exotic-looking nurse from the main floor came walking through the door pushing the medicine cart.

I knew I had already taken my medicine; however, I wanted to see what the chart had to say about me, "Could you give me my medicine?" I asked. She leafed through the chart unable to find my name.

"Oh, you're an ICU patient," she observed. "I can't dispense your medicine; you'll have to wait for a nurse from ICU instead." I was pissed. I wanted to find out what they said about me.

"All the nurses are busy and I'm dying to get some breakfast," I tried to be especially sweet. "Do you think you could get my medicine for me just this one time? Please," I said.

"I can't do that," she replied.

"But I've been waiting half an hour and my poor stomach is growling. Just this once, please," I pleaded.

"All right, but if I get in trouble, I'm coming after you," she said in her quaint accent as she went into the nurses' station. Seconds later she returned with my chart in hand, "Looks to me as if you've already had your medicine this morning," she said.

"I don't remember taking any medicine. Let me see," I said glancing at the chart. I scanned the page quickly, looking at everything except the medicine timetable. Suddenly my eyes were caught by the words, "A-Typical Bipolar Disorder," directly under this was, "Personality Disorder, Schizophrenia Disorder."

"What! What's A-Typical Bipolar Disorder?" I exclaimed. She grabbed the chart away from me.

"You're not supposed to be looking at this without your doctor," she snapped, closing the chart. But I had seen what I wanted.

She brought the chart back inside the nurses' station and I stood there totally bewildered. *What does it mean? Am I crazy? What's wrong with my personality?* The nurse returned, "I can escort you to breakfast if you like," she said.

Silently preoccupied with the newly attached labels, I stood waiting for her to put the medicine cart away. *They must think I'm a Sybil with multiple personalities. Am I?*

I didn't realize that the nurse was back and trying to get me to the elevator until she shook my arm saying, "You want to go or not?" I returned to reality long enough to get onto the elevator, then my thoughts fled.

A-Typical Bipolar. Personality Disorder. Schizophrenia Disorder. They had labeled me crazy. Death would have been better for me than having to live my life in a mental institution with such a label. Numbly I tried to take it all in, my eyes focused on nothing, my mind in turmoil. *How can all this be true?* I asked myself, and received no reply.

FOURTEEN

A-Typical Bipolar, Personality Disorder, Schizophrenia Disorder. The words resounded in my head. Slowly, I groped my way into the dining room and sat alone at a table. When Angela joined me, I didn't try to make jokes as I normally did. I spoke hesitantly and barely heard her words.

All my hopes for getting out of Brookhollow had been smashed by seeing the label they'd given me. My mind whirled from thought to thought. Nothing seemed to help. I was condemned.

Suddenly, an idea struck me and I bolted upright in my chair. In that instant, all the pain I had been living with for so long momentarily disappeared. Along with this feeling of well-being, my idea also disappeared; however, I felt too good to worry about it.

My head was clear, my mind working, and my body limber. My hopeless attitude changed automatically. If I felt well I could get out of here. I could do anything. I threw my feet up on the chair across from me and relished the lack of pain.

After Angela left I stayed seated, watching as most of the dining room emptied. "I'm getting better," I murmured happily.

I had to be kicked out of the dining room before I

would get up, in case movement would dissipate this wonderful feeling of wellness. Unfortunately, the pain in my bones and aching in my head returned during my walk back upstairs.

By the time I reached the Quiet Lounge my mind was cloudy and my body sore. All I wanted to do was lie down on the couch. I stayed there until Marty came in to recruit me for Group. I went to please him. I felt listless, pain-ridden, and depressed.

During the entire group session, I stayed silent, never saying anything. Right after it was over, I walked back to the lounge and lay down again, trying to find a quiet place, where I could think.

Within minutes several strange faces appeared. I tried not to notice them but then an incredible commotion came from somewhere in the hall. Lagging behind, I watched everyone head out the door to see what was going on. Soon they were all trooping back in with Jean, a nurse, edging them on.

When everyone was assembled, Jean announced, "You're not allowed out of the Quiet Lounge until further notice." The room resounded with our questions, but the nurse wouldn't give us further information.

We made up our own stories and the room became alive with chattering, ". . . someone has a knife . . . someone smuggled drugs in here . . . he's fighting with the nurses . . . he's holding a doctor hostage."

I wonder what will happen? Who is it? I hoped whoever it was won the battle. The idea that a staff member would be in trouble pleased me, gave me a chance to vent my hostilities. They all thought they were gods.

As someone started taking bets on who it was and what the outcome would be, Jean returned and told us we were free to leave. We all rushed to the Main Lounge to gather information.

Angela sat on the couch, moping. "It's Henry," she said softly. "He's uncontrollable. It took three male nurses and two State Troopers to get him out of the building. They're sending him to the state institution. He's too wild for Brookhollow."

I didn't know whether to be glad or sad that Henry was gone. He always scared me, but the fact that he'd been sent to a state institution scared me more.

Finally, I went back to my room, staying there until Dr. Kamari came to see me. We strolled to our usual room. He held the door wide open for me and waited until I entered before he did. This seemed to be his way of making sure I didn't sneak off on him.

All day long my mind had been running over the questions I wanted to ask him; however, when it came down to it, I wasn't able to think of even one. It was so hard to concentrate, and as I looked at Dr. Kamari, he seemed encircled by a cloud. His words seemed to emanate from a long tunnel, and in the middle of one sentence I blurted out, "Am I going to stay this dizzy in the head forever?"

He said something in reply; however, I couldn't make it out.

"What are you saying?" I implored.

His voice grew louder, "No, we'll bring you back."

I understood him clearly this time. Not only his words, but what he meant. He thought I was completely crazy. "Look," I tried to explain, "the lights are hypnotizing me, that's why they have to bring me back."

Inside I thought, *I shouldn't let them do this to me. I wish my sister Jackie were here, she wouldn't let them do this to me.* I began banging on his desk saying, "I want Jackie. I want Jackie." He made no reply. *He's not going to let me see Jackie.*

I leaned over his desk and repeated over and over, "I want a new doctor."

"You can have one if you want," he said, getting up to leave. I followed right behind him. By the time we were in the hall I had forgotten why or what I had said minutes earlier.

Back in my room I lay on the bed, immediately falling asleep. Later that night I awoke suddenly. My vision was blurry as I opened my eyes a crack. Something was walking across the room in a red robe with a red hood over its head. "The devil," I murmured. I flew out of my bed screaming at the top of my lungs.

Pushing open the door, I hurled myself into the hall, right into Dutch, one of the attendants. He grabbed me by my arms and hugged me to him.

"What's wrong Fran?" I didn't reply.

"Let's go back to bed now," he said leading me back to my room.

I stood my ground firmly, saying, "No. I won't go back in there. You can't make me."

"You have to go back to bed somewhere," he said.

"Not in there! Don't you have another room?" I replied.

"You can sleep in Cindy's room. You're not afraid of her," he said.

I didn't understand. He helped me to the door of her room. It was pitch black inside, it was eerie. I took a deep breath and cautiously lay down on the bed. Cindy's words echoed in my head, "I know why." I jumped off the bed and ran back into the hall.

"Do you have some place else?" I asked.

"There's a mattress in the empty room you can sleep on. That's the only other place," Dutch said.

"I know that room. That's the room everyone talks about. The one they lock you in if they can't control you. I don't want to go there." I said.

I sat down on the floor in total confusion. I didn't want to go into any of those rooms.

"You'll have to make up your mind soon Fran, we can't have you in the hall all night," Dutch demanded.

Standing up, I decided to go back to my room and then changed my mind. In utter confusion, my body swaying, I stood in the middle of the corridor.

"Fran, we're going to make up your mind for you very soon if you don't hurry up," Dutch said.

I turned in a panic, screaming, "Please don't lock me in there. Please!"

Patty, another nurse, walked up to us. "We're not going to lock you in anywhere. We want you to go to bed. Now go somewhere right now," she said.

"I'll sleep on the mattress if you go get my blanket and stay in that room with me until I fall asleep," I said.

She got my blanket and then walked into the empty room with me. As soon as I lay down she left. I watched the door to see if they were going to close it. They didn't. I finally fell asleep.

Early the next morning I checked the door, it was still open. I was hesitant about going back into my room. My body ached, my head was sore. Wrapping myself in the blanket, I went to the lounge instead.

Once there, I lay down on the couch; somehow it wasn't comfortable. I tried a chair. It wasn't any better so I went back to the couch. Fifteen minutes later I was back trying another chair. All morning I went back and forth from chair to couch, trying different positions. Nowhere made me feel better.

Finally, I went to the empty room and lay flat on my back on the bare mattress. It was the spot I had been hunting for. My body seemed to relax. The cool air in the room momentarily cleared my head, I was actually able to think. Even my vision didn't seem as blurry as I lay there.

However, a few minutes later, my left side became cold. This seemed strange because the other side had turned boiling hot. Feeling first my left and then my right side, I tried to ascertain what would make such a difference. There seemed to be no answer. But this scared me enough so that I left my comfortable resting place to find a nurse to question.

Jane was on duty. I tried to explain the strange feelings passing through me. She was totally bewildered.

I tried harder to make her understand, "Early this

morning one side of me felt different than the other side, as if they weren't part of the same body. Then, when I lay down, I felt comfortable for a few minutes. But afterwards one side of me was freezing and the other side of me was boiling hot. Is there something wrong?"

"You probably didn't have the blanket on evenly," she replied.

Was I an idiot? Did I belong at Brookhollow? I stormed to my room, vowing I would never again tell anyone how I felt.

Hours later Jane came in. "Don't you want to go to lunch?" she asked.

"Not really, have my lunch sent up here," I replied listlessly.

"You don't want to walk to the dining room. This isn't like you Fran," she said.

"I can't do it today. I really want it sent up," I replied.

"All right," she said, and left.

When lunch was delivered, I finally got out of bed and sat Indian style on the floor with the tray in front of me. Removing the cover from the tray, I gagged at the sight of the grotesque gray-green food. I didn't even know what it was. I drank the juice and played with the rest. Mixing the vegetables and meat together, I tried to take a bite.

Nausea attacked me, I ran to the bathroom and threw up. *This isn't like you Fran. You never do this.* Every time I got up to leave, my stomach churned and I found myself kneeling in front of the toilet again. Finally I was able to leave, although I went only as far as my bed, where I stayed.

First thing the next morning, Jane came in, "You're moving to a room in the main area." I was thrilled.

"They must think I'm getting better," I murmured.

She nodded, "You'll be moving right after lunch." The rest of the morning dragged by.

Finally, Timmy and Jane moved my things. My new room opened new vistas. My new roommate was younger, more alive. The room was bigger and brighter. More was happening in the main area. The first thing I wanted to do was go for a walk outside. I asked Timmy if he would take me.

"I'll have to check with Dr. Keogan first," he said. Several minutes later he returned, "Sorry. Dr. Keogan doesn't think you're up to it. You just got out of ICU," he said.

"You're kidding. Where is he? I'll ask him myself," I said.

"He's in the nurses' station," he said.

I flew to the nurses' station. "Dr. Keogan, can I please go? I feel good. It won't be a long walk. I think the air would do me good. Please?" I said.

"I don't know Fran," he said.

"Please. I promise it won't be long," I begged.

"All right, you can go," he relented, "but only a short walk."

"Thank you. Thank you," I said and ran back to my room to tell Timmy.

Another girl joined us and we headed downstairs. The buzzer rang and freedom followed. The March wind iced my cheeks. The air was brisk and fresh. Timmy and the other girl, Janice, started walking ahead of me. I tried to catch up with them; however, they were going too fast.

Then pins and needles shot through my feet. They stung each time I stepped forward. My pace slowed but I wasn't going to give up. After a few steps, though, I stumbled.

"You guys, help me!" I screamed.

They both turned and ran toward me. I grabbed hold of Timmy's arm, "I gotta go back. I don't feel good," I said.

We started back toward Brookhollow, then a car screeched around a corner. I jerked my head wildly toward the street. Suddenly, I couldn't breathe. I gasped for air and tightened my grip on Timmy's arm.

"Let's get you back to Brookhollow," he said.

In the reception area, I pulled my boots off, my feet ached. "I wanta take the elevator," I sobbed. I hobbled to the elevator, my grip tight on Timmy's arm. Completely leaning on him as we rode the elevator up, my body felt lifeless.

He helped me to my room and I fell limply into bed. I stayed there motionless for hours. "What's wrong with me?" I kept murmuring. Nurses wandered in and out, no one said anything.

Then someone knocked. Dr. Kamari entered. His motions portrayed confidence, control.

"This is my case," he said definitively, his face grimly set. "We're going to try some sleep therapy," he said.

"What?" I asked.

"I'm going to have Alf give you a shot of Thorizene. You're not to get out of bed for any reason. This means pajamas, under the covers, the whole bit," he said.

"All right," I replied.

Why is he doing this? Why am I saying all right?

"Alf will be here in a minute," he said walking away.

I changed into my pajamas and waited for Alf. He came striding into my room with a big grin as he held a huge needle straight up in his hand.

"Ahaha!" he said.

"You're weird," I said.

"You're going to have to roll over, Miss. This shot goes in your behind," he said. I rolled over on my stomach and bared my bottom. Soon enough it was over and Alf left.

In a few minutes Dr. Kamari and Alf returned.

"I don't want you out of bed for any reason. Do you understand," Dr. Kamari said.

"Not even for a cigarette?" I asked.

"All right, you can get out for a cigarette, every once in a while. But as soon as you finish the cigarette you have to go straight back," he said.

"What's Thorizene?" I asked.

"It's an anti-psychotic drug. We're starting you on

high doses of it. It's going to make you very sleepy so we can't have you walking around. If you want anything at all, have someone get it or do it for you," he said.

"All right," I replied.

"I'll give you a bell, Fran, if you promise not to abuse it." Alf said.

What does he mean? They both left again.

Half an hour later, Lydia walked in, "Time for your medicine, Fran," she said. *Of all people, why do they have her coming in here?* She handed me a cup filled to the brim. It looked like orange juice but tasted bitter.

"What is it?" I asked.

"More Thorizene," she said and then left.

In a little while another nurse came in, "Time for your medicine," she said. I took the cup and swallowed the medicine in one gulp. It sent shivers through me. She left.

As time passed I began feeling zombie-like. My head was too heavy to lift off the pillow. My mind moved away from me.

Then another nurse walked in. "Time for your medicine," she said. I had her place the cup in my hand so I could stay lying down.

Sipping at it, I pursed my lips, "Ugh."

"Just gulp it down," she said.

"Am I going to die?" I asked as I pulled the blanket over my head. Without replying, she left.

Dr. Kamari was the next one to walk in, "Do you still think you're going to die? You're not going to," he said.

The only thing I could do was moan in reply as I remained lying on my stomach. Time passed in and out of my head. The next thing I knew the nurse was back wanting me to take more medicine. Then I passed out.

The first thing the next morning, the nurse was there with more Thorizene. All day long, they kept medicating me. I was only conscious when they delivered meals, but I couldn't lift my head to eat. For the next four and one-half days, I just lay there.

Then, on the afternoon of the fifth day of my sleep

therapy, I got out of bed to have a cigarette. My steps were that of a drunkard. I met Dr. Kamari right in front of the lounge.

"What are you doing out of bed?" he asked.

"You said I could have a cigarette," I replied.

"So I did. But then go right back to bed," he said.

I really wanted to talk to him, there was so much I wanted to ask him, so much I didn't understand.

"Am I crazy?" I asked.

"Yes, you are," he replied.

My mind went blank, my body numb. "I gotta go," I said and stumbled away. *I'm not crazy and I'll prove them all wrong.*

I ran into Dr. Keogan. "Dr. Kamari says I'm crazy. Do you think I'm crazy?" I said.

"I don't think this is the place to discuss that, come with me," he pulled me into a quiet corner.

"Fran, I have to tell you this," he said looking at me intently, "I don't think you're crazy. I'm determined to do some tests on you. Just bear with me for a little longer. It's a bit too complicated to explain."

There was something in his voice that gave me hope. I didn't question him further. Later that afternoon Alf stopped by to see me.

"Don't stay up late, you have a busy day tomorrow," he said.

"What am I doing tomorrow?" I asked.

"You're scheduled for an MRI scan," he said.

"What's that?" I asked.

He sat down and said, "It's a big machine which takes pictures of your head."

"How does it do that? And how big?" I asked.

"It's complicated, I don't think you'd understand. There's nothing to worry about though. Just go to bed early," he said.

FIFTEEN

I had the best rest I had in a long time, that night.

The next morning Lydia marched in, "Mary will be taking you to your appointment," she said stiffly. "It's in a half hour, you better get moving and dressed. Go to the nurses' station as soon as you're ready," she said. *I get to go outside again.*

Mary was waiting for me outside the nurses' station door as I approached. "You ready to go, kid?" she said secretively.

"Oh, yea!" I replied. "I can't wait to go outside."

We drove for twenty minutes before reaching our destination. During this time Mary and I talked. She was nice, but cautious. I picked up her mood. I made sure to choose my words and actions carefully. We pulled in front of a two-story white building. She parked and we walked to the door together.

Other than the receptionist, Mary and I were the only ones waiting. An attendant soon came for me. He said, "Hi, I'm Bill. I need you to change into a gown. Everything except your panties are to be off, even your jewelry. When you're ready, come into the room over there, I'll be waiting for you."

I went off to change and afterward found Bill. He walked me to an adjoining room. In the middle was a huge silver machine. It looked like a space shuttle that had landed in the solitude of a spotless white lab.

"What is that?" I asked. "Do I have to go in that thing?" I stepped closer, "Can I look at it?" I asked.

"Sure, just don't touch anything," he said.

I walked over and peered inside. It was nothing but a tunnel about a foot and a half in diameter.

As I walked studiously toward its back, my head started vibrating rapidly, a sharp pain shot quickly through it. I stumbled back, I threw my hands up, clasping my head, and said, "It hurts!" I began creeping against the wall, the furthest I could get away from that thing, back to Bill. "My head," I said.

"Are you all right?" Bill asked, concerned.

"I'm not sure," I said slowly.

"Do you think you could hop up on there for me?" he asked. "Or do you need help?"

Somehow I managed to pull myself up.

"We just have to get a few things in order and we'll be ready to begin," Bill waved.

He moved behind me and attached two wires to my back. "Lie down," he said, making sure my head was positioned correctly in the brace. When he was satisfied, he began pulling two straps across my forehead.

"It hurts," I objected as he tightened it.

"There, is that better?" he asked and connected the straps more loosely. They made my head feel heavier. I didn't want him to go on, but I didn't say anything.

Then Bill put a hard piece of foam between my head and the brace on both sides. I couldn't move my head even a fraction of an inch. "I'm going to leave now," Bill said softly. "You'll feel a few jerking motions but don't let that scare you, we're just getting you into position. Later, we'll be able to talk to each other," he said.

"I don't think I can do this," I moaned.

"Sure you can. How about if we put something over your eyes?" he said.

"I'll try it," I said. He put a piece of cloth over my eyes and then left.

A few minutes later I felt a jerk and then I started to glide backwards into the tunnel. I prayed to God as I went, *please don't let this thing collapse on me.*

"Hi," a voice said out of nowhere. I felt better as soon as I heard his voice. "You'll be hearing some knocking noises every once in a while, don't let it alarm you. I'll keep checking with you and if you don't think you can continue just let me know, all right? You'll be hearing that noise right now," he said.

Clicking and banging started. My body tensed. The noise went on for a good five minutes. Then Bill's voice returned, "How are you doing?" he asked.

"All right," I replied.

"There'll be some silence and then the knocking noise will return," he said.

This sequence continued on for the next twenty minutes and then Bill said, "We're all done. We're going to start you out." As soon as I was out Bill appeared and started taking the straps off.

When I was free to sit up I asked, "Can I go back in there without the blindfold?"

"Sure," he said.

I lay back down, waiting to find out what it was really like inside. The table jerked and before I knew it my body was back inside. There wasn't anything to it, only a mirror on the top. *Why were you afraid Fran?* I asked myself. I headed back out.

Before I knew it, Mary and I were on our way back to Brookhollow. Back on the floor, I went to my room and picked up my pillow, then straight to the kitchenette for my usual cranberry juice. Next, I walked to the lounge for a cigarette. I stayed there all afternoon, listening to MTV, and shooting the bull with everyone. My thoughts were on nothing but the test. *What had it shown? What was wrong with me?*

After dinner, Dr. Kamari walked into the lounge right
to the couch where I was lying, "Would you like to
come talk to me?" he asked. I wanted to say no because I
was pretty fed up with him; however, I went, pillow and
all.

As we entered his room, Dr. Kamari asked, "Do you
always carry a pillow with you?"

"Smart ass," I murmured.

"What?" he asked.

I didn't reply as I plunked into a chair. Sitting behind
the desk, Dr. Kamari began, "How are you tonight?" he
asked noncommittally.

"How are you?" I replied in the same tone of voice.

He began to write in my file. I leaned over the desk to
see what it was. Then he looked up at me and said,
"There's a thing on your brain."

"What?" I asked, frightened.

"There's something on your brain," he replied.

"I don't understand," I gave him a bewildered look.
An eerie silence filled the room. Pondering his words, "It's
a tumor or a blood clot?"

"We don't know yet," he replied.

I sat there with a blank stare, still confused. Dr.
Kamari was silent. "What's going to happen?" I asked.

"Maybe surgery," he replied.

"Who's going to do it?" I asked.

"Not me!" he said.

Silence filled the room once more. I began staring into
an empty corner of the room. "You're lying," I cried.
"There's nothing wrong with me." Tears formed in my
eyes. "There's nothing on my brain, nor am I nuts. You just
want me to be like that guy in 'One Flew Over a Cuckoo's
Nest.' "

"I'm sorry Fran, I know you want to talk but I have to
go," he said rising. "I have an important meeting."

I sat there completely numb. "First, I'm crazy and
now I have something growing on my brain." I could

hardly fathom it all. *What was the truth and what was a lie? Am I going to die?"* I asked.

"I don't know," was his reply as he walked out the door.

SIXTEEN

Tears filled my eyes. When I was able to navigate, I walked blindly into the lounge, which was packed with patients and visitors. I pushed past several groups of people as though they were furniture. Then I threw myself on the couch, my feet slammed into the coffee table, and my arms wrapped around my chest as if to hold myself together. Tears flowed.

What did this new revelation mean? Was a growth better or worse than being crazy?

Angela came over and sat down next to me. "How are you doing, Fran?"

"Get away from me. Just get away from me," I cried. She got up and left. *This can't be happening to me. I gotta get out of here.* I rose, started for the door, and bumped right into Dr. Kamari.

"You've been crying," he said. I moaned and kept right on walking.

"Steve will get me out of here," I mumbled. I stopped at the phones and tried Steve's number. His answering machine answered. No one was home. I slammed the receiver down. "God damn it, just when I need him," I sobbed.

I started for my room. In the corridor I ran into Dr. Keogan and asked, "Am I voluntary yet?"

"Not yet," he replied.

"How am I going to get out of here?" I groaned. He shook his head as I started walking again. Once in my room, I crawled into bed. Using my pillow to muffle my sobs, I kept repeating, "I don't want to die." It was almost a mantra. Soon I was fast asleep. The night passed.

When I woke up I walked to the nurses' station to ask Alf to open the lounge for me. "It's four-thirty in the morning," he shook his head. "Isn't it a little too early for a cigarette?" I went inside the station and sat down on the chair in front of his desk.

"There's a thing on my brain," I said quietly. Only his eyes moved from his papers. He responded quietly, matching my tone, "I know." Neither one of us spoke another word. I sat there for the next hour watching Alf do paperwork.

Finally he said, "Come on, Fran," he patted my arm, "I'll open the lounge for you."

In utter darkness, I sat smoking cigarette after cigarette. I was on my last cigarette and still in my nightgown when the room began to fill with other patients. I ignored them all.

Then Nancy came over and sat down next to me, "How are you doing, Fran?" she asked.

"All right," I said morosely. Several minutes of silence followed. "I gotta go," I said jumping up to leave.

Back in my room, I crawled into bed. Two hours later I remembered Steve was coming for a visit and forced myself to get up and shower. I wanted desperately for him to be there right then, to hug me and tell me everything would be all right. It was all so terribly confusing.

While I was in the shower there was a knock on the bathroom door. "Group is starting in a few minutes, we want you to come," Marty said.

"Maybe," I shouted. Stepping from the shower, I remembered Dr. Keogan was going to be in charge of Group. Hurriedly, I threw on a pair of sweats, an oversized football jersey and my slippers, and went to find them.

I took the last seat in the room, right next to Dr. Keogan, who smiled at me. The conversation was so noisy that I was unable to concentrate. Finally, Dr. Keogan asked me to explain to the group why I was at Brookhollow.

"I was in a car accident," I began.

Martha interrupted me. I smiled at her. Suddenly I was too weak to continue. As I sat there listening, my left arm began to droop at my side. I grabbed hold of my upper arm in an attempt to steady it. Then my head grew heavy and it dropped to my chest. Martha's words began to fade. I began trembling.

"Excuse me, I have one thing to say," Dr. Keogan interrupted Martha, "We're so sorry," he said looking directly into my eyes. His words were clear, but nonintelligible.

What does he know? Is he trying to warn me that something is going to happen to me? My head ached as I tried to figure the comment out. Then someone tapped my shoulder.

I turned to discover Jane standing behind me, "There's a Dr. Mahar here to see you," she whispered.

I left Group immediately. I was met outside the door by a strong, big-boned and ruddy-looking man with blue eyes which showed directness and authority. He extended one hand toward me and held an oversized briefcase in the other.

"I'm pleased to meet you, Ms. Deitrick. I'm Dr. Mahar," he said respectfully.

I shook his hand saying, "I'm pleased to meet you. Call me Fran."

His polite attitude shocked me, no one had addressed me—the crazy one—with respect in ages. His words made me feel as if I was a real person. Automatically I liked him.

"I'd like to examine you in your room, if you'll show me which one it is," he said.

I had no idea what kind of a doctor he was or why he wanted to examine me, but replied, "Sure, I'll show you."

Dr. Mahar closed the door behind him as we entered

my room. Placing his briefcase on my roommate's bed, he opened it, revealing a dozen instruments I had never seen before. Each one was held in place by a form-fitting piece of foam. They looked intimidating. Jane walked in.

"Will you get me a hospital gown, please?" Dr. Mahar asked her. She turned and left immediately.

When she came back with gown in hand, Dr. Mahar directed me into the bathroom to change. "Little Orphan Annie," I murmured as I saw myself in the mirror drowned by my new outfit. Walking back from the bathroom, I clutched the back of the gown together.

Dr. Mahar was at my side immediately, "Here let me tie that for you so you won't be embarrassed," he said.

As soon as he finished he continued, "Walk over to the window and back please?" I did as he told me and then he said, "Okay, let's go sit down."

I sat on one bed, he sat directly across from me on the other. Reaching into his briefcase, he retrieved one of his instruments and a second, which he screwed on top of the first.

"Please close the drapes," he said to Jane.

A bright beam of light came shining from the silver instrument he held, "Keep looking into the corner for me please." He positioned his face inches from mine and moved the light from one eye to the other.

What's going on here? I wondered.

"Okay, you can draw the drapes," he said motioning to Jane. He put that instrument down and took another, a tiny hammer, knocking it against my knees, ankles, wrists, and elbows. Then he had me watch as he pulled a striped piece of material before my eyes. As soon as this was done, I had to squeeze two fingers from each of his hands as tight as I could.

Next, he said, "Close your eyes as tight as possible and try to keep them shut." He tried to open them. I wanted to ask him what this was all for; however I didn't, I just let him go.

Then he pulled a tuning fork from his briefcase and

said, "Close your eyes." A horrendous noise filled the room. I screamed and jumped forward. "I'm not here to hurt you, I'm here to help you," Dr. Mahar said.

I sat back down and let him continue. He placed the vibrating tuning fork on each of my hands and then on each foot as he asked what I felt.

When all this was over he asked, "Can you tell me about what happened?"

"I got in a car accident," I said.

"What happened in the accident?" he asked.

"I don't know. I was at a stop sign and then I was spinning around. My car was in the wrong direction when I got out. I never saw the truck coming," I said.

"What side was the truck on?" he asked.

"My right side," I said continuing with, "They took me to the hospital. I kept complaining that my head hurt, but no one listened. They thought I was crazy. Finally I went home but the pain got worse and I had all kinds of funny symptoms. Since then nothing went right, that's how I got here."

"I see," he said, nodding his understanding.

"Is there anything else you can remember?" he asked.

"Why do you want to know all this?" I asked. He didn't reply and I went on. "After the accident, the police officer gave me some forms to fill out but I couldn't see them very well. I don't remember being in an ambulance but I do remember being in a hospital," I stopped. I wasn't about to tell him another thing, I didn't know if I could completely trust him.

Still, he seemed satisfied with what I told him and said, "Stick out your tongue for me." After I did he asked, "Close your eyes for me." Then he stuck the side of my forehead with a pin and said, "Sharp." I shook my head noncommitally. Then he gently touched the same spot with something soft and said, "Dull." Again the same head shake.

He continued with, "I want you to tell me what you feel every time I touch you with one of these." He pricked me with the pin and lightly touched my face, legs, and feet, alternating the two as he went.

"Okay," he said as he finished, "now I want you to run the heel of your right foot up and down your left shin." I did as I was told as he watched intently. "Very good."

"Now I want you to lie down on the bed for me," he said, taking something out of his pocket and running it along the bottom of my foot. My foot didn't flex an inch. *Isn't it supposed to move?* I wondered.

Even with my curiosity as high as it was I didn't ask one question. I only stared at him more intently. Dr. Mahar picked up both my legs at the knees and let them drop to the bed. *What is this for?*

He immediately went over and closed his briefcase saying, "You can get dressed and then we'll talk." He disappeared and I went into the bathroom.

I sat on the bed waiting for his return. Walking in, he stood against the wall nearest my bed and said slowly and clearly, "You should never have been committed, you should have been admitted." I was taken back. I didn't fully understand his comment and stared at him in bewilderment.

"You'll be *admitted* to St. Elizabeth on Monday so we can run some more tests and find out what is wrong exactly. You have to promise you won't try and run away," he said.

I nodded. Someone finally understood all that had happened to me. At that moment I wanted to get up and kiss Dr. Mahar. I loved this man; however, I restrained myself, "I won't run away, I promise."

Feelings of euphoria filled me. *I'm getting out of Brookhollow! I'm not crazy! I knew it!*

As soon as Dr. Mahar left I started packing. A smile covered my face as I tossed my clothes into the air, "I'm free!" When all my clothes were piled on my bed I ran to the nurses' station to retrieve my luggage.

"I'm sorry, we can't let you have your luggage until you're ready to go," Lydia said.

"Oh, all right," I replied. I wasn't going to let anything ruin my day, not even Lydia.

I didn't understand how I got to Brookhollow, why I was getting to leave, what the doctor saw, what it all meant as far as my future; but I didn't care. All I cared about was not being crazy and now I knew I wasn't. My confidence soared, my attitude became positive.

On my way back to my room a voice from behind called, "Hey there, cutie."

I turned and saw my ex-fiancé, Steve. For a moment I couldn't move. Tears flowed down my cheeks as I looked at Steve's tall blond good looks. He came walking toward me and I started running to him. "I'm not crazy!" I exclaimed.

"I never thought you were," he said softly.

"Are you allowed out for a while?" he asked.

"I don't know. I'll have to ask," I answered. We walked together to the nurses' station.

"Can I go out this afternoon?" I asked Lydia.

"You don't have those privileges," she said.

"I thought I did. What happened?" I asked.

"You may have had them but you don't now," she insisted.

I was ready to scream at her when Steve took hold of my arm and said, "That's all right, I'll visit with you here."

We went to my room. An uneasiness filled the air as I tried to decide if and how I should tell him about the thing on my brain, and about having to go to St. Elizabeth on Monday. I sat on the bed almost in tears.

He walked over to my side, "What's the matter, babe?" he asked.

I put my head on his shoulder and whispered, "Thank you for coming. You don't know how much it means, how much I need you."

"I wanted to come and see you," he said quietly.

We looked at each other searchingly, both trying to fathom what we now meant or didn't mean to each other.

"There was a Dr. Mahar here this morning," I said.

"Yeah," he said.

I gulped and continued, "He told me I should never have been committed. You see, what happened was they found this thing and that's why he said that," I said.

"What thing?" he asked.

"They found this thing, this thing on my brain. I'm being admitted to St. Elizabeth on Monday," I said, the tears flowing now. He held me tighter in his arms.

The realization of what was happening finally hit me. I became limp in his arms and sobbed, "I don't want to die Steve. Please don't let me die," I repeated as my face dug deeper into his chest. He held me closer.

Neither one of us moved until Lydia came storming into the room, "The door isn't supposed to be closed and he's not supposed to be in here," she said.

Steve bolted to his feet. And I said, "We're not doing anything. Can't I have any privacy around here?" I wiped the tears from my eyes.

"You can have privacy in the lounge," she said, motioning us out.

"She's a bitch," I told Steve as we walked to the Quiet Lounge. We were the only ones there and made ourselves comfortable on the couch.

"So what kind of a doctor is this Dr. Mahar?" Steve asked.

"I don't know but he's real nice. He impressed me, he was very professional," I said.

"Well why didn't you ask?" Steve asked.

"I don't know," I replied.

"How did he know there was a thing on your brain just by examining you?" he asked.

"They took pictures of the inside of my head the other day," I replied.

"Why didn't you call and tell me all this?" he asked.

"I tried but I kept getting your answering machine,

and you can't leave a message when you call collect," I said.

An hour later Steve got up to leave, "Call me anytime," he said nonchalantly and then kissed me goodbye. I watched until he was out of sight. He had been very nice, rekindled many of my old feelings, but his departure left me empty inside. Now I had the distinct impression that it all had been a mirage. Our relationship had really ended.

I went back to the lounge. Thoughts of Dr. Mahar and St. Elizabeth crowded my mind. Funnily, I was scared of what lay ahead, of leaving Brookhollow.

Then Dr. Lee came into the Quiet Lounge, "Hi, Fran, would you like to meet . . . ?" I interrupted her.

I began, "They found a thing on my brain. I think it's a tumor but I don't really know. I don't understand anything. Would you explain it to me?"

"I know all about it. The MRI scan you had the other day showed an abnormal growth on your brain. They won't know for sure what it is, or what to do about it until they study it further. Dr. Keogan called in Dr. Mahar because he's the best one to handle this," she said.

I asked trembling, "What kind of a doctor is he?"

"He's a neurologist."

"How long will I be in the hospital?" I asked.

"It all depends," she said.

"Dr. Mahar told me I should never have been committed, what did he mean?" I asked.

"He thinks a lot of your behavior was caused by the growth," she said.

I still didn't understand exactly what was happening or going to happen, but I felt suddenly angry at them all. *Look what they've done to me.*

Instead of pursuing it, however, I asked, "Is it all right if I leave now, I want to call my family."

"Sure it's all right. Before you go, I do want you to know I'll be thinking about you while you're in the hospital and I wish you all the best," she said.

"Thanks," I said dryly and walked away.

I went directly to the phone and dialed home. "Hi, Mom, something has come up," I said.

"I know," she interrupted.

"How do you know?" I asked. "Dr. Kamari called," her voice broke, "Fran."

I didn't want her to weep or sympathize. If she did, I didn't think I could hold together. Instead I rushed on, "I'm going to St. Elizabeth on Monday. Do you think someone can come over tomorrow and pick up my things?" I asked.

"When are Sunday visiting hours?" my mother pressed.

"They start at two."

"We'll be there around two tomorrow," she said definitively.

"Thanks, I'll see you then," I replied and hung up.

I sat at the phone, numb. *I want to go home. How do I know they're telling me the truth? Maybe it's not. They probably are going to turn me into a zombie and I'll spend the rest of my life here. They started with the lights and have now moved onto this.*

I stopped and other thoughts crowded in. *Maybe it is really a tumor. Is a tumor cancer?* Then I reversed, *It's going to be nothing. I know it. Don't let it bother you, Fran, think of it as going to a dentist.*

I began to cry. *Why me, I wanta live! Please God help me. I promise if you get me out of this I'll be a better person, please. What did Dr. Kamari say to my mother when he called? I wish he hadn't told them, they'll worry. What's going to happen to me?*

I dialed Steve's number and got his answering machine. I let the phone drop and stared intently at the receiver as it dangled by its cord. *You could wrap it right around your throat, Fran. You'd be free of this mess anyway.* I shook the thought off, picked up the receiver, and placed it carefully back in its cradle.

Head down, looking neither right not left, I walked

back to my room and crawled into the security of my bed. I lay there staring into space for the rest of the day.

I was helpless, my life was now in the hands of Dr. Mahar. I hated the feeling of not being in control of my life, of having to depend on others. Yet I had no choice.

As the hours passed my emotions flew back and forth: anger, fear, and dread vied with each other. I gave myself up to self-pity, feeling the very depths of my despair. But as I lay there my old spirit began to surface. *Damn,* I thought, *they were all wrong, I wasn't a mental case. I was sick. And if you're sick you can get well.* Suddenly, I came alive once again, my mind in full motion. I was determined to beat the odds, treat the tumor, the commitment, everything. Nothing was going to grind Frances I. Deitrick into the ground.

Slowly I drifted into a deep sleep, dreaming of a life free of doctors, free of pain, free of confusion, free of misunderstandings, and most of important of all—free of control.

The next morning, the dawn broke and I showered, dressed, and ate breakfast. No other patients were awake. I savored the solitude. Now all I had left to do was get my luggage and wait for my family's arrival.

I had to plead with Lydia in order to get my luggage in advance of my family's arrival, but finally she gave in. "There may be a real person in there after all," I mumbled. It took all of five minutes to pack. Afterward I went to the lounge.

Watching the clock tick, I smoked cigarette after cigarette and waited. It was Sunday, the day when everyone would either go home or go out venturing, a privilege I was unfamiliar with. It was depressing sitting there.

As two o'clock edged closer, I kept getting up to scan the corridor to see if my family had arrived. Exactly as the clock struck two, I saw my mother, father, and sisters—Eileen and Connie—walking down the hall. Running past the nurses' station to greet them, I pulled them into my room.

"This is for you Fran," my mother said handing me a blue box.

"What's this for?" I asked.

"You're going to the hospital," she replied.

"What have I been in?" I asked.

"You know what I mean, you're going into a real hospital," she replied.

The air filled with awkwardness. Tears fell from my eyes; I had to force a smile onto my face as I unwrapped the paper.

"It's beautiful!" I said as I drew the nightgown from the box. Its dusty pink color twinkled in the sun's rays. The delicate lace bodice and cuffs gave the simple gown an elegant appearance. I kissed my mother in appreciation.

"It's from your father also," she said. I drew back for a moment. My father had been staying away, obviously embarrassed by his daughter being confined to a mental institution. I decided, however, to take this gift as a peace offering.

Walking over to a suitcase, I tucked the nightgown inside. As I was doing this Connie noticed my new housecoat in another bag and asked, "Aren't you taking this with you?"

I never told them about Cindy and how she had imitated me when I had worn it. Shivering, I stared at the robe and replied, "It'll be way too warm in the hospital for a housecoat."

Nothing further was mentioned and I was glad. I didn't want to risk the chance of further questions and the exposure of any of my experiences at Brookhollow. They knew nothing other than that I was there and I wanted to keep it that way.

We visited for the next hour until my father said quietly, "Fran, we need to go so we'll be home before dark." We said our goodbyes and I watched as they walked to freedom. I felt they'd deserted me, as one would desert a caged animal at a zoo. How I wished I could go with them.

I went back to the lounge and resumed my smoking.

Little by little the lounge filled with returning patients. Each would rant and rave about their experiences during the day. I felt apart from them all, these people who had shared my imprisonment, but with whom I could not share my fears of tomorrow. After a while, I retreated to the solitude of my barren room. Here I stayed for the night, not daring to sleep.

The next morning my stomach churned as I paced the floor of the lounge, waiting to go to St. Elizabeth. I was apprehensive about going, yet excited about leaving. When Mary came in to tell me it was time to leave, I began to cry. I flew to my room and gathered my things. On the way out I stopped right before the door, looked back, and said, "I won't miss you at all."

The buzzer rang and I stepped out into the light, taking a deep breath of the cool, fresh air.

SEVENTEEN

I was out of Brookhollow; it was not out of me. I was afraid of how I would be treated, what people would think. It seemed to me I had been branded with the words, "Mental patient." Indeed, all pride in myself, all confidence in myself and in my ability to gain people's respect, and the motivation needed to rebuild a life was gone. My biggest fear was how easy it might be to be recommitted.

During the drive to St. Elizabeth, I didn't speak. I retreated into myself to gain protection against what lay ahead. Finally we arrived. Slowly the car made its way up the horseshoe drive and stopped halfway to the top. The sight of the huge brick building made my heart beat faster. It looked mysterious and foreboding.

As we entered the building, Mary grasped my arm to assist me; however, her efforts made me feel like an invalid, reinforcing my already shaky self-image.

"Please Fran, cover up so you won't get a cold. Now walk slowly."

Being treated so patronizingly made me rebel, "Don't say another thing; you're here to deliver me and that's it."

I regretted my words instantly; however, there was no way I could take them back.

The receptionist handed me some forms to complete and we sat down to wait for my escort.

"You don't have to stay around," I said.

"Yes, I do. I have my orders," she replied haughtily.

Staring at her, I knew right then that Brookhollow would linger in my life. Finally, a male attendant appeared to escort me, and Mary left.

He dropped me off at a nurses' station on the fourth floor. A plump blonde woman called out, "Hi, you must be Fran. I'm Becky and I'll show you to your room."

"Hi," I said, handing her my bag and purse as we were required to do at Brookhollow. She looked surprised.

"You can bring those right in with you," she said.

She's not going to search them? I thought amazed. She brought me into a room right across the hall and showed me to my bed. It was right next to a window. As I peered through the glass I discovered, to my delight, that there weren't any iron bars.

"The doctor will be here in a minute. In the meantime you can change into this," Becky said handing me a hospital gown.

She left and Dr. Mahar came in, "Hello Fran. Oh, you're not changed yet. Well, do that and I'll be right back in," he said.

"You want everything off?" I asked.

"Yes," he replied.

Five minutes later he returned, "Okay, please lie on your left side, curl your knees as close to your chest as possible, and tuck your head into your chest," he said.

What is he doing? I wondered.

As if he had read my thoughts, he began to explain, "I'm going to draw some fluid, so you'll have to lie as still as possible," he said. There was a prick at the base of my spine. Turning my head to the wall, I squeezed my eyelids together and gritted my teeth against the pain.

"You're doing fine Fran, keep it up. It'll only be another minute," Dr. Mahar said encouraging me. I lay there wondering what all this meant.

Then I heard footsteps. They stopped at the side of my bed. "I'm sorry you didn't have the chance to do this spinal tap but it had to be done right away," Dr. Mahar said to the unseen people. Then he went on to explain what he had done in medical terminology I only half understood.

"The fluid is clear Fran, that's a good sign," he said and then pulled the needle out. I didn't ask what it meant, I assumed clear fluid signaled that I would be okay and I was too afraid of hearing something different.

"Now, I want you to lie flat on your back for the next six hours," he said. I flipped my body over to assume this position, and then I saw two people, one a woman, the other a man. Both wore white jackets. She was middle-aged and plain, but he was gorgeous. My eyes widened as soon as I saw his thick dark wavy hair and blue eyes.

"I hope he's going to be my doctor," I said.

Dr. Mahar laughed, "This is Dr. White and Mr. Harrington, they'll be assisting me on your case," Dr. Mahar said.

"I'm pleased to meet you," I murmured.

"I have to go but they'll be staying to ask you some questions, okay Fran? And, no pillow," he said as he took the pillow from the bed.

"Can I get something to eat?" I asked.

"She has her priorities," Mr. Harrington smiled. "I'll see what I can do for you," Dr. Mahar waved and left.

Dr. White and Mr. Harrington approached the side of my bed. "Can you tell us what happened?" Dr. White asked. I was clear and graphic as I began to explain the episodes which led up to my admittance to St. Elizabeth's.

I was cut short by Dr. White, "Did you have headaches?" she asked.

"Some," I replied. Then she went on to ask me about my coordination, vision and hearing. I tried to answer as many as I could. Meanwhile, I pondered the whole scene and ended up more confused than ever.

When a silver tray filled with covered dishes was delivered, my thoughts shifted, "How am I ever going to get this food into my mouth?" I asked. The nurse placed the tray on

the bed next to my head; however, there were mashed pota-
toes and salisbury steak, hardly edible if one lay flat on her
back.

Clumsily I maneuvered the spoon into the meat. It
splattered. But after several tries, I got some to stay on the
utensil and slowly brought it back to my mouth. The food
fell off halfway there and I tried again. This time I was
successful. Unfortunately, it tasted disgusting. I decided all
the hard work wasn't worth it and just drank the juice.

Half an hour later Becky, the friendly nurse I'd met
earlier, came in. She took my pulse and blood pressure.
Then she put a needle in a vein on the back of my hand and
stroked my upper arm sympathetically.

"What's this for?" I asked.

"It's an IV," she said, attaching it to a tube which led
into a bottle of yellow soupy liquid.

"I don't feel sick, don't they do this to sick people?
What's in it?" I asked lumping my questions together.

"A saline and vitamin solution," she replied.

"A lot of good that does me," I observed. "I'm starved
and it hurts."

Becky clucked sympathetically in response and then
walked out, leaving me alone. To pass the time, I started
counting the number of IV drops dripping into my arm.
The longer I lay there the worse I had to urinate, and the
more tempted I was to get up by myself and go to the bathroom.

I didn't know what would happen if I did and decided
to ask. I spotted a bell, and feeling strange, rang it. Becky
soon appeared, "Can I get up? I only want to use the bathroom."

"Sorry you can't do that. You'll get a headache you
wouldn't believe and it probably won't go away for a few
weeks," she said.

Headache; the word made pictures flash through my
mind. Once again I was at First Memorial, right after the
accident. I was scared to death Becky was going to use a
catheter, just as they had.

Instead, she brought in a bedpan. But I couldn't seem to use it. Pushing it into the corner, I talked myself into waiting. An hour later I put the bedpan back in place. And, as soon as it was, Dr. Kamari walked in. Never was I more embarrassed. I tried to remove it without drawing his attention to it.

He smiled awkwardly and asked if he could sit down. "Of course you can," I said.

He drew a chair close to my bed, "How are you today?"

"Fine, how are you?" I replied.

Explaining the events of the day I asked, "What is going to happen to me next?"

He nodded, "Dr. Mahar is an excellent doctor," he said firmly. "You'll be in good hands."

I watched him intently.

Dr. Kamari, who had caused me so much pain with his assessment of me, now spoke reassuringly as he tried to convince me to trust Dr. Mahar. It surprised me, he actually seemed human. Still, I could not forget the past and remained polite and aloof.

"I'll see you tomorrow," Dr. Kamari finally said as he pushed the chair back into the corner.

"I'll be here," I replied sadly. In truth, I didn't want him to leave. I was more secure about being at St. Elizabeth if someone, anyone was with me. But at the same time, I was afraid to show this weakness to him.

For the next two hours I lay motionless, thought after thought entering my mind. Then the urge to urinate resurged. This time I disregarded the nurse's warning and edged my way out of bed. Stumbling along, I pushed the IV with me. My body felt weak and I was lightheaded, though no headache appeared.

Once I navigated back to the bed though, I was glad I had taken the risk. My independence mattered so much. Still, after all the activity, I was weaker and soon feel fast asleep.

The next morning an elderly stout nurse prodded me,

"You have an appointment for your CAT scan this morning. After I take your blood pressure and you take your medicine, you'll need to start getting ready," she said.

I began to ask her if she would retrieve my things for me when I realized they were all in my possession. A privilege not allowed at Brookhollow. This insignificant achievement filled me with pride.

Searching through my suitcase, I picked out some things, razor included. There wasn't any hydrogen peroxide, which I liked to use as a mouth rinse, so I asked a nurse for some. She told me she didn't have any immediately available, but would order some.

Was there any further meaning to her response? I wondered when she didn't question me as to why I wanted it. Intense questioning was something Lydia at Brookhollow surely would have done, and in the process she would have gained pleasure from the humiliation she was causing.

This nurse just smiled and wrote the order down. I shook my head. As difficult as it had been getting used to life at Brookhollow, it was just as difficult getting used to life again outside. I walked away uncertain of myself.

Uneasily I began freshening up, certain my privilege would soon be revoked with a reprimand following. Before I had a chance to finish dressing, a wheelchair was pushed through my door by a grayhaired, ebony-skinned attendant, who asked, "Is Frances Deitrick here?"

"That's me, where do you want me?" I replied.

"Right here," he said cheerfully as he moved the wheelchair forward, "I'm Al," as he moved the wheelchair forward.

"By the way, where are we going?" I asked sitting down.

"To Lechmere Laboratories," he replied. Then he gently tucked a blanket around me.

We stopped right in front of the door which led outside and I was transferred to a stretcher. As he was tightening the belt around my waist, I became frightened at being tied down. I desperately wanted to go back to my room. I didn't trust him anymore.

The doors opened and the bracing winter wind snapped across my face. The fresh feeling of the wind suddenly brought life and confidence back into my body. I was sorry when it was replaced by the medicinal odor from inside the ambulance.

The waiting room at Lechmere was full of people and Al pushed me on the stretcher through the thick of it, IV and all. My embarrassment grew as I sank deeper and deeper under the blanket. Everyone watched intently as Al transferred me back into a wheelchair.

There was no use ignoring the eyes riveted on me, so after a while, I started explaining to those around me where I had come from and why. They were fascinated and began asking further questions. I was enjoying myself until a little old lady with a squeaky voice asked about the symptoms I had and where I'd been.

I withdrew sullenly, not wanting to tell anyone about Brookhollow. I didn't understand how I could have been committed and labeled without a cause and a treatment, and how a growth fit into all this.

Doubts flitted through my mind about Doctors Kamari, Keogan, and Mahar; the doctors whose conflicting opinions had confused me. All the whys and hows ran rampant through my thoughts. I wondered if they still thought I was Bipolar, what had happened to my nervous breakdown, and on and on.

If a freckle-faced redhaired nurse hadn't interrupted my thoughts I would have surely driven myself crazy trying to understand all that had happened to me. "I need to move you into another room," she said cheerfully and began pushing my wheelchair. The room she had in mind was full and she parked the wheelchair in the hallway.

"How long will it be before I am seen?" I asked.

Shaking her head, she said, "You don't have an appointment so we're going to try to squeeze you in."

After a while I began to squirm, my body sore from

sitting in the wheelchair. Looking over the immediate area, I searched for a place to stretch my legs. In a corner was a worn, red leather recliner. No one could have held me back. I was out of the wheelchair and resting comfortably within seconds.

Patient after patient filed by, each giving me a half-hearted smirk. But snug and comfortable, I just smiled back. Unfortunately, a short time later a nurse ambled by, spied me, and chased me off.

I found myself perched in an out-of-the-way room. Hours passed as I flipped through old magazines and anything else I could lay my hands on, growing more and more tired of waiting as the time passed.

Then a grim-faced nurse appeared and silently moved me into another room. By this time my body ached and I was starving. On top of that I was so lightheaded I wasn't able to concentrate enough to read. I spent the next several hours sitting there with my head drooping into my chest.

Finally, my name was called. Inside the X-ray room I stared at the strange machine which would do the testing. It wasn't at all similar to the one where I had the MRI scan done. This one reminded me of a ring used in a circus by the daredevils, the one they would set on fire and then go through on their motorcycles. It looked terrifying.

A matter-of-fact and uncommunicative middle-aged technician moved a stepstool to the side of the machine and motioned me to get on it. When he was satisfied with my position he left. As I lay on the table it began to inch backwards. The machine stopped when it was centered directly over my head.

Coming from the other room I heard someone's husky voice, "We're going to do two sets; one without dye and one with. There'll be beams of red light directly over your eyes; do not look at them."

When the first set was complete, the technician and a muscular dark-eyed doctor came in to prepare me for the next. As the dye was entering through my IV tube my vision suddenly began to blur, my throat began to close, and my heart palpitated at twice its normal rate.

Hysterically, I cried out, "Stop." Instantly the technician ran from the room and the dye stopped flowing. The doctor replaced the flow of dye with that of another drug and my body slowly returned to normal. Then the door flung open and four other doctors rushed in and encircled the table where I lay.

"How are you feeling?" asked one doctor with strong gray-green eyes, the one closest to me.

"Better," I replied.

"You had us scared. We have a word for people like you," he said.

"Yeah, dizzy broad," I replied.

Everyone laughed as he replied, "Not quite." *I had them scared! What did they think they had me right now, standing around staring at me?*

"And you thought we were ignoring you all day," another balding, round-faced doctor piped up. One of the other doctors patted me on the leg and they left.

"If you ever have to have this test again, better tell them you're extremely allergic to the dye," the technician said.

"Is that what this is all about?" I asked breathing a sigh of relief. He nodded.

"As long as we have you here and the dye in you we're going to continue. Is that all right with you?" the muscular doctor asked.

"I guess so," I replied.

He left and the dazzling red lights soon appeared. Fifteen minutes later I was walking back to the waiting room.

The receptionist called the ambulance to pick me up. Again the waiting period was long. I watched as lights were turned off and people started going home for the night. Nine hours had passed and I was exhausted. My hand was all red where the IV had been attached. All I could think of was how much I wanted to soak in a hot bath.

Then the stretcher came rolling in. Was I ever glad to

see it! Stretching out on it, as though it were a feather bed, I relaxed, not caring who saw me being brought out.

Once inside the ambulance the attendant hooked up a portable heart monitor. It stayed in place until we were back at St. Elizabeth, where he ripped the patches from my chest. I never thought I'd be glad to be back, but I was.

The first thing I asked for once I was back in my room was something to eat. Even though it looked gray and disgusting, I was so hungry I didn't care and wolfed it down, then asked for more.

As soon as I finished eating, I begged to take a bath. Because of the test, the nurse had to call Dr. Mahar to ask his permission. Still, I hated even the momentary dependency. When the nurse returned with Mahar's approval, I soaked for an hour until a nurse knocked and asked how I was doing.

A wheelchair was waiting for me when I finished. Al, the attendant, reminded me, "You have an appointment with X-ray. And if you don't mind, I'm your escort." I nodded and was whisked away.

Afterward, the last thing I wanted was to go back to my boring old room; however, I had no choice. Inside was a new roommate, a rumpled, silk-skinned lady, who had to be in her nineties. She must have weighed no more than seventy pounds and was unable to get out of bed.

There was a hole cut in her throat and she was only able to speak to me by placing a mechanism under her chin. The resulting voice sounded like a computerized toy talking and scared the hell out of me. But I talked to her politely and then pulled the curtain around my bed.

Looking at her frailness and helplessness made me think about the inevitability of age and death. I wanted to avoid the thought, and read the same magazine three times before I fell asleep.

I awoke with thoughts of Steve. Before doing anything else I went to the pay phone.

"Hi," I said.

"Hi," he said.

"Oh, Steve, I miss you. I hate being here. This isn't supposed to be happening to me. I don't understand anything. All I know is, I need you," I said sobbing.

"Fran," he said kindly but distantly. "You have to pull yourself together. You're going to be all right Fran, I know you are. You're a special person, strong enough to make it through this. I know you're scared, you have every right to be, but you'll be out of there before you know it and you'll find someone who cares about you and loves you."

He rushed on before the full impact of his words hit me. "You're going to walk out of there the healthiest person around. If anyone tells you differently, tell them they don't know what they're talking about," he said.

"I want to believe that, and do when I'm talking to you. But I need you to remind me, it isn't easy without you. You make me forget, think differently. Here all I do is think and live this burden," I replied.

"I know it's tough but I'm only a phone call away," he insisted.

Then he continued, "There's one thing I've been meaning to ask you, Fran. Have the doctors mentioned anything about what may have brought on your symptoms?" he asked cautiously. "I mean, did what happened this past summer have anything to do with it?" He pressed on. "Have you told anyone about it?"

"I haven't mentioned it, although I doubt very much it has anything to do with you." I said slowly. I stiffened, suddenly realizing his interest had as much to do with self-preservation as with me.

I'm sure none of this has anything to do with you." I said, painfully. "If you're thinking about the time you lost control of your temper and began slapping me, forget it."

"I regret it Fran. I don't know what happened and I'm ashamed. You know I wish you all the best."

"Thank you," I said humbly.

"Well, I have to go now," he said abruptly.

"Of course," I softly answered, and hung up.

Now I was more upset than ever. Steve was a jerk, yet

I was afraid of losing him, afraid of being with him. I went back to my room and smothered my face in my pillow, sobbing hysterically. "How do you get yourself into these things?" I murmured and lay back.

Not long afterward, Dr. Mahar, Mr. Harrington, and Dr. White appeared.

"Good morning. Dr. White and Mr. Harrington want to examine your eyes," Dr. Mahar said, drawing the curtains closed.

I sat up straight in bed and listened to Dr. White's instructions, "Just look over in the corner for me," she said pointing into a corner.

Then Mr. Harrington took control and I asked, "Everything all right in there Mr. Harrington?"

"You can call me, Dave, and I don't know yet," he replied.

He was so cute; I didn't really care if everything was all right, I just wanted to say something to him. When he was through they both left and Dr. Mahar moved to the window.

He drew the curtains open and then leaned against the sill. A very serious look covered his face as he ran his thumb and forefinger along his chin.

"Fran, we are pretty sure there is an abnormal growth in your head. It can be one of two things: a multiple sclerosis plaque or a pontine glioma, which is a tumor. I'm going to start you on Decedron, which is a steroid. We'll use this to reduce the swelling in your head."

He nodded slowly, "We would follow this course of treatment in either case, so we're safe there," he said, as if thinking out loud. I was unable to reply, so I stared at him morbidly: *multiple sclerosis?*

I felt like I would burst into tears; however, I was frozen, unable to blink an eye. The thought of having multiple sclerosis, or being paralyzed, was more than I could handle.

He was blunt and direct, yet his voice was gentle, caring. "A specialist will be reviewing the results of your tests later today. Then I'll be back to talk with you," he said and then left.

At that moment, I wanted to drop everything, leave that instant, and enjoy what little life I had remaining. I had left the comfort of my bed, ready to do just this, when Mr. Harrington suddenly returned.

"If you have a minute there are some questions I have to ask," he said.

"All right," I replied gloomily, crawling back into bed. As I shook my head yes or no, he ran through thirty or so questions relating to my medical history, my drinking and smoking habits, and how I had felt during the last few months.

Then he said, "I know you are concerned about your diagnosis and I wanted to tell you Dr. Mahar is one of the best. Whatever you have, you'll be well taken care of."

"I'd rather have a brain tumor," was the only thing I managed to say.

"No you wouldn't," he replied, his voice grim.

Pondering the future, my dark thoughts drifted. I stayed in bed the rest of the day, wrapped in my own cocoon, barely talking to the nurses who flitted in and out of my room.

At about eight that night, Dr. Mahar came back. Once again he leaned against the window sill. The way his glasses were positioned at the end of his nose told me he meant business, serious business.

"I, and several others, have studied the results of the MRI, Fran," he said pausing for a moment. He looked directly into my eyes, "The growth on your brain is a tumor," I nodded.

"There are two options for its treatment," Dr. Mahar said quietly. "One is surgery, the other is radiation." Again, he paused, "I have to tell you because of the tumor's location."

I interrupted him, "Where is it?"

He took a deep breath and said in a grave voice, "It's on the brain stem, Fran, and surgery could cause blindness or death."

I swallowed. This had to be happening to someone else. I looked away. Outside the window, it was already dark. There were rumblings from the sky, as it a storm were beginning. The night fit my mood. I pushed away my morbid thoughts and fought back tears.

"Because of the tumor's location I don't recommend surgery." Dr. Mahar continued, "With radiation, on the other hand, you'd have to receive the maximum allowable dosage to the brain. We hope this would terminate the tumor."

"Have others gotten well that way?" I asked apprehensively.

He shook his head negatively. "You would be breaking new ground." He regarded me with clear gray-green eyes and said. "But both the radiologist, Dr. Perrine, and the surgeon are excellent and they can give you the very best treatment possible."

Again he stopped, as if gathering together his own thoughts, and then added, "I want you to think about all this before you make a decision." I nodded, not trusting myself to speak and he left. Silence filled the room.

Afterward, I dazedly sat up on my bed. I was alone, alone to think about a worse fate than I was already facing. I trembled in fear. Pictures of wheelchairs flashed through my mind. Pictures of brain surgery, of my skull being bored into flashed by. Pictures of being bald, of braces on my legs, and of a meaningless life flashed by.

This was followed by pictures of First Memorial, Brookhollow, grocery shopping, the accident, Christmas day, and the Ninth Ward. Flashing glimpses of my own death followed. I shuddered: Too much had happened to me and I knew much was yet to follow.

Suddenly, Dr. Kamari can sauntering in and sat in the chair next to my bed. "How are you today?" he asked. I made no reply as I sat listening to the winter winds whip against the windows. For a few minutes Dr. Kamari sat in silence with me.

Tears formed in my eyes as I looked up at him and said, "It's not fair." "No, it's not, you're too young," he replied. The silence returned. Tears flowed steadily down my cheeks.

Even though no more words were spoken a feeling of concern and understanding filled the air. I was glad that at last Dr. Kamari understood without my having to explain. I had no words to convey what I thought and felt at this time. In truth, right now I didn't think or feel a thing, though earlier I had thought and felt too much.

I had been lightheaded for days but now it grew worse. I felt distant from Dr. Kamari, the rest of my room, the world, as though I was locked in a bubble. "I don't feel good. I want to lie down," I said.

"Sleep is good for you Fran," he said softly and tip-toed out.

EIGHTEEN

I could see Dr. Mahar's grim-set face clearly in the morning light. "I'm going to take my chances with radiation." I paused, and he was silent. "At least it's not multiple sclerosis. At least with this I have a chance."

Dr. Mahar didn't speak at first; instead, he leaned over the bed and patted my cheek. "We're going to give you the very best care we can Fran," he said gently.

I spent the rest of the morning looking at magazines. It wasn't boredom but self-pity which kept me rapidly turning the pages and wiping tears away.

And Dr. Kamari ambled in asking, "What are you reading?" No words came. I was only able to stutter. He sat down until I gained control of myself.

Then I said, "Dr. Mahar was in." He nodded.

"Did you call your family?" he asked.

"No, I don't want them to know yet," I replied.

"Why not?" he asked.

"Because I don't."

He passed a hand across his forehead. "Well, I think Dr. Mahar has already been in touch with them," he said.

"Why?" I demanded.

"He always lets the family know, the same way I do," he replied.

I was furious and our conversation ended. Dr. Kamari

stayed for a while watching my tears, his face grimly set as if he was observing penance.

As soon as he was gone I wished he were back. I wanted his company, even if he couldn't provide the answers I needed. Though he represented Brookhollow, I had grown to depend on him. Despite the fact that he hadn't believed me, he obviously now felt badly. The signs of strain were on him. And his discomfort did not make me feel victorious, only more lonely.

Around seven, another doctor, a tall withdrawn fellow in his mid-forties whom I had never seen before, came striding in. "Hello, I'm Dr. Sanders," he said in a throaty voice. I felt vaguely uneasy.

"I've studied the results of your MRI scan and I'm sure Dr. Mahar has informed you of the results. There's a tumor on the brain stem in a very delicate position. An option open to you is surgery and that's why I'm here— brain surgery is my specialty," he said. Shivers passed through me.

"Surgery. I've seen what they do! They shave your head, bolt it to your body, and then they drill into your skull. In my case, I understand there's a lot of risk. No thanks. I don't think I'm going to opt for surgery," I replied.

"Well, I just wanted you to know I was here," he said abruptly and left.

A half hour later, another doctor I had never seen before walked in. "Hello, I'm Dr. Perrine," she said, pushing back a lock of gray-brown hair from her eyes.

"Hello," I replied.

"From what I understand you may be undergoing radiation therapy. And I'm here to discuss it with you," she said softly.

I had no idea what radiation therapy was; however, I replied, "Yes, I am."

"You'd be receiving the maximum radiation allowable to the brain over a six-week period, five days per week.

You'd have the weekends off to allow the brain cells to rejuvenate because some good brain cells are affected," she said.

Then as she began to stroke my hair she continued, "You have beautiful hair. You may lose some during the course of radiation; however, it should only happen in the immediate area which is affected by the radiation." I grimaced.

"There are ways to get around this—you could buy a wig."

Twin streams of tears coursed down my cheeks. "I don't want to lose my hair and have to wear a wig. *Lose my hair!* God, I don't want this anymore."

Dr. Perrine looked up, obviously weighing her answer. "Fran, you have to. I've studied your MRI scan and have discussed it with Dr. Mahar. The sooner treatment begins the better," she said quietly but firmly.

I nodded. "I guess it has to be this way," I replied.

"That's good Fran. I'll get started right away. Before I leave I'd like you to explain to me some of your symptoms," she said.

I leaned forward and said, "It's like I'm in a bubble all the time."

"That's a good description," she replied. I never expected this type of response and jerked my head back as my eyes widened. *She thought it was good? She understood?*

"I'll be seeing you soon," she said as she turned to leave.

Although I had only spent a few moments with this Dr. Perrine, I had been impressed and felt better about her taking care of me. Her professionalism, tone of voice, and especially her belief in my words put my mind at rest for the moment.

I slept better that night and woke later than normal the next morning. I discovered my medicine sitting on a tray and no nurse in sight. "At Brookhollow they would have never done this," I murmured. "You had to take medicine as someone watched."

I detested the medicine ritual, but was accustomed to it. Now, in more normal circumstances, I was confused over what to do, what to think. I left the medicine there until I could find out more about it. When Becky came in I immediately asked, "Why is this here?"

She inclined her head, "It's your medicine. You were asleep last night and they didn't want to wake you so they left it," she replied.

I breathed a sigh of relief, people were treating me normally again. "I like this place." She smiled. "Should I take it now?" I asked.

"Yeah, you can. And then you better go answer your phone call," she said.

"A phone call for me?" I asked. Again she smiled. I forgot about the medicine and ran out of the room.

"Hello," I said.

"Hello there," Steve said.

"When are you coming? I can't wait," I said.

"Fran, I have a lot of work. I'm just calling to see how you are. You know how it is when you're in business for yourself," he rushed on. I said nothing. "Fran, you still there?" he asked.

"You're not coming," I whispered.

"I can't, I'm sorry," he replied. I slammed the phone down.

I went back to my room, to boredom. *He's not coming. He's not coming. The old Steve would have been here every minute of every day.* I spent the balance of the afternoon reading magazines and playing with my bed's remote control. When the nurses came in and asked questions, I mumbled replies.

My family's visit the next afternoon was the first time I cracked a smile in days. That smile erupted into laughter when my sister Eileen commented, "I love the outfit Fran, where can I get one? The hospital gown goes so well with those green booties and those hairy legs. What do you call it, the bag lady look?"

My laugh rang out. "Most definitely, and believe it or

not, I'm the only one who is alive on this entire floor. I swear to God there isn't another patient here under the age of seventy," I replied. Then I took another hospital gown and put it on backwards for a robe.

"That makes the outfit, Fran," Eileen said laughing. I tried to keep a straight face but soon was laughing even harder than her. I looked ridiculous.

Our visit lasted for another hour and I treasured it. It made me feel alive again. My mother observed how glad they all were that "I was sick." I knew what she meant, what they all meant.

Having a tumor was concrete, tangible, an illness with which they all could sympathize. Unlike being crazy, which had been the cause of so much awkward feelings, the feelings of shame and mistrust, which had filled my family for months.

Those negative emotions were all gone now. Love, laughter, and concern had taken their place. Before they left, they each kissed and hugged me, and then my mother handed me a bag full of red-striped candy—which she usually hated me eating.

It would have been picture perfect, a reuniting of our family if my father had been there, but he wasn't and I knew why. He was still having trouble accepting what had happened to his buoyant, physically-fit daughter.

After they left, I realized that it was too bad a tumor had to be the cause of this new understanding. Some of my own bad feelings toward them lingered on, even after their apologies. Though I had put them through a lot, they had put me through more by not listening and believing. Rightly or wrongly, some of what had happened seemed their fault. As hard as I tried, I couldn't let go of the past few months.

Lying there, my thoughts about everything we—as a family—had gone through, grew more and more emotional until I was drenched in my own tears. I blamed and then I didn't blame. I hated and then I didn't hate. I understood and then I didn't understand. I wanted them to visit again and then I didn't. I wanted to forget but I knew I would always remember.

That night I dreamed vividly. Not of Brookhollow, nor of my family, but of radiation, baldness, pain, and of death. Shaking myself violently awake, I was unsure of my surroundings. As I looked around, realizing I was at St. Elizabeth, I felt a strong need to escape, escape a fate I had no control of. Wrestling with this impulse, I decided the opportunity was non-existent. Slowly, sleep returned.

The next morning, as I lay in bed watching the light play on the trees, Dr. Mahar strolled in. "Radiation is going to begin on Wednesday," he said, his craggy face serious. "And, because it is such a rare tumor, I want to be able to keep a close eye on you.

"Therefore, during the course of radiation I want you to remain in the hospital. This way if anything should happen there'll be someone right there who can handle it," he said.

"Six more weeks in this hospital? There's nothing to do and no one to talk to." I replied dispiritedly. I wanted to disagree, to plead to go home, but there was no use so finally I agreed to stay.

As soon as Dr. Mahar was gone, Becky knocked on the door, "You have an appointment at the Radiotherapy Associates in a half hour so you need to get dressed," she said. I didn't ask what the appointment was for, I had given up trying to get answers and planned on just doing as I was told.

Being outside didn't have the same uplifting effect on me as it usually did, even though it was a beautiful sun-clad day for February. The attendant pushed the wheelchair, not to the ambulance, but to a mini-van. He slid the side panel open and removed a ramp. *Just what I needed to see! I'm going to be treated as if I were a goddamn invalid.*

He pulled the chair backwards up the ramp, and then using tie downs, attached it securely to a metal bar which had been previously bolted into place. Then he strapped a seatbelt around me. I was glad I wasn't near home for, if anyone had seen me, I would have died from embarrassment. Still, I tried to huddle down lower as we drove just to be safe.

We soon reached our destination and Dr. Perrine took control of the wheelchair as soon as I was inside. "How are you today?" she asked cheerfully as she closed the door of the room we had entered.

"Fine," I replied dispiritedly.

"Not really," she interjected, "I can see that." I nodded my head in agreement.

"Fran, we all know how you must feel but you have to try to keep your spirits up." I nodded more from habit than conviction. She flipped a switch and said, "Come here Fran, I'd like to show you the tumor."

She slid three different negatives into position in front of the bright lights she had just turned on. My brain appeared on each negative, although in different perspectives.

"Is that my brain?" I asked.

"That's your brain and here is the tumor," she replied. I expected a huge mass but if I hadn't looked hard enough I would have missed it. The tumor was no bigger than a fingernail.

"But it's so small," I said in amazement.

"Big enough to do a lot of damage Fran, as you've learned."

Then Dr. Perrine picked up a square plate with what looked like a teardrop made of metal in its center. In the center of this was a hole a little bigger than a half dollar.

"This is one of the shields we're designing specifically for you. There will be one of these on both sides of your head during radiation. They'll be used to streamline the radiation into the exact location, while protecting the immediate area surrounding the tumor," she said.

She put the plate away and brought out a contraption which reminded me of the MRI scan headpiece. "This will be used to support your head while keeping it in position.

Here, lie down on your stomach and you'll be able to see for yourself," she said.

She placed the headpiece on the table and I lay down placing my head in it. Dr. Perrine touched an area of my head right above my earlobe and said, "This is where the radiation will be centered. You're going to lose hair in that area, however your other hair should cover it up rather nicely."

"It better," I replied.

When I was back in an upright position she helped me into my wheelchair. "Now I want to show you where this will all take place," she said.

We went to a room on the other side of the reception area. On the door was a danger sign. The inside of the room was spotlessly white with a huge machine in its center. I should have been used to sights such as this by now but I wasn't.

I stared at it and began shaking. Dr. Perrine moved a stepstool over to the table extending from it and said, "Come see how it feels, that will make you less afraid." Hesitantly I did.

She paused. "The treatment itself lasts less then five minutes each day and you shouldn't feel anything," she said. This wasn't much of a relief—the danger sign was still flashing in my mind.

"Do you have any questions?" she asked. I had a million of them but at the moment couldn't think of one.

"No," I replied. "Then we'll see you Wednesday," she said.

After we returned to the hospital I went to bed, thoughts swirling through my mind. Once again I awoke screaming in the middle of the night. My forehead and palms dripped with sweat. My heart pounded. My mind raced with the afterthoughts of my nightmare.

I ran my fingers through my hair to make sure it was still there. Then I got up to look in the mirror to make sure the frontal lobotomy I had envisioned hadn't been performed. Even though I was satisfied I was still in one piece,

I couldn't get back to sleep. Fear swept through me. Something could happen as I slept, or another frightening nightmare could come, which I didn't need—I was living one.

Placing my robe around my shoulders, I sat in a nearby chair, waiting for morning. The moon's rays filtered through the window and streaked my face. Teardrops slowly made their way down my cheeks. *What am I? What's going to happen to me? Will I ever be free?* I stayed there for hours, motionless, mindless.

At seven thirty A.M. my wheelchair was at my door waiting to take me to radiation. The attendant left me in the reception area at the Radiotherapy Associates.

Once again I was the odd ball of the group and could feel everyone's eyes on me. *I should make up a hell of a story to tell these people.* I was about to enrich the person sitting next to me with my fable when Dr. Perrine appeared.

Once at my side, she slowly and delicately lifted my chin as she said, "You have a pretty face." I took her statement to mean radiation was going to disfigure it. I wanted to run. I made no reply, shivering with fear.

She led me into the room with the danger sign and said, "Someone will be right in." After she left I began examining the room in more detail. The room was white and sterile but hardly forbidding. I didn't know why I had been so frightened the other day. I found my courage again. And just in time, for the technicians had arrived.

They assisted me into position and then started maneuvering my head, an inch down, then half an inch up, a little to the left, then a little to the right. When this stopped, one of them said, "Don't move."

In truth, I was afraid to breathe, much less move. Then each started parting and reparting my hair. "You better not cut it," I said half jokingly, staring at them as they marked my head with something and left.

A few minutes later, a dark-haired girl was back to move my head once more. "Now don't move," she said. A low whirring noise began after she left. It stopped and then they both strode back in.

"You can get up now," the dark-haired one said.

"That's it. It's over?" I asked.

"That's it," she replied.

"Holy shit," I said, "there was nothing to it." I had expected flashing lights and ear-shattering roars.

"Don't wash your hair for a few days so we'll be able to find the marks," one technician instructed. I nodded.

Back in my room at St. Elizabeth, the first thing I did was check my hair. It was still there. "I haven't lost any yet," I murmured. Still, I knew I would and that it might not be the worst thing that would happen to me.

Whenthedinner tray came that night, almost without thinking twice, I quietly took the small steak knife and placed it in the drawer beside my bed. "Just in case," I murmured thoughtlessly, "just in case it all becomes unbearable."

By the next morning, I had decided that I wasn't going to let things get to that extreme. I wanted to restore everyone's life to normal so I decided I would talk to Dr. Mahar about stopping my treatments. That way I would be able to return home and start rebuilding. I tried not to think of what else my idea could trigger.

While I waited for my wheelchair, I felt excited over the fact that it might be the last treatment I had. Once at the Radiotherapy Associates I asked Nancy, a technician, "What would happen if I stopped radiation now?"

"All the hard work done so far would be wasted and your tumor would still be there," Nancy replied.

"Would it get worse?" I asked.

"You never know Fran, you should stop thinking so irresponsibly. There are no quick solutions," she said seriously.

"You're not planning on stopping, are you?" she said almost as an afterthought.

"No, I just wanted to know," I mused and pushed away the persistent thought of just ending my misery.

When my name was called, I tried to relax. I even joked with the technicians as they positioned my head and rearranged my hair. When the radiation treatment was over I asked if I could wash my hair. I was thrilled when I was told I could.

"Just don't wash the sides of your head," the technician said. I nodded. That was better than nothing.

Back at St. Elizabeth, I let the whole floor know I had been given permission to wash my hair. This small privilege gave me hope and I danced in circles as I headed for the bathroom. The nurses didn't know what to make of my twirls and turns, although they looked amused. Washing my hair made me feel more like a normal person again. For me, it was a small but positive sign.

Afterward, lying down on the recliner, I waited for Dr. Mahar's visit. Hours later I was still waiting. I didn't understand why he hadn't come, he was usually in by mid-morning, and I went to ask the nurse on duty.

"He's already made his rounds and has left the hospital," she said. Strangely, I liked the idea of his skipping over me. It was another sign, making me feel as if I were getting better.

However, the next morning when I made my way to the bathroom in order to prepare for radiation, the face that stared back at me in the mirror horrified me. It looked swollen and there were black bags under my eyes, and a mustache of black hair which added an evilness to my appearance. I tried to rationalize the change in my appearance by telling myself it was only due to my tiredness, and once my face was washed and I had makeup on, my looks would be back to normal. But they weren't.

Later that morning before treatment began, the technicians once again began positioning my head. Then they started rummaging through my hair.

"Did you wash your hair?" one asked.

"Yes, why?" I replied.

"I can't find the marks. We're going to have to mark you again. You can't wash your hair," she said.

"I'm going to wash my hair, so you better do it," I replied. I heard snipping noises. "What are you doing?" I asked.

"We have to cut away some of your hair in order to mark you properly," was the response.

"You didn't tell me that." Tears filled my eyes. "How much are you cutting off?"

"Not too much and besides your other hair should cover it up," she said.

"My hair!" Then they began marking the sides of my head with something.

"It's not going to hurt," one said.

My head was rearranged a last time before treatment began.

When Dr. Mahar came to see me I was standing at the nurses' station in tears.

"Would you like to come talk to me?" he asked.

"Sure," I replied. We went to our meeting room.

"They marked me today," I said my voice breaking.

"Did they?" he quietly replied.

"And they cut my hair off to do it," I added miserably.

"May I see?" he asked.

I lifted my hair on one side. "Oh," he said. "It's not too bad Fran, really."

"Really it is," I replied. Suddenly there was a horrible churning sensation in my stomach, I thought I was going to throw up. My head started to throb and I felt weak. "I don't feel good, can I go now?" I said.

"If you like," he replied.

I didn't think I was going to make it back to my room, but I did and that crummy old bed never looked so good. Slowly I lay down on my stomach. As soon as I got comfortable I felt like the bed started to shake. I grasped its edge to keep from falling.

"What's going on?" I murmured. Several minutes later the shaking stopped and I got up and headed for the bathroom. I stuck my fingers down my throat but nothing came up. *I gotta feel better.* I stuck my fingers further down my throat and everything came up. I didn't feel any better though and went straight back to bed.

After that, the treatments made me feel worse and worse. I tried not to lose all hope but it was difficult. I'd thought all my troubles were over when they had discovered I wasn't crazy, but little did I know they were just beginning.

A few days later things deteriorated even more. On my way to take a shower, I stopped dead in my tracks as I passed the mirror. "What's wrong?" I mumbled. I began pinching both my cheeks in an attempt to make them look normal.

It looked as though my face was rounder and fuller. I started making motions with my face as though I was about to kiss someone as I tried to regain its long and narrow appearance. *What happened to my high cheekbones? I look like a chipmunk.* Tears started to form.

Then, as I wiped the tears from my eyes, I brushed the hair away from the side of my head and saw not only the tattoo but a bald spot as well. *Oh my God!* I became hysterical. Not only did I have chipmunk cheeks, but I was almost bald.

I hurried into the shower and began washing my hair. Soon I started to notice strands of hair falling. I tried not to think about it, but then a clump went sailing to the tub's bottom. I froze, my mouth gaped, my eyes widened. "My hair," I yelled. Then another clump fell.

I shut the shower off and flew to the mirror. I was scared, and trembling, I lifted my hair to see the damage. I shrieked in horror, "Noooo!" My skull shone. I was as bald as a baby's behind and the area it covered was almost as big as one.

The floor became saturated with the water from shower and tears. I closed the toilet lid and sat down, trying to collect myself. *I want to go home! I want this to stop! This is not happening, it can't be. I've turned into a big, fat, ugly, bald woman with chipmunk cheeks. How can I ever let anyone see me like this. Steve! Oh my God, Steve! He'll never come close again. Why me! Why me!*

Quickly I went to get my housecoat, pulled it around me, ran to the phone, and dialed Steve's number.

"Hello?" I said.

"Hi," Steve said.

"I've been trying to call, where have you been?" I asked.

"Working," he replied.

"So much has happened Steve, I need you," I said.

"What's happened?" he asked.

"I started radiation and now I'm bald. I'm scared. My face is swollen. And, I have a tumor. I don't even know if I have a future," I replied.

"So what if you're losing hair, Fran, we'll just have to call you Baldy. Fran, you have a future," he said. "You have to believe that."

I started crying and said, "Oh Steve, I don't know what to do, I'm so confused."

"You know what to do, keep smiling. You're going to be fine. Look Fran, I have to go now but do keep in touch."

Sobbing, I hung up.

Sprawling across the bed, I fell asleep. Several hours later, I awoke trembling and out of breath. For a few minutes I didn't know where I was. At first I thought I was home in bed, that Brookhollow and the tumor were dreams. But then I ran my hands through my hair and felt the bald spots. My stomach writhed. I began tossing, turning.

Whatever had awakened me was quickly forgotten and replaced by fears of reality. I didn't know how this had happened, how I was going to put the pieces of my life back together, or whether I'd be alive a year from now. My stomach churned. A chill ran through my body.

Never before had I felt this alone, this scared. Once more my stomach writhed. I wanted Dr. Mahar, I wanted my family. I wanted someone. My stomach rumbled violently. *I want it to stop! I just want everything to stop! I can't do it anymore, I can't!* My stomach convulsed, nausea hit me and I flew to the bathroom.

In the pitch black I knelt before the toilet. My fear of life was more intense than ever before. I scrambled to turn the light on in order to help myself.

Suddenly the truth came to me. *That's all I had, me. I was the only one who knew, cared, and understood. Everyone else only pushed, shoved, questioned, poked, prodded, and labeled.* I cried hysterically as I splashed cold water onto my face.

If there were such a thing as a miracle I wanted it to happen right then. I wanted these memories, these thoughts wiped out forever. But nothing happened. No one came. There was no help. I was exhausted and crawled on my hands and knees back to bed. Life didn't seem worth living. Nothing would ever be the same.

Almost by instinct, I reached blindly into the drawer next to my bed and clasped my fingers around the knife I had hidden from the long-ago dinner tray. *You can't think about it Fran, you can just do it.* I sat there staring into space.

You're not crazy Fran, you're not. Why won't they listen? Too many things are wrong with you, your life won't be anything anyway. I slashed out at my wrist.

You asshole, I cursed myself. *You can't even do this*

right. The side of my hand was cut. A streak of red marked the spot. *You didn't want to die Fran,* I cried silently. *If you had, you would have been successful, or at least you'd try again.* Sobbing, I lay down and fell asleep.

NINETEEN

When Dr. Mahar came to visit me the next morning he picked up my arm to take my blood pressure.

"Ow," I exclaimed, the sound slipping out before I could stop it.

"What's this Fran?" he asked fingering the long red streak across my wrist.

"Nothing, just nothing," I said pulling my hand away. "I don't want to talk about it."

He stared at me for a few long minutes, then got up and left. A few hours later I had a surprise visitor, Dr. Scott Keogan.

"Long time no see. How are you?" I asked.

"I should ask you that. How do you feel, Fran?" he responded. "Dr. Mahar is worried about you. He called me after he saw you earlier today, and said you're showing signs of acute depression. Can I help in any way? Would you like to discuss anything?" He looked at me intently.

"I'm okay, I think," I said dispiritedly lifting my hand to my forehead."

He sat down and gently took my hand, fingering the bloody scratch. "That's some cut. Fran, how do you feel about the tumor? Are you having trouble dealing with all this?" he asked.

"Yeah," I paused, "did you know that I have to stay in

this hospital or go to a nursing home during radiation? That's six weeks!" I said. "Look around you, there's nothing to do but lie here and think. I don't have anyone to talk to."

"I know," he replied.

"I'm terribly frightened because of all this. What's happening? How can something so small be so bad? Will I ever look like me again? My hair is falling out. I don't understand all this. Why don't they leave me alone?"

"Fran, we're all worried about you. Dr. Mahar says he's afraid you're behaving like someone severely depressed."

"I don't understand," I said.

He responded, "He means you're acting like someone very confused and unhappy."

"Wait a minute, Dr. Keogan, are you saying . . ." I paused and then yelled, "I'm not crazy, I have a tumor! Isn't that right?"

He quickly responded, "The combination of your tumor, radiation therapy, and medicine are making you feel bad. They're making you act like someone with acute depression. But no, Fran, you're not crazy."

"I don't understand." I said hesitantly, "I'm scared."

He smiled, "We can discuss it later, Fran. In fact we could talk easier, as long as you want and as often; if you'd come back to Brookhollow . . ."

"To Brookhollow," I echoed his words.

"I'm not crazy, you said so yourself. Why should I go back to Brookhollow?" I quickly asked.

He responded, "You're not crazy, but the tumor is affecting your behavior. St. Elizabeth is not equipped to take care of patients that are depressed. They're not used to treating people like you that need special care. They don't have the training or the experience, not like we do at Brookhollow . . ."

"I don't understand. I don't like it here, but I hate Brookhollow. Why can't I just go home?" I asked. "What do you think I should do?" I replied.

"I think you should come back to Brookhollow for a little while. We can help you better there. If you are unhappy or confused, we can work with you easier. And you do have friends at Brookhollow." He stroked my hand. I pulled my arm back and stared at the wound. *I did that to myself?*

There was a long silence. "All right," I replied hesitantly. "Brookhollow?" I repeated half to myself after he'd left. I was surprised that the place I had so badly wanted to flee from before, now seemed a sanctuary.

Hours later I was still debating my decision. *Brookhollow? It's for crazy people. But, at least I can get dressed, not have to lie all day and night in a tiny room with only my family's visits to look forward to. It's so boring here. There'll be people my own age to talk to. Maybe I will go. I'll even be able to go for walks, go shopping, and watch T.V. But what will people think?*

Back and forth my mind flew. *I'll go. Maybe not. Dr. Mahar did say I should never have been there. But then why did he say I should go now? The food is better at Brookhollow and I do like Dr. Keogan. But I like Dr. Mahar too and the nurses here are nicer. If I go to Brookhollow I'll be able to go outside. I'm definitely going. But Lydia is there. I don't know.*

Dr. Kamari stopped by to visit a little later. "There's a bed available at Brookhollow, Friday afternoon."

"I don't know if I'm going. I might stop treatments altogether," I said.

He gave me an eyebrow raising look as he said, "What?"

"I want to go home," I replied.

"You can go home after the treatments," he replied.

"I want to go home now," I said.

"If you go to Brookhollow I can give you a pass and

you can visit home. I think that would be better," he replied.

"That's not the same," I said.

"But Fran, if you stop your treatments, you could become much sicker and you'd probably have to go back into a hospital with a terrible prognosis. If you keep taking treatment and take care of yourself, you might be able to go home and stay home afterwards. You should do that," he said nodding his head yes.

"I don't want to stay here or go to a nursing home, or go to Brookhollow," I insisted. "I have too much to do," I said.

"You can do it after," he replied. "Nothing is that important. This is your life we're talking about. I promise you can go home on visits and on those visits you can take care of these things," he diplomatically replied.

I stopped and realized it was a no-win situation. My voice broke, "If you promise I can visit, I'll go," I said.

"Good," his lips clenched and his eyes hardened for a moment, "because you were never actually discharged from Brookhollow," he said. *Was it a threat?* I wondered.

"What do you mean?" I asked.

"Just what I said, you weren't discharged." He recovered himself and his facial muscles softened again. "However, we no longer can make you stay and you'd have to return voluntarily. It will be much better if you go back that way," he replied.

I wondered if I had been tricked? But he seemed so concerned that I put the idea out of my mind.

When Dr. Kamari left I returned to my thoughts. I was glad he had made up my mind for me, because I really didn't know what to do. I was so confused about everything.

Most of the time I was throwing my thoughts out to see the reactions they would get and nothing more. I thought that by doing this, I would be able to understand them and see whether or not they were normal. Most of the time I felt as if I was grabbing at thin air and needed to have my ideas confirmed as normal.

Even though each confirmation brought some confidence back, I continued to doubt because of my experience. After all, some had seen me as crazy and I couldn't help thinking others probably saw me that way as well, even now.

At six o'clock my family, including my father, came for a visit. They all wanted to see the tattoo marks and oohed and ahhed in amazement. They asked question after question about radiation and the tumor. I had no idea how to answer many of them.

It was as if it were all happening to someone else. Actually, the attention I was receiving confused me. They were all being too nice, as though I was fragile, and might disintegrate at any moment. I shivered and tried to think of other things.

Connie was the first to spark my interest when she said, "There's a family meeting tomorrow with Dr. Mahar."

"What about?" I asked.

"I'm not sure," she replied.

"How dare he . . ." *He never mentioned it to me. I don't want my family involved.* I paused then I added, "Am I invited?"

"I guess you can go if you want," she replied. "We're only discussing your condition because we care so much." Connie bit her lip. "And we want to do what's right for you, Fran," she paused, "The doctors know what's right."

"Damn right I'm going. What time is it supposed to start?" I asked.

"One," she replied.

Later I changed my mind and decided I didn't really want to go after all.

Our conversation shifted. They knew the news of the meeting had upset me. For the next half hour we all tried to lift each others' spirits; however, for different reasons. I was doing it to keep them from asking me more questions about the tumor and the hospital. I didn't want them so involved. I didn't want them to worry, they seemed even more upset than I was. They had no ulterior motives.

I should have been appreciative that they cared, but at that moment I wasn't. The fear we all felt individually mounted. Once they were gone the tension of their visit began to lessen. Instead, an overwhelming sadness came over me.

This whole thing had torn my family apart. At one time I was the favorite. Now the stress I had caused was taking its toll on everyone, particularly my mother. She looked and acted as if she hadn't slept in months. And she had lost so much weight her bones showed.

I would have done anything to save her from any more agony, although at the same time I was causing her more agony because I was shutting her out. I knew it, I felt it, but couldn't help it. I also knew none of us would forget these months; life would never be the same.

The next day when Dr. Kamari showed up for the meeting with Dr. Mahar, he asked, "Where is everyone?"

"I don't know," I shrugged.

"Let me call Mahar," he said in an exasperated tone.

When he returned he said, "The meeting is at Dr. Mahar's office downtown, not here. But when it is over your family is coming to pick you up and take you to Brookhollow. I'll be there later to see you," he said.

"I'm sorry about all this," I said. Although I wasn't sure what I was sorry about.

"That's all right," he said and gave a tight smile.

Filled with nervous tension, I waited for my family's arrival. I was glad to be leaving the claustrophobic hospital room but apprehensive about what lay ahead. When I finally saw my mother, father, Connie, and Eileen walking up the corridor, the biggest smile came onto my face.

As we came face to face, everyone started talking to me at once about what Dr. Mahar had said. My head moved frantically as I tried to catch their every word. He told them things I had never heard, or maybe had heard but couldn't remember.

Before we were about to leave, they needed to bring a wheelchair. We left as soon as it arrived. It was strange being in my parents' car for the first time in a month. However, my freedom didn't last long—we were at Brookhollow's door before I knew it.

And as the horrendous buzzing noise sounded, my heart sank. I had come so far only to return. We had to wait in the reception area for Dr. Keogan. I tried to reassure myself. *The food is better here. I get to watch T.V.* I said over and over to myself in an attempt to stay calm.

I watched closely as Dr. Keogan walked toward us. His fast pace and erect stance bespoke confidence. When he was close enough, he extended his hand to me and said, "Well Fran, it's nice to see you again."

I stood up, shook his hand, and said, "It's good to see you again too, Dr. Keogan." After introducing my family, Dr. Keogan and I went into the room I called the interrogation room and they left.

"I guess I'm glad to be back," I said haltingly. "There's more to do here and the food is better too."

"I think so," he genially agreed. "And, we have carpets on the floor."

"I'm going to be here for six more weeks," I said sadly.

"I know and I'm sorry you won't be able to get out more but you're only allowed ten hours away from here a week," he said.

"It's better than being in the hospital or a nursing home. That's where Dr. Mahar said I was going to have to stay, either St. Elizabeth or a nursing home," I replied.

He nodded, "And we're glad to have you here instead. You have a pretty good reputation around this place. Besides, Lisa and Eric Lee, Dr. Kamari, and I will be here for you. Now, I have some forms to fill out. Can you tell me what medicine Dr. Mahar has you on?" he said.

"Decedron and K-lyte," I replied.

"No wonder you feel so good, Decedron is legalized LSD," he said.

"Holy shit. I didn't know that." I shook my head and said, "I have to go to radiation every day."

He nodded, "That's no problem. You should think of all of this as having a wart removed. There's a wart on your brain and radiation is going to remove it. We'll be in constant touch with Dr. Mahar," he said.

I shivered, feeling particularly vulnerable, "I'll try not to be too much trouble," I replied.

"But Fran please, if you don't feel good tell one of us right away." He looked up and gave me a kind look. "We can finish this later, it's almost dinner time and you're probably starved," he said as he gathered up the papers.

Then he escorted me to the unit. My luggage and purse were searched at the nurses' station and they kept a lot of my things. It was like seeing a movie in reverse. Then I was assigned a room in the main area, not ICU. I was honored. Dinner was waiting for me on my bed when I arrived, stuffed chicken breast. Thinking I was hungry, I tore right into it but ended up eating very little.

As I was setting the tray aside, Martha strode into the room. Her toothless grin, straggly greasy hair, polyester highwater bellbottoms, and K-Mart top startled me. *She's my roommate? No way.* I walked right past her without a word and ran to the nurses' station.

"I request a new roommate immediately," I said.

"Why? What's wrong with Florence?" asked a nurse I had never seen.

"What do you mean Florence? Martha is in my room," I replied.

"Florence is supposed to be your roommate. What number room are you in?" she asked.

"Two thirteen," I replied.

She looked into a folder and said, "Sorry about this, I gave you the wrong room number. You're supposed to be in two fifteen with Florence."

Without saying anything more I went to move.

The new room looked exactly the same as the one I had left; however, my roommate was much better. She was in her middle sixties, small and cheerful, in fact, extremely nice, and best of all she was immaculate. I didn't stay long though, I was too curious about who else was there. And as soon as my belongings were put away I headed for the lounge.

Dr. Keogan stopped me in front of the nurses' station, "I was going through the papers you brought from St. Elizabeth's and I noticed Dr. Mahar has put you on a special diet, no cholesterol, sugar, or salt. Do you know why?" he said.

I shook my head negatively.

"Well, I'll call the dietician and you'll start on it tomorrow. Then I'll talk to Dr. Mahar," he said.

"That's all?" I asked.

"That's all," he replied. Once again I started for the lounge.

Though most of the faces in the lounge were new, a few like Angela and Nancy I knew. I avoided Nancy like the plague and sat down next to Angela.

"How have you been?" I asked.

"Good. What are you doing back here?" she asked.

"I have to undergo radiation and am going to stay for six more weeks," I replied. I didn't think she heard my reply for she was staring into space, then holding her pillow she huddled deeper into the corner of the couch.

"You okay?" I asked. There was no response. I didn't know what would happen if I continued to prod so, anxious for a cigarette, I kissed the wall.

I sat back down next to her. When I was almost through with my cigarette she said, "What happened at St. Elizabeth?"

"Not much. I'm kinda glad to be back," I replied. Her eyes were glazed as I looked at her for a response. *I wonder what's wrong?*

Several seconds later she said, "They're not going to

do anything about your tumor?" I had just told her the answer a few minutes before but I repeated myself.

"I have to go for radiation treatments every day for the next six weeks. I didn't need to be here, but I either had to go to a nursing home or stay at St. Elizabeth, some choice, huh?" I replied.

"I'm going to be here for a while yet too," she said. Then she started singing a song from "The Sound of Music." I had no idea what was going on and had no intention of asking. Instead I got up and left.

Friday night meant a movie in the cafeteria. This was better than sitting around bored, and I made my way there. The room was dark and there were only two people inside. I squinted to see who they were and found Dr. Keogan and Jack, one of the attendants. Immediately I started toward their table.

"Do you mind if I join?"

"Hi Fran. I don't mind at all. Sit right down," Dr. Keogan said.

"Hi Fran. How are you?" Jack asked.

"Good. How are you? I missed you," I replied and hugged him.

As soon as I sat down Dr. Keogan's beeper went off and he left. Jack turned to me, "I heard about the radiation and I'm sorry."

"There's nothing to be sorry about. This thing is going to blow over. It's kind of like having a wart removed, or so I've been told," I replied, my voice shaking a little despite my efforts.

"Well, if you ever want to talk, I'm here," he said.

"It's nice of you to offer. It's nice to know you care. I'll remember," I replied and tried to change the subject. I felt awkward about having him know so much, I didn't want him or anyone else to treat me differently. Others started flooding in and Jim got up to put the movie cassette in.

Nancy was the leader of the pack. All decked out in a yellow silk dress, she looked as if she was going out on the town. Then I got a whiff of her exotic perfume. It smelled as if she took a bath in the stuff. I laughed to myself at this, and at myself. I also was a sight in bedroom slippers, jeans, a sweater three times too big, no makeup, and ungroomed hair. We were hardly in fashion.

"Hi Fran. How are you, babe?" Nancy asked sitting down next to me.

"Good," I replied.

"You want a piece of gum?" she asked.

"Sure," I replied taking a piece.

"I missed you. Where were you anyway?" she said.

What is she up to? She might be apologizing? You're only going to be here six weeks, put up with her. "I was at St. Elizabeth," I said.

"What did they do to you?" she asked.

"I had an MRI," I replied.

"I had one of those and I had a bunch of tests too. They didn't find anything though," she mused.

Like I really care. "Really," I replied.

She nodded her head and then she went on to tell me about her family, what she's been doing, and about her almost-wedding, almost-rape, almost-murder. I nodded in agreement as I took it all with a grain of salt.

Then her hearty laugh broke loose. I couldn't help myself, I joined her. Our laughter evolved into senseless conversation and before I knew what happened we had our arms around each other. I was having a good time, glad she was there to lighten my load. By the end of the movie we had vowed our friendship.

Walking back to the unit, we flung our arms around each others shoulders. Stopping in the lounge for a cigarette, we promised each other we would spend the next day together. Then we hugged and said good night. I needed a friend who would laugh with me and Nancy was perfect.

*I*t's Valentine's Day. I wonder if Steve remembered? I lay in bed longer than normal that morning as I thought of Steve.

Then I knocked myself in the side of the head for doing this and got out of bed to busy myself and to forget.

I went straight to the shower. I hadn't taken a shower in two weeks, only baths. Nothing made me feel as good as a shower. Without thinking, I lathered up my hair. When I realized what I had done it was too late.

For a minute I was concerned over what would happen. But my good feelings overcame it. *They'll just mark me again.*

I met Nancy in the hall and we went to Group together. Dr. Lee was surprised to see me, especially because I was with Nancy. In Group I told Dr. Lee I'd be staying until chemo was over. I figured I had to tell something, but the less people who knew, the better. The last thing I wanted was questions.

Then, after Group, Nancy and I took turns doing what the other wanted. I even told her about the tumor and she didn't once say she was sorry. And she didn't ask a million questions. I liked that.

Dr. Lee walked up to say she wanted to meet with me. We went to the room and I told her all about St. Elizabeth and the tumor. When I finished she said, "I'm sorry."

"There's nothing to be sorry about. I just have to ride this out," I replied trying to sound confident. When our time together was over, we set up an appointment for the next Wednesday.

At five, the next morning, I was at the nurses' station. "Alf, will you please open the lounge for me?"

"It's too early, you know that," he replied.

I went in and sat down on the chair in front of his desk. I wasn't completely awake yet as I said, "Do you think I belong here?"

He shook his head, "You're normal except there's a thing on your brain," he replied as his eyes shifted from his papers.

"Some people don't think so," I said imploringly.

"Some people can be dumb."

"Even doctors?" I said hesitantly.

"Especially doctors," he smiled.

I returned the smile. His words had reassured me for the moment. Then he told me a story of how he had broken his neck and had his head bolted to his body on both sides. His point sunk deep into my mind. It could be worse, and I was not alone.

Still dressed in the nightgown my mother had bought, I stayed with Alf until he was ready to open the lounge. Once inside, Alf sat down to talk to me.

We made small talk for a while and then he said, "Fran, I'm so sorry. You're too nice a girl for all this to happen to you."

I knew my reply verbatim and it flowed with my hopes, "There's nothing to be sorry about. Everything will be all right."

After Alf left, my insecurity returned. I went to the phone to try Steve. It rang two or three times, then I hung up and tried again. *He has to be home on a Sunday morning.* Still no answer. I tried again, letting the phone continue ringing. This time I got his answering machine; however, the operator wouldn't let me leave a message on a collect call no matter how hard I begged. I shuffled slowly back to the lounge with my head hung low.

Throwing myself down on the couch, I felt frustrated. Then Nancy came over and sat down next to me. "Hi Fran. You know what? Dr. Keogan won't let my mother come and visit. He won't even let me take her phone calls," she said.

"There's probably a reason for it," I interjected. "You want to talk about problems, I'll tell you about problems! Compared to some of mine yours aren't anything. So why don't you shut up and make the best of it," I snapped.

"What's your problem?" she asked.

"I don't have any problems. Except I don't belong here and if it weren't for that stupid tumor I'd be home right now," I replied.

"Does having a tumor scare you?" she asked.

I didn't expect her question and had no answer ready. *She probably thinks having a tumor made me snap and not what she said.* "It's not having the tumor but the fact I might die, that scares me," I said.

She put her arm around my shoulder and said, "Stay with me, I won't let you die. I take care of my friends and you're my best friend."

Tears welled up in my eyes. Her words made my mood change for the better, "You want to go exploring with me?" I said.

"No. I'll get in trouble," she replied.

"So will I. But you know what they're having for dessert today, butterscotch sundaes. We could go exploring for a while and then stop and have a sundae. No one will ever know we're gone. I'm sick of being cooped up here, are you?" I asked.

"They're having butterscotch sundaes?" she said licking her lips.

"Sure are," I replied.

"Let's go," she responded. And we were off.

We made it downstairs and began poking in and out of different rooms. We discovered nothing interesting though. So we went to claim our sundaes.

Our eyes danced with delight when the waiter placed the ice cream, swimming in sauce, before us. Neither one of us spoke as we devoured them. We both asked for another as soon as we had finished. Just as the waiter was serving these Lydia approached the table.

"What do you think you're doing, ladies?" she snootily asked.

We both looked up innocently and said, "Nothing." "Neither one of you is supposed to be down here. And you Fran, you're not supposed to be eating sweets."

"I'm not supposed to be here? Why not?" I asked.

"You know you're on twenty-four hour check and not allowed off the floor," she replied.

"I didn't know," I said.

"You did too," she insisted. "Now, both of you put those spoons down immediately and go back upstairs," she said.

"I'll go when I'm done," I said.

Obediently, Nancy got up to go. "You're not eating that sundae," Lydia turned toward me.

"Yes, I am," I said. I picked up my spoon and took a few bites. The muscles in her face tightened as she watched. I looked at her from the corner of my eye. "That's good," I said when I finished.

"Take another bite and you're going into ICU," she said steaming. I picked up my spoon and drove it into the ice cream. Half of it was on my spoon as I moved it to my mouth. Lydia grabbed the spoon and the ice cream went sailing to the floor.

Her voice rose, "Your doctor said you're not supposed to have it. Now you better get back upstairs before I really get mad." Her teeth were clenched, as were her fists.

"I'll go upstairs when I'm ready," I said quietly. "No one told me I was on twenty-four hour check." I countered. I looked toward Nancy who was grinning from ear to ear and giving me the "thumbs up" sign.

"You're my patient for the afternoon and I have read your file. You are not allowed down here," Lydia yelled.

"I'm not a patient. I'm a visitor. I don't need to be here and I don't need your stupid rules," I replied.

Lydia grabbed me by the arm and pulled me out of my chair, "I've had it. You're going upstairs right now." I became dead weight.

She began pulling me along with her as she walked. It started to hurt so I began walking on my own. "Wait till I tell Dr. Kamari, you're going to be sorry.

"I wasn't doing anything other than eating ice cream. There's no reason why you have to be rough," I said. She made no reply as she continued to hold onto both Nancy's and my arms.

At the lounge she pushed us forward and then let go. "I have my eyes on both of you."

"Good for you," I said. When she was out of sight both Nancy and I broke out laughing.

"I'm in trouble now," Nancy said.

"Why are you in trouble? She's the one who started it. She didn't have to be such a bitch," I replied.

I went and kissed the wall and when I turned I saw my mother and sister Connie walking past the door. I butted out my cigarette in an ashtray and ran after them. "Ma!" I screamed. She turned, saw it was me, and they both started back.

"What are you doing here?" I asked when we were face to face.

"We came for a visit. Are we allowed?" my mother said.

"Sure, let's go to my room," I replied.

"This is your room?" Connie said as she flopped onto the bed.

"I know, it's not much," I replied, "but it's better than St. Elizabeth."

"Here, these are for you," my mother said as she handed me cigarettes and gum. "Sugarless gum," she added.

"Thanks," I replied.

My mother's face suddenly lit up. "They said you could go home on some visits. How would you like to go home this afternoon? Tony and Michele are coming. They're bringing dinner just for you," my mother said.

"All right! But I don't know if I can, I'll have to ask Dr. Kamari and he's not here. But if you wait here I'll see if they'll call him," I said walking toward the door.

"Lydia, will you call Dr. Kamari? I have to ask him something," I asked as I stood three inches inside the nurses' station door. "I'm not calling anyone for you as long as you're in here," she snapped.

"What?" Then I realized where I was and stepped back a foot as I said, "Now will you call?"

Her face tightened, "Dr. Kamari doesn't like to be disturbed on a Sunday unless it's important. Why do you want me to call?" she replied.

"You bitch," I murmured under my breath. "I want to know if I can go home for a visit," I replied.

"Why?" she asked.

"Just call him, all right," I said.

She picked up the receiver and dialed. After a few seconds she looked up at me and said haughtily, "No one is answering. I guess you can't go." She hung up.

"Try again," I said.

"I don't think it's necessary," she replied.

"I do. Please try, it's important."

"All right, but I don't want any more trouble from you," she replied. This time someone answered and said Dr. Kamari wasn't there. Lydia left a message for him to call.

"I can't wait, my family is here now to take me home. Will you call Dr. Keogan?" I asked.

"Fran, you're not a privileged patient, you're just a mental case, you can go home some other time," she hastily replied.

I paid her no mind. "I want to go home today. Please call," I said. As she tried Dr. Keogan I stood tapping my fingers and toes. *Why does she always have to be so difficult?*

Finally she was on the phone with Dr. Keogan. I only got one side of the conversation and it didn't sound optimistic. I wanted to talk to him; however, Lydia wouldn't let me. Then she was off the phone and half smiling as she said, "Dr. Keogan doesn't think you're up to it, you just started radiation." My heart sank.

At that very moment the phone rang. It was Dr. Kamari. I watched Lydia's facial expressions darken as she listened. After she hung up she said, "Dr. Kamari said it would be all right. He thought it would be good for you. But he wants you to take your medicine with you."

"No problem," I replied.

I ran back to my room to tell them I could go. Seconds later we were on our way. Before we left the floor we stopped for my medicine. The nurses took their time in getting it and I grew more and more impatient as every second passed. I couldn't wait to go outside.

When Lydia finally handed me the medicine she said, "I can't believe he's letting you go. You're still on forty-eight hour check." I flashed her a smile.

In the car, on the way home, we joked and enjoyed each other's company. I was excited about seeing Tony, and all other thoughts were forgotten.

The surroundings of my street looked foreign. Even the house I had lived in for twenty-five years appeared changed. I grew uneasy as I entered, leery of what and who were inside. I was afraid suddenly; afraid of how I would be treated. Since I didn't understand what had happened I didn't think anyone else could either. I drew a deep breath as I turned the kitchen door knob.

Eileen, Jackie, and my father were in the kitchen. Tony was nowhere in sight. When Eileen and Jackie saw me they shouted greetings as they came toward me. They both hugged and kissed me, but as if I were a China doll.

This eased only some of the tension. They didn't seem as if they were the same and home didn't seem as if it were home. "Where's Tony?" I asked.

"He and Michele stopped to do an errand but then left right away to go visit you. I'm surprised you didn't pass them. Since you're here, they should be back soon," Eileen said.

We all gathered around the kitchen table. Then I asked, "May I go upstairs? I want to get some clothes."

"Listen Fran," Eileen said, her face reddening. "What are you asking for? This is your house. You can go anywhere you want."

I bit my lip and shrugged in response as I got up. Before I was out of the kitchen, Tony and Michele came in.

"Hi Fran!" Tony said.

"Hi," I said opening my arms. We hugged as if we

hadn't seen each other in years. I felt normal in the safety of his arms. Then I greeted Michele with the same kind of enthusiasm.

"I have something for you, Fran," Tony said. He went into a knapsack and rummaged around for a moment. He pulled out a T-shirt he had won during a New Year's Eve race. The instant he handed it to me, I loved it, for it meant he cared and was glad to have me home.

What I had been trying to avoid since leaving Brookhollow suddenly became the main topic, the tumor. I had no answers for Tony's questions; however, the rest of my family did. They informed him from start to finish about me, the tumor, and what Dr. Mahar had said. They talked as if I weren't even there and when I did try to interject they ignored me.

Then they started talking about the accident, the Ninth Ward, my radiation therapy. How much we'd all been through; I wished I wasn't there.

Finally, dinner was ready. I tried everything I could to keep the conversation diverted but as the main course was served, my father raised his glass high in a toast, "Thank God," he said emotionally, "it's only a brain tumor."

TWENTY

Back at Brookhollow, there was nothing I wanted more than to stay in bed. I was exhausted even after ten hours of sleep. My radiation appointment at eight A.M. was the only rationale for getting up.

Yawning, I made my way to the bathroom. My reflection in the mirror caught my eye. I edged closer and gasped. Each day the face I stared at looked more grotesque—swollen and misshapen. I could no longer rationalize the change in my appearance by telling myself it was only due to tiredness, that once my face was washed and makeup put on my looks would return to normal. I had used up all excuses. I was hideous—a freak—and would have to accept it. Still I struggled on.

At the nurses' station, Jess announced that my escort, Mary, and I couldn't leave until eight for radiation. That worsened my mood, I hated being late. When our car finally pulled into the Radiotherapy Associates' parking lot I was out and on my way before the engine was off.

"Good morning," I said waving my hand to all the technicians.

"You're out of the hospital, right?" one replied. His voice was so normal as he glanced at me that worries over my horrendous looks dissipated.

"And I love it," I replied.

Mary caught up with me then and said, "Don't ever do that again. I'm supposed to be with you at all times outside of Brookhollow. You might get dizzy or feel faint."

"I just walked in the front door. Hardly an endurance test." I replied.

"It doesn't matter. Next time it would be better to wait for me," she said patronizingly.

"Give me a break." I sighed and picked up a magazine, attempting to ignore her.

The technicians eyed us suspiciously. Shooting them an exasperated glance, I rolled my eyes in an effort to explain and to let them know she was being ridiculous. They smiled and winked in understanding.

Jan, one of the technicians, came up and took my picture, then he asked me to go into the treatment room. Jumping up I asked, "Mary, aren't you coming with me? I am going into the next room."

She scowled, "It's dangerous in there and you know it."

"Dangerous!" I said, "But you just said I wasn't allowed anywhere without you. Will you please make up your mind," I added. Mary turned away in silence.

Before treatment began, Jan, the other technician, began positioning my head. Then he rummaged through my hair. "You washed your hair, didn't you?" Jan asked.

"Yes," I replied.

"I can't find the marks we put there last time. We'll have to tattoo you permanently, unless you don't wash your hair again," she said.

"I'm still going to wash my hair so go to it," I replied. I began hearing the familiar snipping noises. "What are you doing?" I asked.

"We have to cut away some more of your hair in order to tattoo," Ted, the other technician, responded.

"How much are you cutting off this time?" I asked wistfully.

"Not that much—and the same as before, your other hair should cover it up," Jan interjected.

"What hair, I'm almost bald already!" They pushed my objections aside and began marking the sides of my head.

Jan leaned over me, "Now, you're going to feel a little prick." I clenched my teeth and squeezed my eyes closed. The needle penetrated my flesh, then struck a bone. Shivers ran up and down my spine. Then they rearranged my head before beginning the treatment. Finally, it was over.

The ride back to Brookhollow was silent. Once there, I ran directly to my bathroom to see what I looked like. Locking the door behind me, even though this was against the rules, I peered into the mirror. My hair looked normal at first glance.

Then simultaneously, I lifted the hair up on both sides of my head. My mouth dropped. There were two huge bald spots, one above each ear. In the center of each was a red bullseye. "Oh my God!" Tears formed, "What did they do to me?" I murmured, letting the rest of my hair drop.

I stayed in front of the mirror staring. Then I lifted one side of my hair back up and leaned closer to the mirror. "Freak," I cried, letting the hair drop. "You can't tell now." I picked it back up. "What's going to happen if I lose more?" I let the hair drop. I picked it back up. I did this over and over again and began to sob. I cried with rage and frustration. *What more could they do to me?*

I was startled by a knock on the door. Marty asked, "You all right Fran? Group is about to start if you want to come."

"I don't think so," I replied wiping tears from my eyes.

"I like it when you come to Group. I'm going to miss you," he said.

"I'm tired. I think I'm going to take a nap," I replied, trying to make my voice sound normal.

"Well, all right. But if you change your mind you're more than welcome," he said.

After a few minutes, I peeked out the door to see if he'd left. At eleven, when Group was over, I went to the lounge to have a cigarette. Marty was still there—our eyes met. I looked away and sat on the opposite side of the room, acting as if he weren't even there. He walked over and sat down beside me.

Putting his arm around my shoulder he asked, "Is it going badly, Fran?" I didn't say anything at first.

Then I turned to face him and said, "Please just leave me alone."

"Don't you want to talk about it? It might make you feel better," he said.

"Nothing could make me feel better now." I got up and walked away. I knew he was hurt because we were good friends; however, I couldn't deal with questions or talking.

I went down to lunch and sat at my usual table. Not talking to anyone, I smoked cigarette after cigarette. Being bald wasn't the only cause of my withdrawal. I felt awful as well. Just when I felt at the depth of despair, Nancy joined me.

Nancy's flamboyant personality took charge. It was a tonic. She began teasing and joking, not paying attention to my silence. In a matter of minutes we were both laughing. We ended up making plans to go shopping and visit each other on the outside.

After a while, we were the only two left in the dining room. I poured myself a cup of coffee and lit a cigarette. Nancy followed suit; however, as she was pouring her coffee she began trembling. Her shaking grew out of control. The coffee flowed over the top of her cup and began running down the sides of the table. I had no idea what was happening and was afraid to say anything.

Puddles of coffee lay around her cup as she sipped. She picked up her cigarette, which was nothing but a butt, and took a deep drag. "Damn," she yelled, scrunching it out furiously on the table.

I tried to say something funny; however, Nancy was now in her own world, mumbling and gesturing to no one in particular. I shivered, not knowing what to make of her behavior. Sometimes Nancy acted perfectly normal and then minutes later something seemed to snap. I tried to ignore it. It wasn't easy, for she began hyperventilating and turning red in the face.

Finally I gathered up enough courage to ask, "Nancy, you okay?" She began laughing hysterically.

"Please Nancy, please stop," I begged looking around for help.

Quickly walking over, Dr. Keogan joined us. He was deadly serious as he grabbed Nancy's arm and marched her out of the dining room, never saying a word.

I wonder where he is taking her. I wonder what is wrong with her. I should be more cautious. Tony's words, "Most of those people are delusionary" popped into my head. *I know what's going to happen. I'm going to become crazy just by being with these crazies.*

Petrified, I sat there unable to move. Finally a waitress kicked me out and I went back upstairs. Mary met me at the nurses' station and said, "You have an appointment with Dr. Mahar in a half hour. I've already called a taxi so get your coat and meet me back here."

Feeling like I'd been through the mill and aching for fresh air I asked, "Can't I walk, it's only fifteen minutes away?"

"No, Dr. Kamari didn't leave permission. So you're to abide by the rules," she said haughtily.

"Couldn't you call him?" I beseeched.

"I can't do that and besides the taxi is on its way. You can just wait until next time," she said annoyedly. "Look Fran, why don't you stop giving us all extra work."

"This is your work. I'm sick and you're supposed to be helping me. You could call if you wanted. You just don't want me to get out of here at all." I objected.

"If you don't stop you're not going anywhere," she said.

Without another word, I went to my room and got my

coat. The five-minute taxi ride to Dr. Mahar's was tense. I needed some relaxation. Some time to recoup, to feel like a human being, not a patient. I blamed Mary for not being able to take that time.

Dr. Mahar's office was on the seventh floor. Getting off the elevator, I tried to escape Mary by speeding up. "Stay with me," she called. "Don't walk ahead."

"Where do you think I could go?" I replied.

"Just do what you're told, Fran," she said exasperatedly.

Hurrying into the office, I approached the receptionist. She'd always been kind to me; I joked with her.

Mary only stared. "Sit down over here," she called. Walking to the other side of the room, I chose a seat as far away from her as I could get. *She better not come into his office with me, it's none of her business.*

Looking around, I concentrated on Dr. Mahar's reception room, which was decorated in an African motif. Statues of Moorish men, giraffes, and other carvings predominated; I spent the next half hour closely examining them. The more waiting time, the better. At least I wasn't at Brookhollow.

Dr. Mahar appeared at the door, "Hi, Fran. Come on in," he said. I shot a quick glance at Mary. She remained absorbed in her magazine. *Good.* I got up and went inside.

In his office, two other people sat at Dr. Mahar's desk. *I'm not that important, am I? Does this mean something is going wrong? Isn't the treatment working?*

Dr. Mahar interrupted my whirling thoughts. "This is Ms. Foster and Ms. Green. They're students from St. Elizabeth. You don't mind do you?" he said.

"No, that's all right," I replied, sitting down in an empty chair, still musing on the meaning of the strangers' presence.

"First thing I'd like you to do is change so that we can examine you. You can go right into there, let us know when you're ready," Dr. Mahar said pointing to an adjacent door.

I followed his directions obediently. I felt differently at Dr. Mahar's than I did at Brookhollow, and didn't mind being told what to do.

Turning the lights off, Dr. Mahar began to examine me, beginning with my eyes. The examination was exactly the same as the first day I had met him. Then he turned me over to Ms. Foster and Ms. Green.

A short while later, Dr. Mahar flipped on the light and said, "Thank you for being so patient. You can get dressed now. And then come back into the office and we'll talk," he added.

As soon as I sat back down in his office I asked, "What happens if radiation doesn't work?"

Dr. Mahar looked up from his papers, "Fran, you have to believe it will—as I do." They were the sweetest words I had heard in months. "Try to have a positive attitude and concentrate on visualizing yourself getting better."

"I'll try." I said, trying to draw comfort from his words.

Then Dr. Mahar shook his head, "In fact, the tumor is slightly smaller now than it was in your last exam. I think it may be a good sign."

I could hardly believe my ears. Was something good finally going to happen? I felt elated but still fearful. Dr. Mahar leaned forward to get my attention.

"I want you to start taking Maalox four times a day. It is very important. I also want to see you once a week until radiation is over. On your way out have my secretary set up an appointment for next week," Dr. Mahar said.

"Thank you," I murmured and got up to leave.

Back at Brookhollow, I didn't feel like talking and retreated to my room. Later, Jess stopped by. "You've been in your room all night. Do you feel all right?" she asked.

"Yeah, I'm just tired," I replied. She handed me Decedron, Thorazine, K-lyte, and Maalox. "It looks like quite a gulp," I wanly joked, and set the liquid medicine on the nightstand.

"You have to take that now, while I'm here," Jess said.

"I can't take it all now," I replied. "I'll throw up."

"And I can't leave it here. You're going to have to take it," she said.

I picked it up and gulped every last drop. "You happy now?" I said. She walked away and my stomach exploded. Running into the bathroom, I vomited everything up. Finally, I crawled back to bed and prayed for sleep, the only thing which would take the pain away.

The next morning I went to breakfast, still feeling queasy. Angela joined me; however, there was no sight of Nancy. "Where's Nancy?" I asked looking around.

"She's in ICU," she replied. "I'm glad she's there, she scares me. And she scares everyone else. Even some of the doctors are afraid of her. I don't understand how you can be friends with her," she replied.

"She's fun. Sure, she has her problems, but so do you and I."

"Not as bad as her. Do you know what she did to get in here?" she asked.

"What did she do?" I asked gloomily.

"She jumped up and down on the roof of Alf's car screaming her head off that if she didn't get back in she was going to kill herself. She returned the same day you did. I'm surprised you didn't know about it," Angela replied.

I laughed as I pictured a two hundred-and-fifty pound Nancy jumping on top of the car. "What happened to the car?" I asked. "Did it collapse?"

"I don't know," she replied seriously, not understanding my joke.

Two new patients, Rose and Kelly, joined us and Angela introduced them to me. Everyone ordered breakfast, French toast and sausage. My diet forbade anything like that, even if I had wanted it, which I didn't—because of my stomach.

Without a complaint, I munched on grapes and orange

slices as I watched them devour the syrup-laden French toast. "You're going to get fat," I scolded.

Before breakfast was over I had to leave to get ready for radiation. Jess met me in front of the nurses' station with my medicine.

"Jess, I threw up last night. I can't take it now, I just finished breakfast. I'll take it when I get back," I said.

"You have to take it now," she replied.

"You know, you're really starting to bother me," I shook my head and rushed off. After treatment she was waiting at the door to Brookhollow with my pills.

"There's no getting away," I sighed.

Later that day, Dr. Kamari showed up, "Would you like to come talk to me?" he asked.

"Sure. How are you?" I said.

"I should be asking you that," he replied.

"You usually do," I pointed out. His use of the same phrases all the time bugged me. *Why the heck does he always say the same thing as if it were for the first time?* I was going to ask but I figured he would respond with his usual "what do you think" reply, and I decided to ignore the whole thing.

"So how were treatments today?" he began.

"Good," I replied, then changed the subject. "What does Bipolar mean?" I asked, looking him directly in the eye.

Shifting, he stared at a spot on the ceiling. "It's almost the same as mood swings only more complicated."

"Well, how about my nervous breakdown?" I asked.

"That's out of the picture altogether," he replied. I was lost.

"Well, what am I?" I asked.

"Bipolar fits but it's not precise."

"It only fits because of the tumor."

He nodded as if annoyed, "That's true."

I moved to the edge of my chair and leaned over his desk so he could not avoid me. "Can I see my chart?"

Then I grabbed for it; however, he was faster. He had it closed and held against his chest as he said, "There's nothing in there that will interest you."

"How do you know? Come on, let me read it." I replied.

"Maybe some other time," he said. He put the chart back down on the desk and I went for it. He yanked it away and then stood up saying, "If you're going to play games I have to leave." *There's something in there he doesn't want me to see. I'm going to read that chart if it kills me.*

Our meeting was over. I wandered from lounge to lounge looking for something to do or someone to talk with. There seemed to be nothing and no one so I went to my room.

That day was not the only boring period during my stay at Brookhollow. The rest of the week dragged as well. I actually began looking forward to radiation, Dr. Kamari, and pottery. At least that was something to do. And with Nancy locked in ICU, any chance of real fun was gone.

Then on Saturday, Nancy was released from ICU. We hugged and screamed during our reunion. In honor of Nancy's release we decided to throw a toga party. She and I sat in the lounge and planned every aspect of it.

The party was going to start at eight that night, when both Nancy and I were going to run from our rooms in nothing but sheets singing, "Toga, Toga! Who loves ya' babe, the garbage man does!" Then we would both dash to the lounge where we would dance. We even made a list of those who would be invited, those to be ignored. Angela was at the top of the invited, Martha headed the list of people to be ignored.

When Angela came into the lounge, both Nancy and I jumped up and started talking about our party at the same time. "Are you guys crazy? They'll never let you do that. And you can bet if you do you'll get in trouble. You can count me out," she said.

Then we told the rest of our guests and got the same

response. Nancy was disgusted with everyone, saying, "No one has any sense of adventure."

I told her, "We'll have the party ourselves."

She hesitated and then said, "I don't know, I don't want to go back to ICU."

"Toga. Toga! Who loves ya' babe, the garbage man does! How can you pass this opportunity up? Toga. Toga! . . . ," I said.

She was in tears laughing; "Fran, you're hilarious but I can't afford to take the chance," she said. I turned and started walking for the door, "Where you going?" Nancy asked.

"Never mind," I replied.

Five minutes later I returned dancing and singing, "Toga.Toga! . . ." From behind my back I brought out two ice cream sandwiches and threw them on the floor. Then I started dancing on top of them. Nancy was rolling on the floor. Pieces of vanilla and chocolate ice cream flew across the room.

"You're crazy, you're crazy," she laughingly screamed.

"I am not and I've been told that by a very reliable source," I replied.

"You better stop, you're going to get in trouble," she said.

"Toga. Toga! . . . ," I replied.

"Who loves ya' babe, the garbage man does!" Nancy yelled. Lydia marched through the door. I scrambled to throw the ice cream sandwiches away before she noticed.

"What are you two doing?" she asked.

"Nothing," we both replied.

"I thought I heard singing?" she said.

"You probably did, but is that against the rules too?" I replied.

"Not as long as that's all you're doing. And believe you me, I'm going to keep my eye on you two," she said and left. In whispers, Nancy and I started laughing again.

I stopped for a moment and chuckled as I ran my fingers through Nancy's hair and said, "You have ice cream all through your hair. I'm surprised Lydia didn't notice."

"You'd be in ICU if she had," Nancy replied in a croaking voice.

"They can't put me in ICU, I'm not crazy. I have everyone confused around here," I replied.

Since our party was on the back burner we had to find something else to occupy us. We searched, but found nothing to do, so we spent the rest of the night in front of the television.

An antacid commercial came on. "Aah," said Nancy, and we started discussing the medications we were taking. "You think that's bad," I said, "I'm on Thorazine."

She asked, "What?" then continued, "My brother was on that for a while and he almost died because of it."

"Nooo?" I replied.

"Yeah, that stuff can kill you." She rolled her eyes dizzily. "If I were you I wouldn't take it anymore," she added.

It can kill me? Why would Dr. Kamari give me something like that? I don't really need it. I don't belong here. I won't take any more.

Before I had a chance to find out what medicine Nancy was taking, Alf came in and kicked us out for the night. Nancy sang one last "Toga! Toga! . . . ," and then left.

"You have medicine to take, Fran. Stop at the nurses' station on your way to bed," Alf said.

I stopped there as instructed, but told the nurse on duty, "No Thorazine." The nurse started to give me a hard time. "Look, I know what it can do," I objected.

"You'd better take it anyway," she said.

"Stick it," I replied and walked away.

Mrs. Clancy, another nurse, was standing in front of my bed as I opened my eyes the next morning. "Time for your medicine," she said.

"Oh please!" I closed my eyes again.

"I don't have all morning," she said. I took the Decedron, K-lyte, and Maalox, but refused the Thorazine.

"Dr. Kamari won't like the idea of your not taking Thorazine," she said.

"Too bad. I don't need it," I said.

"Why don't you take it until you can talk to Dr. Kamari tomorrow," she said.

"Why don't you just get out of here," I replied.

Her face was tinged with anger as she turned and left.

Afterward, getting ready for my radiation treatment, I decided to be as late as Mary normally was. At exactly eight o'clock I started back upstairs to get my shoes, coat, and medicine. At eight-fifteen I started for the lounge, and now with my shoes on my pace had become a slow hobble. I expected to see her tapping her foot at the door; however, she was nowhere in sight. I sat down on a couch to wait.

Ten minutes later Mary appeared. "What are you doing here?" she asked.

"I'm supposed to meet you here," I replied.

"Patients aren't allowed in the lounge unescorted," she said emphatically. "And that means you." Other people stared at us, my face reddened, and I stood up to leave. *What is she doing, she told me to be here?*

"Well now that you're here, let's go," she snapped.

In the car I asked, "Can you stop so I can get a pack of cigarettes?"

"That's not my job. And besides, you made me late," Mary replied, tapping her red fingernails on the steering wheel.

"It's only going to take a minute and if you're already late, what's the difference? You have time," I said quietly, "you could act human."

Mary floored the gas pedal and I went flying forward. "What the hell is your problem," I said.

She glanced at me, her voice flat, "I don't have a problem but I know all about yours. You're in denial right now and are being a total ass," she replied.

Anger spread through. "You have a lot of nerve! Just

because you're late don't take it out on me. You've made me late plenty of times," I said. She didn't say anything more and neither did I.

At the Radiology Associates, when Jan greeted me she said, "You're kinda late this morning so you'll have to wait for these people." Five other people were sitting in the waiting area.

I knew we were going to be there quite a while and asked, "Is there anywhere around here I can buy a pack of cigarettes?"

Mary heard my question and sprang over to me, "You're not getting any cigarettes, so forget it."

"Why not?" I asked.

"Because I said so. And because you can't go unless I go, and I'm not going," she replied.

"We have all this time to wait, what's the problem?" I asked.

Shaking her head Jan said, "Look, I'll show you how to get there."

"Thanks," I said as Jan pointed the way. I walked over to Mary to get my coat. She tightened her grip on it as I asked, "May I please have that coat?"

She whipped it out of my reach and said, "You don't have time to go anyway. I just called Brookhollow and I'm taking you back. Someone else will escort you back here. I'm late."

Despite my objections, she insisted on leaving. "By the time we get back there and then back here I could've been done," I said.

"Well, if you hadn't made us late we wouldn't have to do it."

"Who made us late?" I queried.

"Look, if you know what's good for you, you won't say another word, and like a good little girl you'll get into the car," she replied, her voice rising.

All eyes were on us. I shot a quick glance at Jan. Her sympathetic eyes said she was as shocked as I was. I wasn't going to lower myself any further and said, "I have no problem with going back to Brookhollow. May I please first put on my coat?"

Mary shoved the coat at me, "If you did things right in the beginning you wouldn't need to be at Brookhollow." My mouth dropped and I felt as if I wanted to melt into the rug.

In the car I sat silently.

Mary's lips were clenched. "Fran, if you say anything to anyone they'll be the last words you ever say." I looked away. "Did you hear what I said?" she asked.

I couldn't hold my tongue any longer. "If you think for one minute you're going to get away with your degrading, demeaning, and downright inhuman treatment of me, you have another think coming," I lashed out. "You don't scare me. And as far as I'm concerned, you don't belong working with sick people and I'm going to see to it that you're not anymore."

"You're dreaming," she said in a savage tone. "You'll be lucky if anyone even listens, you're only a patient. A case we work on!" she replied.

I wanted to cry. I didn't want to be thought of as crazy even if it was only by her. "You bitch!" I retorted. I heard her slam the gas pedal to the floor and the wheels screech.

I gasped as the car hurtled forward, alongside, and in between the other cars. I held on to the ceiling handle for dear life. We flew around a curve and the speedometer hit over one hundred. I cringed. Since the accident I was a bundle of nerves at fifty-five miles per hour, now I was a complete basket case.

When the car finally stopped at Brookhollow, I jumped out without a word and ran right inside and to the nurses' station. "Is Dr. Keogan here?" I asked Alice, the attractive black nurse on duty.

"Not right now. He should be in by the time Group starts, he's directing the one downstairs," she replied.

"Who's taking me back to radiation?" I asked.

"You're lucky, you've got Timmy, and he's putting his coat on right now," she replied. Five minutes later I was on my way back to radiation. I was still on edge as Timmy tried to joke and make conversation, and seldom replied.

Later that day at Group, Mary's obnoxious behavior was a hot topic for me. I explained, using every adjective I could think of, what I thought of her and what they should do about it. A guy in the group who thought he was Mr. Macho said, when I had finished, "Hey gorgeous, you shouldn't wait for them to solve your problem, do it yourself." For a minute I thought I was going to get up and throttle him.

"Don't call me gorgeous, I have a name, and you know what it is. So if you want to say something to me, say it right," I replied.

Dr. Keogan took control and the discussion soon came to an end with nothing resolved, as always. As everyone left, Dr. Keogan stood at the door. Still feeling shaken, I was the last in line to leave. I was wobbling as I passed him and squeezed myself through the doorway, because there was less room than I had thought.

Suddenly, I got a strange feeling. It was as if the doorway were a mile long and I was being suffocated as I went. When I was finally in the corridor I gasped for breath, losing my balance and falling into the wall.

"Are you all right Fran?" Dr. Keogan asked.

"Yeah, I just lost my balance, don't a lot of people do that?" I quickly replied and began walking away, using the rail for support.

Dizzy and nauseous, I wanted to go to bed but at the same time I was furious and unable to wind down. Finally, bed won. I tossed and turned as I tried to connect everything. *Do I feel sick because of the tumor, radiation, or do I just not feel good? Why was Mary acting as she was? Am I at fault? Should I say something to Dr. Mahar? Will I be showing him my craziness if I do?*

It was as if I were a caged animal, damned if I did and damned if I didn't. I wanted more than anything not to be afraid to say what I felt or thought. But I didn't know what would happen if I did.

Would my words be construed as something connected to the tumor or would they add to my psychological diagnosis? My confused thoughts ruled, I knew they were the cause of my silence. *Maybe I should forget what happened with Mary, I'll be leaving soon anyway. Look how she degraded you, don't stop now.*

A million ideas ran through my head but I was unable to come to a conclusion, let alone take action. So much had happened to me. So much I couldn't understand.

At dinner, my bad mood continued. I didn't speak and was toying with my food when Drs. Kamari and Keogan walked over. Dr. Kamari broke the silence saying, "Dr. Keogan tells me you had an exciting ride this morning?"

My heart pumped furiously and I replied, "Yes, and I want to talk to you about it now," as I began to get up.

"No, no, no, we'll talk about it later. I want you to eat first." He continued, "You know, if you were still taking your Thorazine, what happened with Mary might not have bothered you. I think you should start taking it again."

I seethed. "I'm not taking Thorazine," I replied. "I don't need it. Besides, someone told me it can kill you."

"Who told you that?" he asked.

I knew Nancy had; however, I also knew Dr. Kamari would've shot down her words in a flash. Moreover, taking Thorazine made me feel like a zombie and I didn't want that. "I don't remember," I replied.

"Well, the amount of Thorazine you were taking can't kill you and you were doing so well on it, you should take it again," he said.

"I'm not taking it and that's that," I replied.

They left and I returned to playing with my food.

Somehow I had expected Dr. Kamari to react to what happened with Mary as if he himself had been put through it. His reaction didn't just demean me, it made me feel betrayed.

I walked back to the lounge feeling as if I would never again be treated as a human being. Not only Mary, but everyone I met would treat me as a crazy person with no rights. This made me hate Brookhollow and everyone in it even more.

The lounge was bustling with patients and their visitors. I looked around, despising my surroundings. It was a mass of confusion. I felt as if they and I were from different worlds.

They were druggies, widowed, divorced, crippled, tattered, illiterate and poverty stricken. What they talked about and lived was, in my world, something you read about in a newspaper and donated to. It scared me to think that now, possibly someday soon, I could be the one to whom donations were made.

Right before I was about to leave, a girl I had never seen before approached me. "Hi, I'm Lizzie," she said as if she was drugged. "Hi," I replied. And I put out my cigarette. She stayed standing at my side, twisting from right to left. I tried to ignore her. "I'm Lizzie," she kept repeating over and over again. I stared at her for a few minutes and then got up and walked away.

The next day, after treatment, I waited to see Dr. Perrine. When she called me inside her office, Mary got up to follow.

"Do you mind?" I said.

"I'm going in there with you, it's my job," she replied.

"You're not going in there. It's none of your business," I said.

"I am too," she retorted. I walked in the room and closed the door in her face. It didn't stop her, she pushed right in. "Didn't I tell you I go where you go?" I slumped down in my chair and folded my arms across my chest.

Dr. Perrine stared at us both and said to Mary, "I don't think it's necessary for you to be here."

"I have to," Mary insisted, "I'll sit right over there." She pointed to a small black stool. "You'll never know I'm here."

"She doesn't have to be here. No one ever goes in

when I see Dr. Mahar." I looked at Dr. Perrine beseechingly.

Dr. Perrine said quietly and calmly, "I don't think
Fran is going anywhere. I want you to leave."

Mary stomped out of the room. "Thank you," I said
humbly to Dr. Perrine.

"It's patient-doctor confidentiality," she said winking.

On the way back neither Mary, nor the driver talked. I
took the opportunity to express my thoughts to Mary in one
simple word, "Bitch," I said.

Her face flushed, "You're a very sick girl," she said
drawing out the word sick. "We all have to remember
that." She flashed me a nasty smile. Silence filled the car.

As soon as the taxi stopped at Brookhollow's door I
escaped, embarrassed and humiliated. *I don't even know
why they send her with me.*

As soon as I was back in my room I went to the mirror
and stared at the swollen-faced stranger's reflection, "Now
what?" I said softly.

TWENTY-ONE

The days passed routinely, the fear inside the same. A different escort daily, a new patient now and then, and this was life. Days turned into weeks; weeks of doctors, of radiation, and of not knowing. Months inched by.

Inwardly I was tired and discouraged. Outwardly I continued to battle the Thorazine, Mary and the environment of Brookhollow. All I wanted was for my treatment and my incarceration to be over. Spring had come, the outside world was green and fragrant.

I was locked in a stale prison; moreover, there was something even more depressing. Brookhollow air was infectious, incestuous. Nancy, Angela, Lydia, and my doctors had become my family. The sterile, white rooms were my home. My world went no further.

Then one evening, as I lay on the lounge couch telling Nancy about my neverending argument with Dr. Kamari over my right to see my file, a nurse summoned me to the hall phone. My sister Eileen wanted to take me to breakfast the next morning.

When I returned to the lounge to resume my position on the couch, there was Nancy, sprawled in my place. "Come on Nancy, stop kidding. Get off the couch," I said. She petulantly ignored me. "Nancy, come on. I was there first and I was only gone a second," I said.

She scrounged up her eyes and yelled, "Get lost." I thought she was just teasing me, "Come on, please get up!" I further entreated. She lifted herself upright, grabbed one of the snack trays from the table next to her. Then she hurled it at me, as though it were a hardball.

"Are you crazy Nancy?" I screamed as it hit me broadside. The tray, once full of dip and fresh vegetables, now lay empty at my feet. My hair and clothes were covered with green, orange, and cream-colored mush, as were my face and hands. I stood there with my fists clenched, trying to catch my breath.

Watching me from the sidelines, Marty came up and patted me on the shoulder. Suddenly feeling strength I never knew I had, I pushed him aside and grabbed some food from another tray. Then I drew my arm back preparing to give Nancy a taste of sour cream.

As I released the handful of sour cream in Nancy's direction, a visitor stepped in front of me and the sour cream landed smack dab on the side of her astonished face.

Vince, who had just walked in the room, stepped forward, and instantly locked both my arms together, "Fran, what do you think you're doing? Do you know what you just did? You assaulted a visitor! She could have you charged."

"I didn't hit her on purpose," I objected. "It was Nancy I was aiming for," I replied.

"That's not any better! I thought you were a much better person than this," he said as he propelled me further down the corridor. As we walked away, I saw the visitor crouching against the wall, terrorized.

She must be scared to death. I should apologize. "I want Nancy locked away until I'm out of this place. She's crazy. And I want Dr. Keogan to reprimand her and make her pay for my jeans," I rushed on all my frustration pouring out.

"I paid fifty-five dollars for them! This place is the only reason these kinds of things happen; it's a lousy influence! And you're not much better. Leave me alone. I don't need you and you know it," I replied, freeing myself and running to my room.

I went directly into the bathroom to clean myself up. There was sour cream everywhere. As I stood in front of the sink wiping off my jeans and cursing Nancy, a nurse's aide appeared, "Can I talk with you a second . . . ," she began.

I was in no mood for chit-chat and slammed the door in her face. "Fran?" she implored.

"Leave me alone. I didn't do anything," I replied. "Go away." Her footsteps resonated down the hall.

I leaned against the sink and took deep breaths to calm myself. Speaking out loud I mumbled, "This place is absolutely unbelievable! You're stupid for ever having come back here. If it ever gets out, your chance at a career is flat over."

Then I glanced up into the mirror. Mascara covered my mammoth cheeks and my radiation-swollen eyelids were red and irritated. "Oh my God!" I cried, "You freak."

I closed my eyes quickly and turned the water on so I could wash my appearance away, while avoiding the mirror at all cost. "Will I ever look normal again?" I sobbed. Frantically, I splashed handful after handful of water onto my face, hoping this would be the cure-all but knowing it wasn't.

With the water still running full force I sat down on the toilet and cupped my head in my two hands, trying to shield myself from the person I'd become. Suddenly, I saw the pink tiles in the shower stall slowly move in and out, it was as if they were breathing. I gasped and sat there stupified. Even after all Dr. Mahar had said, I was still afraid these occurrences signified my craziness.

Sometime later a knock came, "Fran, I would like to talk with you," Vince said.

"Well I don't want to talk with you. All I want is for you to keep Nancy away from me," I replied.

"Fran, I know you didn't do anything. Marty told me

she saw everything. All I want to do is to make sure you're all right. Please," he said.

"Go away," I replied. "I need Steve." Vince left.

Now, with Steve on my mind, my thoughts slowly evolved into mass confusion. *I don't want him but I do. I don't want to be here, but I am. I don't want questions, but I get them. I want to understand Nancy, but I can't.*

The sound of the flowing water broke my trance. *This is ridiculous. I shouldn't hide away. I have rights! I should demand immediate action.* I got up off the toilet, turned the water off, and stormed into my room. From my dresser I took pen and paper and began writing a letter to Dr. Keogan about the punishment Nancy should receive and how I expected reimbursement for the jeans she ruined.

When I was finished, I boldly sauntered into the nurses' station and flung my letter onto Lydia's desk, "I want this put into Nancy's file and brought to Dr. Keogan's attention. She will not get away with her behavior. For that matter, this whole place won't get away with how you've treated me," I said and immediately turned on my heel.

Before I had walked more than a few feet, I heard Lydia snarl, "It's not going into her file, it's going into yours."

On the way back to my room I ran straight into Vince. Giving him a cold stare, I started to walk away again. He grabbed my arm and said, "Fran, Nancy was put into ICU."

I gave no indication of feeling anything over his statement and continued walking. Tears filled my eyes. *Good. She should be locked in there forever.*

Vince turned and began following me. I stepped up my pace, I didn't want anyone next to me. And once in my room I slammed the door behind me. Now that I was alone once again, the strong protective shield I tried to gather about myself withered into nothingness. I sobbed uncontrollably as I lowered myself onto my bed. *I don't understand people.*

The next morning the faces I saw in the halls seemed

solemn and grim. I felt as though they were blaming me for Nancy's explosion and tried to avoid everyone. Then, when I went into the lounge for a cigarette, I met up with my roommate.

"I just want to thank you, Fran, for getting Nancy off this floor. She scares me. I wish I were more like you and able to stand up to her," she said.

I looked directly in her ice-blue, dazed eyes. "So, I'm a hero. A hero I'm not proud to be. I liked Nancy. I don't know what's wrong with her but I'm not glad."

Storming out, I went back to my room and began getting ready for my sister's visit. Several minutes later Eileen walked in. "Let's go!" I said grabbing my coat. I was out the door before she was even completely in. As soon as we were in the car I told her about Nancy.

"Fran, I can understand you're being sorry for her, but it sounds like she has real problems. You ought to keep a wide distance between you. After all, Nancy will be out of your life soon enough."

I shook my head, "Easy for you to say, but for now, Brookhollow is all the life I have and Nancy's pranks have made it bearable."

As we entered the restaurant I thought everyone seemed to be staring at me. "They must know I'm from a mental institution, Eileen," I said feeling odd and embarrassed. "I can't live my life like this. I just can't," I murmured.

Eileen kept trying to reassure me that it would all soon be over. "Look toward the future," she implored.

But as I sat watching my sister eat her waffles, and sipped on my coffee, new and fearful thoughts about my future entered my mind.

A future of not knowing if I were to live one more year, one more day. A future of wondering if radiation had worked, if the tumor would come back. Was it to be a future of doctor after doctor? Of fear after fear?

I was sinking further and further into this frightening

world of new, projected images and I couldn't seem to control it. I wanted to fight against my fears but didn't know where to begin.

I stared off into space as Eileen continued to speak. For some reason, something she said reminded me of Steve and now my mind turned to him. It was another dead end. I couldn't stand it, I wanted it to end. *Thoughts like this never come at Brookhollow. Maybe I don't belong in the real world anymore?*

"Let's go," I said to Eileen as I stood up. She got up, paid the check, and followed without a word.

I was quiet on the way back and didn't say anything as we kissed goodbye. Immediately I strolled down the hall, desperately looking for something to do to get my mind off myself. Then, glancing at the clock on the wall, I realized Dr. Keogan was directing the last twenty minutes of his Group.

Flinging open the door to the lounge, I expected to be warmly greeted. No one looked up. The only ones in the room were Dr. Keogan, Marty, and a patient I didn't know.

Marty finally came through, however, exclaiming, "The sunshine has arrived!" I forced a wide smile in reply —luckily he was satisfied. I waited for a chance to enter the conversation. It never came. By the time Group was over, I was upset at being ignored and fled.

As I walked away, I suddenly felt tired so I went directly to my room to rest. Soon I was dead asleep. Suddenly I awoke hearing, "Pow! Pow! Pow!" My eyes opened a crack to see Nancy standing in my doorway with her arms extended like a bodysnatcher.

"What's wrong with you?" I said sleepily.

"I'm going to kill you, Fran," she screamed as she started walking toward my bed. With each step closer, her sinister laugh grew louder. I froze, paralyzed. I sunk my head deeper into my pillow.

Now, she was inches from my side. She leaned over, put her hands around my throat, and started squeezing. I gasped, unable to breathe. Then directly into my ear she loudly screamed, "You're dead." I began to black out.

Suddenly, Lydia and Jess appeared and pulled Nancy off me. Nancy was still screaming curses as they dragged her from the room.

After they were gone, Robin, a nurse's aide rushed in, "Are you all right?" she called out.

"What is Nancy doing out of ICU? She's crazy! Keep her away from me," I cried, my whole body shaking.

Robin sat down on the edge of my bed. She was young and sympathetic and very gently took hold of my wrist. Being touched again, however gently, sent shivers through my spine. Flashes of being dragged into Ward Nine ran through my mind. I panicked.

"I didn't do anything. Leave me alone," I yelled.

"Everything is all right Fran. Calm down," Robin replied.

"Leave me alone," I repeated. She got up and started walking toward the door; but before she was gone, she turned and said, "What Nancy did is called deadly assault. You should call the cops. I'll stand up for you."

"Right," I said miserably. "Call the cops from inside here, they'd laugh."

TWENTY-TWO

Finally, sleep returned, a sleep filled with dark whirling thoughts and hands fastened about my throat. Early the next morning Dr. Kamari woke me. He sat in a chair beside my bed.

"Will you tell me exactly what happened?" he asked.

I told him. Then added, "And I don't feel safe in this place with Nancy out to kill me."

"No one is going to kill you as long as I am your doctor and Dr. Keogan backs me up, he assured.

For a long time I stared, "You've told me a lot of things, very few have turned out to be true." A sharp, angry look came on his face, quickly replaced with a calm, reasoned one.

"Look Fran, I know you're angry and confused. I'll give you floor privileges, but you'll sleep in ICU. That way you and Nancy will be kept apart."

"Why don't you put Nancy in there?" I asked. "She's the one who attacked me, not the other way around."

"I'm not her doctor," he replied in an icy voice. I felt safer but mad at the injustice of it all.

He leaned toward me, honey seeping into his tone, "And, I think we should try some sleep therapy again," Dr. Kamari said.

"I don't think so," I firmly replied.

"It'll make the rest of the time you have here go by much better," he said getting up to leave.

I started to follow, then my legs and torso buckled and I collapsed on the floor.

"Are you all right?" Dr. Kamari asked, helping me up.

"I'm fine," I stiffly replied.

Dressing in my usual sweat suit, I started cautiously down the hall. I opened the door to the Main Lounge— there stood Nancy. Immediately she lunged at me, going for my neck. Several patients stepped between us, allowing me to flee. I wanted to find Dr. Kamari and get out of Brookhollow that very minute. I met up with him in front of the nurses' station.

"I want out of here and *now!*" I said.

"You can go back to St. Elizabeth if you want," he replied coolly.

"Fine," I said and turned to go. I sidestepped the room where Nancy was and went into the Quiet Lounge. It was full and I left to try ICU. On my way I ran back into Dr. Kamari.

"I have made all the arrangements for you to go to St. Elizabeth." His voice sharpened, "You'll leave in the morning. Your parents are coming to take you there. I've reserved a room for you in the Psychiatric Ward," he added.

I was startled and my face went white. "The Psychiatric Ward, what are you talking about?"

"I don't think we should discuss this here," he replied tautly, some of his irritation surfacing. "If you'd like to say something to me, we can go down the hall."

I followed him down the corridor and into our usual room, my eyes blinded with tears. As soon as we were seated I said, "I'm not going to any psychiatric ward."

"You will have to if I say so," he replied.

"I will not," I said hurriedly, with a look combining horror and disbelief.

"There's only one way you'll be able to stay here and that's if you take Thorazine," he answered fiercely. I tried to calm myself to gather my thoughts. "I've already called your parents," he added.

"What did you say to them, or is this another threat?" I replied.

"I told your mother you were refusing your medicine, that I was going to put you back into the hospital, and you needed a ride," he said.

I looked at him in agony. He had all the power and I had none. Under my breath I mumbled, "You bastard." Then, with an effort—words emerging between sobs—I said, "If you call my mother and tell her that everything is all right and she doesn't have to come anymore, I'll take the Thorazine."

"Do you promise?" he asked.

"I promise," I replied, "just call."

In front of me he telephoned her. Then he got up to leave. As he stopped to shake my hand, a glint of triumph came into his eyes, "You'll start on Thorazine tonight."

With shoulders stooping and head hung low I made my way back to ICU. I had been defeated. I was met at the door by Sam, holding a cup with Thorazine.

"Can't I have it in pill form? All this liquid, plus the radiation, is making me sick to my stomach," I said, playing for time.

"No, Dr. Kamari wants you to have the liquid," Sam replied.

"Please call him and ask him I can't take the pill and tell him why," I replied. She nodded and walked away. A few minutes later she returned with the Thorazine in pill form. I took it from her and pretended to swallow it, instead I kept it under my tongue.

There's nothing wrong with my mind, I repeated to myself.

"Dr. Kamari said I had to check to make sure you took it. Please open your mouth," she said.

"I'm not going to open my mouth. I said I took it and I did," I replied quickly walking away and into my room.

I went right into the bathroom, spit the pill into the

toilet, and then flushed it. Then I put on my sweat pants and lay down on my bed. Soon after, there was a knock on my door and Dr. Keogan poked his head in, "Can I talk to you for a minute, Fran?" he asked.

"Sure, come on in," I replied. He walked over to the other bed and flopped down on it. We were both lying flat on our backs staring at the ceiling.

"It's a pretty neat ceiling with all those square tiles," Dr. Keogan said. I made no reply. "Dr. Kamari wanted me to talk with you."

"I'll just bet he does," I laughed sarcastically.

"You know you have a very serious illness and you need medication right now," he said.

Tears flowed down my face as I turned to Dr. Keogan and said, "Maybe I'm sick, but making me a drug addict isn't good for me either. I can't take any more."

"You have a lot going for you, Fran, and we all see it; however, you're ill. You need drugs to calm you."

I covered my face with my hands and started crying even harder. "Drugs and people trying to kill me."

"Nancy was punished for what she did," he replied, "And now she would like to be your friend again, she likes you and so do I." He got up, walked to my bed, patted my cheek, and left.

"Like a dog," I muttered as he went out the door.

When Dr. Keogan was gone I went into the lounge. I was still mad at being forced to take Thorazine and I felt nauseous and in pain.

Tears flowed uncontrollably. *I want out. Not only from here but from my life.* As I sat there staring out the window, feelings of imprisonment grew in my mind, or what was left of my mind. I went closer to the window and pressed my face tightly against it, feeling the screen imprint itself on my face. I became lost in my own world.

First thing the next morning I was handed Thorazine. I took it the same way as the night before and walked out the door. In the Main Lounge, I spit it into a wastebasket. While I was in there Lydia came in to take my temperature.

Dr. Mahar had ordered my temperature to be taken four times a day, and since *he* had ordered it, I had no problems complying. Although I never looked at Lydia as she was taking it, I knew she was giving me a cold stare. I didn't care.

After Lydia left the lounge, I felt alone, desperately alone; and automatically walked to the window. My arms crossed angrily against my chest as I stood there watching life. *Will I ever belong? Will life ever be worth living?*

Any progress I had made in improving my sense of self-worth had been completely shattered by these doctors' attempts to make me take Thorazine again. I saw what it did to people—maybe it calmed them but it dehumanized them also. Made them obedient slaves. *Why did they want to do it to me?*

Then slowly and gently a hand clasped my shoulder. It was Timmy. I gave him a quick glance and then returned to staring out the window. I wanted nothing to do with anyone.

"Fran," he said quietly, "I'm going to be your escort this morning and I'll be ready to leave in a minute. Why don't you go get your coat and meet me back here," he said. Without looking or saying anything to him, I complied.

My head bowed, I stood in the doorway of the lounge waiting. When he was at my side we silently started on our way. Once at therapy I found an out-of-the-way spot to wait. I did not greet the receptionist that morning. I couldn't even mumble the words, I felt so miserable.

Treatment came and went. And I walked out as though I had never been there. Not even Dr. Perrine was able to remove the frown from my face. I simply could not believe the things which were happening to me.

Back at Brookhollow, I made my way into the Quiet Lounge and lay down on the couch. I fell asleep. Sometime later I awoke to see Jack standing over me.

"Get off the couch. You're not supposed to lie there. There are other patients," he said.

My eyes weren't completely open as I tiredly replied, "I've seen plenty of others doing it."

"Well, don't."

He left and I closed my eyes once again. Several minutes later Jack was back with Lydia, "Get off the couch now," she said. My eyes opened a little wider but I didn't move. I wasn't given a chance to do any more before Jack had me by one arm and Lydia had me by the other. They pulled me off the couch.

I ran to my room and stayed there for hours, never moving from my bed until Dr. Kamari came in.

"I want to see my file," I said.

"It's still in the other nurses' station. If you come with me, we'll see what we can do," he said. Reluctantly, I got up to go with him. Though bed seemed a sanctuary, I wanted to see what they were saying about me. Once we were in the main unit, Dr. Kamari started walking right past the nurses' station.

"What about my file?" I asked. He gave me a strange look. I stopped and leaned against the wall, "I'm not going anywhere until you have my file." He gave me another strange look. "All right," he said and then went into the nurses' station.

When he came back out he flashed my file in front of me and I followed him down the corridor to our meeting room. Watching my face intently, he put the file on top of the desk. Eagerly I snatched it up and began slowly flipping through the pages, trying to find out what had been said about me. The room was silent.

Then, leaning toward me, Dr. Kamari grabbed the file back, "I'm here to talk, I'm not here to watch."

"But I haven't had time to read the contents," I objected.

"There's nothing in there you don't know about. Maybe I'll let you read more later if you take your medicine and behave. Now I have to go," he said as he began to get up. *There is something in there they don't want me to see.*

Back in my room, I felt an eeriness which I had never

really felt before. Inside I was empty and hollow. Thoughts of doom, decay, and death filled me. These seemed to be battling for the right to be the first to enter my soul. I turned on every light and opened the curtains as far as possible. The moonlight only enhanced the features of my mind's coffin and I drew the curtains closed once more.

In bed I tried to flush all thoughts away. I listened to my heart beat, trying to quiet myself; but soon the beat quickened. Thoughts kept rushing in to remind me of who I was, of what was happening to me. I didn't know how to stop them. All I wanted right then was to die—what kind of life was this? Somehow the night passed.

Moving methodically, I forced myself to rise out of bed, shower, and get ready for my treatment. Then Sue appeared with my medicine. Neither one of us said anything as I took it and turned away.

"I can't stay here," I mumbled.

On her way out Sue turned and said, "I'll be escorting you this morning." Then several minutes later she returned with a tray in her hands and placed it at the foot of my bed, "Breakfast," she said and left again.

Without thirst or appetite, I drank the coffee and spooned down a few mouthfuls of cereal. Slowly walking to the nurses' station I announced, "I'm ready to go."

"You are going to stay with me at all times, right, Fran?" Sue said.

The way she said it, as though she were my master, sent me into a fury and I screamed, "I'm not coming back, though."

"That's it," she said pulling her coat off. "I'll have to call Dr. Keogan."

"What for?" I asked.

"To see what I should do," she replied.

"About what?" I asked.

She made no reply, but strolled over to the phone. Several minutes later she returned to me and said, "Your appointment is cancelled by orders of Dr. Keogan. That means an extra day will be added to your treatment time."

"That's not fair," I objected.

"You said you weren't going to come back and Dr. Keogan doesn't want to take any chances," she replied and then walked away.

I ran to the phone, looked up Dr. Kamari's number, and frantically tried to call him. There was no answer at his office. I tried him at the hospital where he worked. They told me he would be in court all morning. Then I called the Radiotherapy Associates and set up an appointment for later in the morning. *I'm going no matter what. I'm not having another day of it.*

I left the phone and went back to the nurses' station. "Please call Dr. Keogan. I have set up an appointment for eleven o'clock and I expect to be there," I said.

"I'll call but don't expect anything," Sue replied. She dialed his number and then hung up, without really listening for an answer. "I can't get him, you'll have to call and cancel the appointment. You're not going anywhere," Sue said with a cool stare."

"I'm going. There has to be a way out of here," I cried. I leaned against the wall fighting back tears. A few minutes later Sue came out to open the door for one of the nurse's aides.

I snatched the opportunity and before they knew what was happening I was out the door and running down the corridor. They were right behind me. *Get to Dr. Keogan. He won't let them do anything to you and then you can talk him into letting you go.* I took the stairs two at a time. They were only inches from me.

"Fran, if you stop now we'll forget about it. If you keep going you'll be in trouble," Sue said. I kept right on going.

I flew around the corner into Dr. Keogan's office. "Help!" I screamed. He was sitting at his desk with another man and looked up, startled. Sue rushed in and tried to take hold of my arm.

I drew it back and said, "Dr. Keogan, I have to go to radiation. She won't take me." He remained seated and said nothing.

Lydia strode in and grabbed my other arm, "Come along, Fran," she said. They half-pushed, half-carried me out of the office.

Back in my room, I lay on my bed sobbing. Finally, Timmy came in. "I'm here on tiptoe to take you to radiation," he said in his usually jovial way. Just the sound of his voice made me cry more. "Hey, I'm not that bad am I?" I shook my head and went into the bathroom to wash my red and swollen eyes.

Later, as we sat in Dr. Mahar's waiting room, I stayed quiet, trying to get my equilibrium back. Once inside the office, Dr. Mahar's comforting, supportive attitude soothed me. "Fran, could you go into the examining room? Let's look for improvements." Absentmindedly I nodded.

My mind was preoccupied with life at Brookhollow as Dr. Mahar began his routine. But then he said something which caught my attention immediately. "Fran," he smiled reassuringly, "the tumor has shrunk."

"You're kidding," I sputtered unbelievingly.

"I told you Fran, we were going to beat this thing."

"I know," I said tears coming to my eyes. "But it's been so hard."

His voice softened, "No one knows that better than I."

We gazed at each other in silence for a few minutes. Then he said, "You know you should never have been committed. All your problems stem from a purely physical cause, the pontine glioma. This is a very rare tumor. It is very common for tumors on the brain to cause hallucinations and the other symptoms you have described." I sat up. Tears washed my cheeks.

"Dr. Mahar," I said, "I don't know how to thank you. You are the only one on my side. You are the only one who has stood up for my sanity, Dr. Mahar, who has helped me regain my life." I sobbed. I tried to quiet myself and took a deep breath, then I went on. "Will I be getting out of Brookhollow?"

He nodded, "Two days from now. This Wednesday will

be your last treatment. You can go home that afternoon or the next morning."

"That afternoon," I said definitively.

"Not anxious or anything," he chuckled.

I laughed wholeheartedly in return. Riding back, feelings of elation filled me as I told Timmy what Dr. Mahar had said. He gave me the "thumbs up" sign. Reaching across the seat, he squeezed my hand.

It was almost dinner hour by the time we got back to Brookhollow. Timmy went upstairs and I entered the dining room to sit at my usual table.

Not long afterward, Dr. Kamari came striding toward me. I could tell by the frown on his face that he knew. "Well Fran," he said color rising in his face, "I understand your radiation treatments are ending and that you want to leave us."

"You're damn right I do," I said angrily. All of the emotions which had been bottled up for so long spilled over. "Your staff has mentally and physically abused me and I am not going to put up with it one day longer than I have to. You'd think someone in my condition would receive better treatment. At least you'd think there would be some form of discipline against the staff member. But according to this place, staff is God."

He cleared his throat. "The procedures are set up here so that you're not involved. We know what is going on and we are handling it," he said.

"Not good enough," I countered vehemently.

His lips tightened, "We don't think you're well enough to go home. You need help, drugs to calm you," he began his usual scenario. "I'll have to call your parents . . ."

This time I cut him short, "Call whomever you want. You're fired," I said loud enough for the whole room to hear. My words caught him off guard. He sputtered, "You have to have a doctor as long as you are here. Who do you want?" he said.

"Nobody. I'll take care of myself," I replied. He left and walked back to the staff's section.

All I had to do now was wait out the last few days of my sentence. They passed by hour by hour, but they passed. During that time I made up my mind that I wasn't going to let anyone bring me that low again. I knew I was overdoing it; however, I figured I needed my own cockiness, at least for a while, to survive.

During this time Dr. Kamari no longer came to see me and I didn't attend any Groups. I loved it. I was regaining control of myself and depending on my thoughts, and not someone else's. Brookhollow still controlled my physical movement, however. At night they still confined me to ICU.

The day before my discharge, Dr. Keogan stopped me in the corridor. Angrily, I told him, "You're fired too," before he had a chance to say anything to me.

"I know you feel that way, Fran, but why don't you come to my Group to get everything off your chest."

"I'm all Grouped out," I said and then walked away.

My discharge date finally arrived—Wednesday, March 23, 1988. I thought I would dance for joy after my very last treatment; however, I was drained of emotion and silently returned to Brookhollow—as I had so many times before.

The instant I got back I began packing my clothes, even though my parents weren't coming for another four hours. Once that was done, I decided to go to the lounge. At the ICU door, I stood quietly waiting for someone to open it. "It's the last time I'll have to do this," I murmured. I passed through without a hint of guilt.

Walking into the Main Lounge, I made myself comfortable on the couch. Every nurse came up to wish me good luck and tell me how much they liked me. Alf, Timmy, Vince, and the other attendants who'd befriended me trooped in and hugged me. Each one grinned and gave me the "thumbs up" sign, as if they'd rehearsed beforehand. I returned the gesture, smiling triumphantly. Then we all stood around talking.

Before our conversation was over my parents walked in. My eyes lit up as I rose, hugged and kissed them both.

Within the next few minutes, I gathered my things and we were on our way out, out of Brookhollow for good.

The horrendous buzzing noise sounded as the front door opened. And then, suddenly, I was *free*! I never once looked back.

AFTERWORD

Almost three years have passed since I came home to regain my strength and life.

During the first few weeks I did little besides eating my mom's nourishing meals and reading. I was still weak and easily fatigued, but gradually I became very uncomfortable with the idea of not working and started scanning the "help wanted" ads in our local newspaper.

I finally came across an entry-level job I thought would be appropriate and called to set up an interview. After a short wait, a gravel-voiced man got on the line and immediately started to describe the position and then asked about my credentials.

He seemed to be impressed, until I mentioned that I had a brain tumor and had been in Brookhollow. Then, by some strange coincidence, he was suddenly called away and left me with receiver in hand. I was pissed! I didn't want to face a life full of closed doors, I had too much to offer.

Of course, I knew brain tumors scared people, no less histories of mental illnesses, but I had to believe in myself once again or fail before I began. This wasn't going to happen to me. Not now, after I'd come so far.

I blue-skyed ways to get around my problems. Within the hour I had found one possible solution. I called my

father's lawyer, who was a judge. We set up an appointment for later that day.

At two o'clock sharp I was in the judge's chambers. We
discussed the situation and then I told him that I wanted
the Brookhollow incident removed completely from my
record.

The judge recommended a practical alternative to the
court proceedings, which he said would cost thousands. He
suggested I have my doctor write a letter stating the fact
that the commitment should never have happened and that
I had no psychological problem at all. It sounded good to
me!

Back at home, I called Dr. Mahar and explained the
situation. Immediately, he offered to write the necessary
letter. When I got off the phone with him I wandered from
room to room, deciding on how to begin my new life. I had
to take my time, I wasn't feeling well enough to work full-
time.

I also knew that if I wanted to do more than survive,
major changes would have to take place. I was determined
to do whatever was necessary to get back on track, and
reach my goals. Nothing and no one was going to blow me
off course again.

My first step forward, while I recuperated, would be to
do something constructive; sitting around the house all the
time just wasn't for me. Since I had gained quite a lot of
weight in the hospital and still had chipmunk cheeks, exercise seemed the best way to start.

I borrowed my sister's stationary bike, intending to
build from there. And build I did. By the end of the summer
I was biking twenty miles on the stationary bike, ten miles
on my ten-speed, jogging three miles, doing a hundred sit-
ups, and performing a twenty minute work-out each day. I
may have looked like the old Fran again but I definitely
wasn't her. I was more quiet, more questioning, more pur-
poseful.

Moreover, I had blown Steve out of my life for good. It
was hard but I purposely busied myself to stay away from

any temptation to get in touch with him, and it was the best decision I made for myself. I was getting to know myself, getting in touch with my feelings and my own strength.

As my energy started to grow, I began volunteering my time with the mentally disabled. The work was rewarding and I could make my own hours. It was a start.

By Christmas, we were all joking about my "escapades" and I had a caricature, drawn up for my mother, of me running with a shopping bag in each hand. Things were getting much better and, except for one short episode of chemotherapy during which I was never sick nor lost even one lock of hair, they have continued on an upward curve ever since.

I am now employed full-time as an insurance claims adjustor. When I told my prospective boss, in our first interview, that I had had a brain tumor, he smiled and said, "It looks like everything is under control." Indeed it does. Even though there are no cures for the type of brain tumor for which I was diagnosed, I have been in remission for two years. Dr. Mahar puts it most succinctly: "You're beating the odds; you're creating your own statistics."

So be it.